my *f*ather
and me

To Kaew.
Best wishes in your
future.   Heaven Cent.
                    1992.

warmwords
         Staff.

my father

New Zealand
women remember

and me

TANDEM PRESS

First published 1992
Tandem Press
2 Rugby Road,
Birkenhead, Auckland 10
New Zealand

© 1992 Penelope Hansen

ISBN 0 908884 117

Produced by Linda Cassells, Auckland
Designed by Jacinda Torrance
Printed by GP Print, Wellington

Contents

✦ ✦

Acknowledgements

The editor and publishers wish to thank the following: Fleur Adcock and Oxford University Press for permission to reprint 'Cattle in Mist' and 'My Father' from *Time-Zones* (© Fleur Adcock, 1991); Jenny Bornholdt and Victoria University Press for permission to reprint 'The Watch', an extract from 'From the Album' in *Moving House* (VUP, 1989); Bub Bridger for permission to reprint 'Long John Montgomery', and for permission to reprint 'Johnny come Dancing' from *Kiwi and Emu: An Anthology of Contemporary Poetry by Australian and New Zealand Women* (Butterfly Books, 1989); Sandra Coney and Penguin Books for permission to use an extensively reduced chapter from *Out of the Frying Pan* (Penguin, 1990); Marilyn Duckworth and Hodder and Stoughton for permission to reprint an extract from *Pulling Faces* (Hodder and Stoughton, 1987); Lauris Edmond and Bridget Williams Books for permission to reprint extracts from *Hot October* (Allen and Unwin/Port Nicholson Press, 1989) and *Bonfires in the Rain* (Bridget Williams Books, 1991), and Lauris Edmond and Oxford University Press for permission to reprint 'At Pyes Pa' from *New and Selected Poems* (© Lauris Edmond, 1991); Patricia Grace and Longman Paul for permission to reprint extended extracts from *Mutuwhenua: The Moon Sleeps* (Longman Paul, 1978); Sheridan Keith and New Women's Press for permission to reprint 'A Christmas Story' from *Shallow are the Smiles at the Supermarket* (NWP, 1991); Jan Kemp and Butterfly Books for permission to reprint 'To My Father, M.H.K.' from *The Other*

Hemisphere (Butterfly Books, 1991); Fiona Kidman and Random Century for permission to reprint 'The First Land' from *Wakeful Nights, Poems Selected and New* (Vintage New Zealand, 1991), and extracts from 'At the Lake So Blue' from *Unsuitable Friends* (Century Hutchinson, 1987); Rachel McAlpine and Mallinson Rendel for permission to reprint 'Before the Fall' from *Selected Poems* (Mallinson Rendel, 1988) and Rachel McAlpine for permission to reprint 'Jane and Heaven' from *The Hum*, a work in progress.

Introduction

◆ ◆

What do fathers mean to their daughters? This book turns back the clock, sometimes a little, sometimes a lot, to look at the fathering experienced in the last seventy years by some eminent New Zealand women. It is a collection of observations in writing — fiction, non-fiction and poetry — from (mostly) well-known New Zealand women about their fathers, or, in the case of fiction, about fictional fathers.

Contributors were asked to write about their relationship with their father, rather than be interviewed. Whatever the method chosen, bias is inevitable, a point of view established. Any bias in this collection belongs to the individual writer, not an interviewer. This admits the danger of embellishment, of putting icing where there was none, of painting a pretty family picture.

But there is little humbug here, and not much delusion either. If anything, the New Zealand voice heard in these pieces dresses things down, not up. It speaks forthrightly — a practical voice with a distinct New Zealand accent, a bluffness and a brevity of expression that echos the wordlessness of some of the fathers. The lifestyles depicted here are quintessentially New Zealand living styles. The points at which relationships are nurtured and flourish are distinctly ours: at the beach, at the bach, in the bush, digging for pipis, fishing, prising open the oysters; doing things for ourselves; walking, climbing, being outside together; holidaying relentlessly.

Why fathers and daughters specially? There hasn't been much written about fathers and daughters. It's an unexplored relationship. But in an age when women are moving more into the workforce and men sharing more — albeit marginally, according to Hillary Commission statistics — in the childcare and the housekeeping which inevitably goes with it, it's timely to look at fathering and its impact on daughters in New Zealand.

Of the women who completed this exercise a number said they found it difficult to separate their father's role from his relationship with their mother:

> My father was the man he was to me, partly because of the man he was to my mother . . . my relationship with my mother was always part of my relationship with my father and vice versa.
>
> *Margaret Mahy*

But having made the effort to write, some discovered that their father was more influential in their lives than they had at first thought:

> Over the years, if I ever thought of it at all, I would have been certain that the parent who had the greater influence on me was my mother. From the perspective of seventy years, I'm not so sure of that . . . I see in myself his weaknesses and strengths . . .
>
> *Pauline O'Regan*

Readers are invited to draw their own conclusions from what they read in these pages. *My Father and Me* does not have psychoanalytic or sociological intentions. No effort is made, nor was one ever intended, to explain or attempt to construct theories of any sort from the stories told herein. It was produced to give readers the opportunity to think about fathering. It may be a book produced for Maurice Shadbolt's 'chattering class', for people with a human, perhaps a daring, curiosity about one of the two most significant relationships in a young girl's life.

No systematic selection of contributors was undertaken. There were, however, some guidelines. On the whole, well known women were invited to contribute simply because they were well known and had spent their childhoods in New Zealand, and an attempt was made to provide a diversity of geographical location, age, occupation and racial background.

In total fifty-eight well known New Zealand women were approached. Contributors were offered the option of anonymity. One chose it but later changed her mind and withdrew. Twelve were too busy to spend the time required to write a piece such as this; four said that they would find the process too painful because of the recent death or illness of their father; two began the piece but were unable to finish because they found it more difficult to write about their 'dreadful relationship' than they had anticipated; three said that they had no relationship with their father, so did not see any point in the exercise. Others who declined gave no reason. In the end the selection depended more upon the willingness of contributors to write about, and have published, details of one of the most important relationships in their lives.

The selection procedure — or lack of it — has in the end shaped a book that is essentially positive about fathers and their relationship with their daughters. While this is certainly not representative of all daughter/father relationships, it probably represents a significant majority — neither perfect, nor irretrievably damaging. The Otago Women's Health Survey (Otago University) whose findings were reported in 1991 show that one third of New Zealand women are sexually abused in some way before they reach the age of sixteen. Of this third, 'One third (38 percent) . . . reported their most serious incident of abuse as being with a relation, and about half of these (18 percent) were abused by a relation who was living in the same house as them. . . We found that the women who had stepfathers were more likely to be abused by them when compared to biological fathers. One or two in a hundred biological fathers sexually molested their daughters, but one in ten stepfathers.' The book in which daughters talk about abusive relationships has still to be written.

Here, only the fiction pieces deal with abuse. In fact surprisingly little fiction has been written by New Zealand women about daughters and fathers. It could fairly be said of all New Zealand women writers, as was said of Tessa Duder, that their fictional fathers are shadowy. In fact, the only New Zealand writer who has delved into the relationship between fathers and daughters is Maurice Gee, and with such intelligence and feeling that it is easy to understand why other writers might shy away from the same undertaking. Relatively, as this collection shows, the daughters who are poets have been much more forthcoming about fathers than fiction writers.

While it is true that no attempt has been made to construct theories from the stories, it is impossible to resist the temptation to point to similarities, things that recur:

◆ the miserable rage of fathers faced with recalcitrant teenage daughters, the fierce struggles, the silent chasms which confront father and daughter as adolescence takes over;

◆ the warmth of men like the fathers of Erin Baker and Margaret Mahy as they, innocently or not, defy the stereotypes;

◆ the certainty and strength of men like the father of Moana Maniapoto-Jackson, who stands up for his daughter, supports her, but quietly, never confusing the manly with the macho;

◆ 'We are not a family that wears its heart on its sleeve,' states Sue McCauley. 'I have friends who are heavily into hugging . . . who can say 'I love you' with the ease of American sitcoms.' In this book, she's not alone. In fact, our contributors write easily of their family reluctance to state love, not as a burden, but as a fact of life, a currency whose value is greatly enhanced by infrequent use. As Sue McCauley points out, words fathers don't use, some daughters make a living from;

◆ the mothers, like Alison Holst's, who facilitate the relationship between father and daughter, and by allowing it to happen enrich their daughter's lives. If these men were mostly 'good fathers', it is at least in part true that they were so because they were married to women who permitted them to be so, women who had lives complete and busy enough to enable them to share their children;

◆ the frequency with which single-minded New Zealand fathers on holiday create worlds for their families which provide daughters such as Sylvia Rands, Joanna Paul, Penny Brothers with sustaining inner lives tied irrevocably to the sea and the bush;

- the number of storytelling fathers who produce writing daughters: Lauris Edmond, Margaret Mahy, Pauline O'Regan all tell of fathers who were magical storytellers — seannachie;

- the frequency of that moment of recognition, when a daughter looks at her father and realises he was not the hero, the perfect human being, she had thought. And the movement then to accept him and love him as a fallible human being;

- for many, the rich intimacies and rituals of family life, mysterious initials, codes between parents which exclude the knowing child from the parental relationship;

- the amazing — today it seems so — predictability of life for middleclass families in the fifties;

- the frailty of fathers as they grow old:

> My father who at 82 . . .
> now frail and thin, frets against
> his uselessness when his eyes cloud up
> his breath coming in fits and starts
> cleaned through an air-pump three times a day
> and then on a good one, perambulates
> the lawn with my mother to survey the progress
> of a troop of new sweet-peas along the trellis
> *From 'To My Father, M.H.K.'* — *Jan Kemp*

- and in the end, the precarious nature of it all:

> Even the happiest family life is also full of terrible dangers because members of a family are so varied, yet live so closely that they become victims of one another's limitations.
>
> *Margaret Mahy*

It's difficult to thank adequately people who are prepared to share the personal with the public. It's not an easy thing to do — to pull out the threads of a private life woven with your father, and to weave them together again for all to see. My sincere thanks to all the women and their fathers who generously and willingly agreed to participate in this project.

I hope this book and the pictures it paints of fathers working with their daughters, of daughters struggling alone, of daughters and fathers learning together, of daughters and fathers fighting furiously, provokes some thought about fatherhood, its importance to daughters and to fathers themselves.

Penelope Hansen

Long John Montgomery

At seventy-two
My father died dancing
And
I don't know
A better way to go
Than that
Life wasn't good to him
Nor he to it
But in the end
He did the thing
With such style
And grace
Dancing an Irish jig
With joy
In his face.

BUB BRIDGER

BUB BRIDGER was born in Napier but has lived most of her life in Wellington. She was married once, and says that was enough. She has four children and seven grandchildren. 'They're all marvellous.

'For eighteen years I lived in the sun on a hill. Now I'm on the flat and though the sun still shines on me, I miss the view of the sea and the sky and the hills.' But to compensate for this, she gets on her bike and pedals around the eastern bays, and picks the wild daisies and feasts on the beauty of it all — that lasts for a day or two, then she has to get out and see it all again.

She writes poetry and short stories. 'I've written for television and radio. I'm now writing a book about a girl called Tussy Bray.'

Moana Maniapoto-Jackson

• •

One day my father and I were walking along the main street of Rotorua, and I said to him, 'Wow, check that jacket out! It's choice!' My father kinda stopped for a moment, and stared at it. Then he said, with a little sigh, 'You know, before you kids came along, I used to wear all the latest gear. . . Ah, well . . .' And we carried on our way. *My* father? A dedicated follower of fashion? I'd never thought about him like that before. In fact, I think that was the first time I realised that Dad hadn't *always* been Dad (if you know what I mean). He'd actually had a life before we — me, my four sisters and my brother — came along. He'd done other things, been places, been a teenager, maybe even broken a few rules, *and* even been a kid.

You know how on the soapies, the father tells the daughter he loves her, and she tells him the same? Well, that's not us. But just because we've never said that stuff, doesn't mean we've never felt it!

You see, my father and his four brothers were brought up strictly. Their mother was a bit of a matriarch — she didn't stand for any nonsense. Mamaeroa (Hamiora) Maniapoto was an intelligent, articulate woman and an inspiration to her son. She fought for our people and our land in the courts and in Parliament. She collected a fat folder of waiata and whakapapa from both sides of the whanau. Our grandfather, Hema, was also a deep thinker — as well as a top fisherman, hunter and sportsman. He worked hard all his life and even up until his death, in his late eighties, could be found pottering around the house with paint and brush in hand.

'Dad and I walked through the whole confusing scenario of my university enrolment day together. I don't suppose many students took their parents through!' Moana Maniapoto-Jackson with her dad at graduation.

My father is a lot like his father. His hands are hardened from a lifetime of hard physical and manual labour: in the bush, on the wharf, in the mills. Dad taught me how to strip varnish, paint, wallpaper, tile, putty, garden — everything. He's also shared with me stories about life growing up in a little village called Te Rangiita, of catching wild horses in the ranges behind the family farm, of his days at Te Aute College, and army life during the Korean War. He's a great storyteller, my father. Loves to tell them. Loves to hear them. Some of the best times we've had were spent in the company of some of our 'old people'. People like Maata and Te Hiri Mariu. And Joe Hoko — all from tiny Waihi Pa. Dad and I loved hearing them tell us of the time when canoe would transport people on the lake.

Like his mother, my father is now collecting waiata and whakapapa. He has passed the relevant information on to me, that I might know who I am, where I come from, and who came before me. Now when I travel through the district of Tuwharetoa and Te Arawa, I recognise many names referred to in my father's accounts. Sometimes I can remember the context from which they sprang. My father taught me how to recognise, from the shape of a hillside, the site of an old pa. He taught me how to conduct myself in a strange district, what to do and say. Cripes — I can recognise the print of a wild pig in the bush. And I can play three chords on a ukelele.

My father and his brothers are one of the most entertaining acts I've ever seen — just ask anyone who has attended a hui at Waitetoko marae. (Of course, my Dad taught me not to 'blow my own trumpet' — but, hey, I'm blowing theirs!) The family custom is nonstop entertainment throughout meal servings. Dad's big dream was for his six children to join him in song after a speech. You know how embarrassed kids get? We used to just about die when Dad got up, let alone ourselves. But now we enjoy jumping up beside him — it's definitely where I got my start in music. My father introduced me to the stage when I was four weeks old, placing me on the back of his famous aunt, Guide Kiri, when her cultural group took to a South Island stage. When I was seven, we both performed in an operatic production of *The Merchant of Venice* — I played a pageboy. Educational stuff, that.

Whenever idiots have asserted that Maori don't support their children at school, I've always thought of my shy parents, who fronted up at school whenever required. It couldn't have been easy for my father, given that only two of us in our class were Maori. Dad could always be relied on to help with homework. (He's still doing it for my university siblings!) He's got a good brain. But he also helped us out with our teachers. There was a nun who terrified me so much I started skipping classes — and we're talking seventh form here. Dad confronted her and sorted out the whole situation. He's great like that — if someone upsets one of his kids, he'll sort it out. If someone annoys him, it's a different matter. He hates conflict and he'll do his best to avoid it. Dad and I walked through the whole confusing scenario of my university enrolment day together. I don't suppose many students took their parent through. Heck, I didn't care. What a culture shock for both of us.

My father is very artistic. He can draw the best horses I've ever seen. I think I got my sketching ability from him. It stood me in good stead when I spent two years researching and illustrating a thirteen-journal series on the historical development of Aotearoa, colonisation and Te Tiriti o Waitangi. My co-worker and I would discuss some of the more distressing factors which our research had revealed. We used to get so fired up about it. I remember Dad saying something like: 'Sometimes I just don't want to know about some things — it just brings out too much anger and frustration.'

My close women friends — Donna, Annette, Kim and Jane — they all adore my father. Donna is fond of saying, 'They just don't make them like that any more. The young men of today just don't compare to those of our fathers' era.' Like her Dad. Like Jane's Dad. And like my father-in-law, Bob. They come from another era, and they brought with them an air of dignity and humility.

Of course, Dad and I haven't always seen eye to eye. There was a time during 1981 when a few family relationships were strained. Ours reached a peak when Dad caught me painting up anti-tour slogans in his basement. He was getting ready to go to the Boks v Bay clash! He didn't really mind driving me into the city, but no way was he gonna let me ride with him to the gates.

We have a good laugh about that one now. Actually my father stars in one of our latest music videos, *AEIOU*. He came up for a Ranfurly Shield clash and our producer, Kerry Brown, talked him into doing a spot.

Now, we call him Elvis.

◆ ◆

MOANA MANIAPOTO-JACKSON (Ngati Tuwharetoa/Te Arawa) lives in her Otahuhu bungalow with 'three men and a baby'. Her husband Willy Jackson (Ngati Porou/Maniapoto) is a sports broadcaster for Aotearoa Radio, a trade union organiser and manages her band, Moana and the Moahunters.

The band plays funky bi-lingual dance music, and tries to incorporate traditional beats and dance movements to make an entertaining show. Their biggest hit to date is for their cover for the women's anthem, 'Black Pearl', which went to No. 2 in the national charts, and then went gold. Their first album was released early in 1992.

Moana is the eldest of five daughters and one son who belong to Bernadette and Nepia Maniapoto. 'These hardworking parents put me through St Joseph's Maori Girls College and helped me through Waikato and Auckland Universities, where I attained a law degree.' She was admitted to the Bar in 1985, but for political reasons chose not to practise. Instead she co-wrote, researched and illustrated a series of journals for young Maori exploring the colonisation and historical development of Aotearoa.

She worked as a daily talkback host on Aotearoa Radio and after eighteen months talking political/cultural/social issues day in day out, was offered a spot co-hosting a live music/games show for children on TV3.

'We lead a full, exciting and varied life and are lucky to have support from some very special friends and families.'

Lauris Edmond

◆ ◆

*M*y father had a crooked nose and a crooked smile; he'd broken his nose as a boy, riding his bike at night without a light, and it had set a bit awry, but the smile was natural. Probably it was like that because he was shy; he wasn't awkward, and talked easily enough about things he knew well — work and politics — but he could never say what was in his heart, and towards the end of his life he realised this, and it was a great sorrow to him.

I think of him now, across all these years — he died at sixty and that was nearly forty years ago — as someone who was part of the pioneering generations; his parents had come to New Zealand on the immigration vessels of the 1870s, and Lewis himself kept and practised the pioneering virtues. He was resourceful, industrious, uncomplaining, shrewd; he had little time for rules and systems, ignored all orthodoxies and proceeded in his own way, making, or making up, what he couldn't find to hand in objects and ideas. A classic 'number 8 fencing wire' man, in fact.

He was a painter and paperhanger, an occupation in which we all had some share. His clients expected him to be designer as well as decorator, and we helped to choose combinations of wallpapers and borders for the rooms he was to paper. The usual practice was to have a main paper, up to about 7 or 8 feet, topped with a narrow ornamental border that picked up on its strongest colours, then a different paper above that. Houses in the thirties all had a 12-foot stud. The family conferences about these choices were long and satisfying. Mum and Lindsay and I said you couldn't have a stripe on the bottom and a floral on top. Nor could you have blue and green together, or blue and pink mixed with orange and brown — each was a separate camp.

I'm not sure what he thought about these deliberations, but most probably it was that Fanny, my mother, would know best. He knew about work and money and 'the men' (an apprentice, an in-between employee, and a senior, a sort of foreman); she would know about style. I didn't realise then — except in the intuitive and strangely accurate way children do know these things — that part of his habit of deference to her opinions came from some half-conscious awareness of a class difference between them.

It was probably little enough. Both sets of parents had come to Hawke's Bay as young people, Fanny's to work as farm labourers, Lewis's father looking to establish a small business, his mother to work as a domestic servant. However it happened, or partly happened, my father, by the time he was my father and we lived together in a family ménage, held the titular power as head of the household, but deferred to my mother on all matters personal, social and, certainly, artistic.

Yet the division was not simple. Though my father's family always seemed less stylish, less worldly, somehow less impressive than my mother's relatives, it was his mother who was known as a seer, with special powers of spiritual vision. Lewis himself (as by the time I was in my teens I was allowed to address him) had an interest in the occult and read books about reincarnation, thought transference (as he called it) and communication with the spirit world. But this didn't interfere in any way with his practical and pragmatic daily life. On the day of the great earthquake he was up a ladder, painting tanks for a farmer on the hills towards Puketitiri. As he held up his brush to dip in the paint pot that hung on his ladder, the tank leaped off its stand into the air and rolled down the hill. He was a phlegmatic man, my father, and told us that his main thought was that if he'd been in front instead of at the side he would have been taken too. It was somehow characteristic that he wasn't.

As time went on, Lewis's interest in extra-terrestrial phenomena was overtaken by another fascination — off-beat politics. The connecting link between these two spheres was probably the idea of a perfect world. Utopia was a dream that stirred many people during the famished thirties. There was extensive literature on the subject, but Lewis wanted practical policies too.

In 1935 the Labour government came to power. For months before the election we, like most families we knew, had the plump and smiling face of Michael Joseph Savage up on the wall, though in our case it wasn't in the house but out in Dad's office, an old fowl house a little distance from the back verandah. There he did his accounts, mixed pots of paint, wrote letters to the newspaper and read, discovering an obsession that was to last all his life for political rebirth or, as he called it at first, monetary reform. He'd always been interested in ideal societies; many of the books lying about the house had titles such as *Equality* (Edward Bellamy) *Looking Backward* (by the same author), and there was H. G. Wells' *A Modern Utopia* and *The Open Conspiracy*. It was sub-titled 'Blueprints for a world revolution'; and it did seem that my mild and often uncommunicative father was excited by such a prospect. Another was called *Perfecting the Earth*. He believed in this possibility, and after a while so did I.

Other Labour Party members including candidates like John A. Lee and William Barnard (our member after the election) also didn't greatly distinguish between the new dawn promised by Savage and Semple, Nash and Fraser, from the more general reform they encountered in their reading. Thoughtful, unschooled and largely self-educated men were common; for my father the focus increasingly fell on Douglas Social Credit, a faith which came to dominate our household. I think we became a bit cranky in the eyes of people in the town, but at first it wasn't so — didn't the whole world want Labour to win? When it happened, the night of the 1935 election, we gathered in the chook house, all of us, and shrieked and laughed with Dad; we'd wanted Utopia to come, and as far as we could see, it had.

Hot October

During the years of the Depression, my father did what many others did — maintained a home-grown industry out of domestic

'He made long trips around the country with an eye for unlikely but lucrative painting projects.' Lewis, Lauris Edmond's father.

living; he made a good deal of our furniture, mixed his own paint, chopped all the wood for the coal range, built sheds and verandahs and made the stretchers we used for our camping holidays. Nothing that could be made was ever bought in a shop.

He made long trips around the country with an eye for unlikely but lucrative painting projects, and he would go a great distance to paint railway stations, warehouses, schools and school houses. It was always profitable because he could offer low prices and engineer the same sort of home-grown meals and accommodation that he later adapted for holidays and foreign travel.

When he was tired he slept — promptly, effortlessly, deeply. He carried a stretcher in the car or truck when he was alone, and travelling to or from a job, and when he felt the need he simply got out and put it up at the side of the road. There he would stretch out and slumber peacefully till he woke fresh enough to drive again. My father's capacity to sleep on the spot, on the instant, when ready, was the cause of some of the few quarrels my parents had. He would drop off in his chair when there were visitors, and this habit furiously embarrassed Fanny; but I don't remember that he was able, or willing, to change it. He was the quiet one, the patient support for her more volatile, more voluble style, but he was quite stubborn too, and clearly reserved the right to decide for himself how far he would go to please her.

By the end of the decade, when war was declared, my father's intense association with 'fringe' politics had given him a touch of paranoia, though I think this may have been an aspect of the espousing of unpopular causes, and not a problem peculiar to him. Certainly he thought of all political events as evidence of international monetary plots. This was a mixture of truth and delusion — armament firms did indeed operate as the first multinationals, financial networks existed and flourished, and there was no overt news of their operations; but the conviction that the directing power was always Jewish was less provable. For him, no further proof was necessary beyond what he read in *The Protocols of the Learned Elders of Zion*, a book we'd had in our house for years; it set out the evidence for an international conspiracy authorised and controlled by the Zionist faction of the Jewish people.

Some people thought the document a hoax, but to my father and his Social Credit friends it rang with authority. The enemy was all the more suspect for being hidden, and as the 1939–45 war dragged on it did seem to me too that only the armament factories profited, and they recognised no national frontiers; whether the Zionist control part was true I could never decide, but on the whole I was on my father's side. Social Credit, however, was to prove itself by justice and fair dealing. Everyone would have equal access to wealth and advantage — consumption would equal production, as we were fond of saying (I gave morning talks at school on the subject, coached by my keen Dad). News of the dumping of cotton and coffee and other crops, while millions starved, came to Social Credit meetings by various means, and outraged and horrified all of us. Out in the chook house/office, Lewis and I had many a serious conversation on the way to the right sort of world. But if the Japs came we would pack up and go into the bush, or up into the hill country where Uncle Bert had his farm.

As I grew older I came to feel that my father's parenting was often a sort of trial by absence. Partly because he worked such long hours, and partly because he was uncommunicative on personal matters, it was possible for me to have all the vital connections between parents and children with my mother — at least for quite long times. It had been different when we were small; then he'd been with us far more. Perhaps he was at ease with small children — as reserved people sometimes are — and became less so as we grew into opinionated and strident adolescence. Certainly there are occasions and habits it is good to recall from the time I was small:

> I think our parents loved each other. They laughed together often, and seemed to have an array of shared occupations that suited both equally. They read to each other for instance, Dad doing rather more than his share because Mum usually had hemming or

'I think our parents loved
each other.'
Lewis and Fanny,
Lauris Edmond's parents.

domes and hooks to sew on dresses or shirts while she listened. Wodehouse's *Jeeves* books were among their favourites; they read the series through and then at intervals did them all again, falling about laughing at Bertie Wooster's wounded dignity and Jeeves's calculated deceptions, his suave 'Yes, sir', 'Indeed, sir? I am sorry to hear that.' They sometimes sat at the kitchen table in the evening with a Jeeves volume, forgetting the time we were supposed to go to bed.

Hot October

Was reading aloud an accomplishment, and a recreation that vanished with their generation? My Dad certainly did a lot of it, and was wonderfully willing to go on and on reading me a favourite story, as adults so seldom are. He was busy — at work, that is — or else he was at ease, with time to spare; even years later when my mother was ill, and he had to do the washing and cooking, I noticed he had a man's, not a woman's, way of doing things — one at a time, not all together. Long after I could read for myself he would sit on my bed at night and go on and on in his quiet musical voice, covering whole chapters of, say, *Alice in Wonderland* or *Through the Looking Glass*. I lay in bed and savoured his way of dramatising characters like the Gryphon or the Red Queen or Tweedledee and Tweedledum. And I have another delightful glimpse in my mind — Dad at the kitchen table writing out recipes that Mum dictated (taken no doubt from the radio or newspaper), and putting 'Steamed Apple and Pig Pudding', and then 'pig' again every time she said 'apple'. A feeble enough joke, but it made them hysterical with laughter at the time, and long afterwards I came across the spattered old exercise book and smiled to find Apple and Pig Pudding there, in his broad, clear, workmanlike writing.

Parents are not seen by their children as individuals in their own right, with qualities and aspirations separate from their function as parents. However, when I think about my father now I can see that he was actually there as a person, a man, even if I didn't think so at the time. He was quite secure in himself I think, confident, and courageous; I don't mean he had physical courage, though he did, and indeed could earn extra money by tackling high buildings and poles and girders that others would not touch — calmly swaying about with his paint pot and brush up there, as though the ground was not hundreds of feet below, but a few inches. But he was brave in less visible ways too, regarding difficulties as risks worth having a go at. His advice to me was always, 'Go on, try it' — with the significant exception of my leaving home for long spells, and that was because as a principle he liked his family near him, and didn't really think much beyond that.

Within his limits — which is to say on his home ground, not among people he didn't know — he was very much at ease with himself, adaptable and inventive. When we had all left home (except our late baby, my young brother), he and my mother decided to travel and began with Australia and Fiji. Lewis took to the nomadic style of life quickly and easily, making a thousand adjustments. He bought cheap vans and when they had served their purpose sold them again; some were old wrecks which he would tinker with, keeping them on the road and fitted out like home-grown dormobiles in which they could explore the country. He plotted and altered their routes according to their shared desires; Fanny by this time had TB and was semi-invalid, so his confidence and flexibility were constantly needed. He did much of the planning, and all the work.

> He was unshakeably loyal to her, he truly adored her all his life, and caring for her now that she was ill was his central preoccupation. However, the day came when he visited us [my husband and I] in our first house, a small rented establishment in an old part of suburban Wellington, and I think he felt a distinct wry pleasure in coming alone. It was Easter. The weather was still hot; we had beans and lettuces in the sandy little patch we called our vegetable garden. Lewis weeded, dug up an untidy corner and planted winter cabbages, mowed the minute lawn, fixed a hinge, replaced a board in the ancient verandah. In his reticent, gentle way he became briefly indispensable: he was our steward, our resident overseer. He was easy to like. Perhaps he asked a shade too little of us, of Fanny, of life itself, and as he said goodbye,

forgot some trifle, came back, said it again, I wondered if he felt
something of this himself. My father. A modest, honourable man.

Bonfires in the Rain

In the next five years, from 1947, he had a great deal of
fulfilment, and was, I suppose, as happy as he had ever been —
and he was a man capable of a calm and untroubled happiness,
who could put doubts and worries away by an act of will. As a
young adult I went to Pyes Pa, the ideal place chosen for his
retirement and their middle-aged leisure, for every holiday I had.
When we began to have our own children they too spent blissful
days and weeks exploring the garden, orchard and bush
surrounding the Pyes Pa house. Since we, the family, or the
people we'd married, were all teachers, there were a good many
of these family idylls.

> Lewis after reading and dreaming of his utopia for years was
> actually building it in this ripe land, the first he had ever chosen;
> all the other addresses, even the Greenmeadows house which he'd
> taken over from his parents, had been accidental. Fulfilment for
> both of them meant having their children there too, at home, with
> the wives, husbands, friends they cared to bring with them. I don't
> think either of them really believed that we might come to have
> other homes, more important to us than the one we'd grown up
> in. At the same time it was extra proof, if any were needed, of the
> fruitfulness of the family that we had acquired partners who came
> with us. In his heart Lewis was an ancient tribal patriarch still,
> self-effacing and tentative though he might be when faced with the
> concentrated volubility of the crowd.
>
> *Bonfires in the Rain*

But Lewis's perfect world, read about, imagined, and now
formed, did not last.

> One by one — or two by two, and in our case four together — we
> left to go home for the beginning of the school year. Within weeks
> of our going, Lewis, sitting on the verandah one afternoon, was
> gripped by a violent pain in the stomach. It went away, and he did
> not ask the reason for a long time (what would orthodox doctors

know anyway?). By the time he did, the diagnosis was cancer of the bowel too far advanced for an operation to be possible, though there was an almost certain cure for cases identified early enough.

Would he have agreed to an operation? It was one of the tragedies of their blind faith in unorthodoxy, his and Fanny's, that it kept them from other useful knowledge. Both were inclined by taste and temperament towards extremes, but they also lacked a milieu which might have encouraged a broader view. In 1951 'natural living' was still the pursuit of eccentrics or cranks.

. . . During the last eight or nine months of his life we — and he — slowly came to terms with the realities of his condition and in the end talked openly about it, though I could never do this without helpless tears. I was pregnant again for most of 1953, and in July Lewis came alone to Ohakune. He wanted to make a last bid for help from one of the natural health experts, Ulric Williams, who ran his own hospital in Wanganui. The first evening he spent in our house was extraordinarily poignant. He was thin, quite shrunken, yet everything he said was alight with the mild kindliness he'd always shown; he sat with his square hands in his lap and asked questions about the children. He found it hard to eat, even a chinese gooseberry I sliced, and could swallow only a mouthful. He had an obvious swelling in the lower part of his body.

'We're alike,' he said to me with his crooked smile, 'you're bulging too.' I sat still and willed myself not to cry.

The next morning Trevor drove him down the Parapara road to Wanganui. 'The poplars will be over,' I said as they left. When we took that road in late autumn the poplars were wonderful, marching over the hills like golden battalions. Now it was winter, on the way to Wanganui it rained, mist obscured the spurs. But it was the journey back that was really grim. Dr Williams had said he could not admit Lewis because he was 'too close to being a bed-patient', and driving north with Trevor at the end of that day Lewis came at last to the end of his optimism. He arrived pale and drawn.

'It's a long way,' he said, and told me over and over, as though it would make sense of things, 'he would have taken me,

29

but he doesn't take bed-patients.'

In August that year I went to Pyes Pa on my own. One day Fanny came into my room to put his washed brush and comb on the windowsill to dry.

'It's all I can do for him,' she said despairingly, 'this, and learn about bills and money. We say I'm his secretary, as though it's funny.'

In bed on the big verandah, round the corner from Fanny, and their shared bed, he talked to me, saying at last what must have been in his mind for a whole lifetime. That he wished he'd known us better, hadn't worked so hard and missed so much of what happened at home, hadn't been so shy. He said sixty was too young to die; he couldn't understand why this should happen to him when he'd been so careful about his health. (One question nobody could ask was about his long exposure to the lead in his home-mixed and, more recently, hand-sprayed paint.) We would have to look after Fanny; we were not to be sad, he would stay with us, in our minds, in our dreams.

Bowed down too by regret for time and opportunity not understood, not grasped, and now lost for ever, I could make no answer.

On the way home I failed to recognise Ohakune station and was carried, ridiculously, on to Waiouru, where I had to wait for a midday goods train to take me back. Lewis, who had painted so many railway stations that he had accumulated a comprehensive lore about them, would have enjoyed my dilemma, but it was already too late to tell him. I had said goodbye.

He died in October. Clive and Dorothy stayed with him for the last week, and Trevor and Doug [sons-in-law] went for the funeral. Lindsay and I were both pregnant, and Fanny insisted it would be too distressing for us. Through that day I worked as usual, played when necessary, but later I lay awake in the dark and struggled to grasp the remorseless finality of what had happened. The months, indeed years of illness were, I saw, no preparation at all. The shock of the event itself was as great as if I'd had no warning. Lewis, dead, was so inexpressibly different from Lewis alive, even if ill, that I could not make my mind take it in.

There was one eccentricity of my father's that, even in our grief, we all found truly bizarre. Not wanting to leave the money he'd earned, and kept for us, to be diminished by death duties or other taxes, he had sealed in tins, then buried, a large amount of cash — several thousand pounds. Fanny alone knew where HT (Hidden Treasure) was, and when Clive had brought it inside (musty-smelling but otherwise undamaged), together they counted the notes and banked them. Each of us was given our share. We made a great many jokes about HT I suppose to express, or conceal, our embarrassment at such a legacy — so affectionately planned, so queerly executed. I spent mine on a piano.

Bonfires in the Rain

At Pyes Pa

My father, a mild and unheroic man,
died bravely; shrunken by disease
and disappointment he lay on the verandah
he had built, seeing across his partly
planted orchard a blue shimmer of sea
and mountain in a country rich, he had
supposed, in continuity. Smiling
at us he comforted his children: death
was not so great a thing that we should fear it;
he could for instance visit us in dreams . . .
His hands, brown as earth, lay on the bed;
we were to care for his trees. We cried
but could not speak — what comfort could we offer,
who felt our good health like an accusation?

LAURIS EDMOND

LAURIS EDMOND grew up in Greenmeadows, a village outside Napier in Hawke's Bay. She trained as a teacher and speech therapist in Wellington and Christchurch, married and went back to small towns as the wife of a high school teacher and eventually, mother of six children. Having written poems as a child, she continued writing in a subterranean and fragmented fashion and emerged, apparently from nowhere, as a new writer when her collection *In the Middle Air* won the PEN Best First Book Award in 1975. She then went on to publish eight other volumes of poetry, winning the Commonwealth Poetry Prize in 1985 with her *Selected Poems*. She has also published a novel, several radio plays and one stage play, and the first two of a three-volume autobiography. *New and Selected Poetry* was published in 1991.

Lauris Edmond was awarded an OBE for services to New Zealand literature in 1986, and an Honorary Doctorate of Literature from Massey University in 1988. She lives in Wellington on a hillside which, she says, provides the perfect combination of town and country conditions.

Pyes Pa

Gaylene Preston

••••••••••••••••••••••••••••••••••

MY DAD

Warm hands and whiskers. A big body to get lost in. You could climb all over him and there'd still be some left.

My Dad.

He killed taipo (big Westcoast wetas) with his bare hands and chooks with an axe. We ate the chooks but not the taipo.

He would pull tobacco out of his Kauri tin, and papers from his Zigzag packet and roll a smoke with one hand as he drove the milk van (Brad the Bradford) down the road to Paroa.

He was never there, yet always present. My mother and grandmother — the real power in the household — maintained his authority in his absence. *Your father* was a mythological beast — as in 'Wait-'til-I-tell-*your father*'. But we knew *your father* was only Dad. He never laid a finger on us. He was a hopeless softie. He approved of me one hundred per cent as long as I didn't stand in front of the television while he was watching it.

My mother seemed to be disappointed and annoyed with him a lot of the time. But my grandmother (his mother-in-law) lived with us and knew what side her bread was buttered on. She maintained he was a 'good scout' and would hear no evil. She lived with us for twenty years and never had an argument with him.

He didn't really go in for arguments. When I got older, I did.

We had a real humdinger the day I watched Brixton burning on the television. I had lived there for a few years and was watching my local go up in smoke. He maintained the Poms deserved all the trouble they got. 'They should never have let them in, in the first place.' I told him not to be so smug. The fires

could be burning in the football park behind his house in just a few months time. It was a bitter argument. We disliked one another for it.

Later that winter he wrote me a letter. I've only had three from him in my life. When he writes a letter it's a project. He has to hold the paper a long way off and he wears his glasses on his nose. He licks the pencil even though puce pencils went out years ago.

His letter just says, 'Dear Gay,' then describes the view from his kitchen window. Barbed wire, army everywhere, helicopters, short wave radios. He never said, 'You were right' or 'I'm sorry.' He just wrote down what he could see. That was all. 'Love Dad.'

He lives in the now, my Dad.

It was only when I asked him to sit down with me and a tape

'He approved of me one hundred per cent as long as I didn't stand in front of the television while he was watching it.'
Gaylene Preston with her father.
Photo: Kate Jason Smith

recorder that he told me about his war.

He volunteered to fight Hitler with a mate from his football club. He says they didn't give the slightest thought to 'King and country' at the time. They just wanted a job and the chance to get to hell out of being unemployed in Greymouth.

He was overseas in the army for four and a half years and spent three and a half weeks of it in combat. The rest of the time was in training, travelling and being held prisoner. After two years in an Italian prison camp he escaped into Switzerland by walking over ten mountains. He was as fit at that moment as the day he signed up.

Only recently I began to understand why. He doesn't worry. My mother does that for him. He only takes on what he can control. He's a lapsed Catholic agnostic. He truly believes that once you're dead, that's it. He wants to see the year 2000 and has paced himself for this event. After that he will work further on his immortality.

He lived in an Anglican household, once he married my mother. When Nan came to live with us (my mother's mother), she brought her own personal hotline to God. If you wanted anything (within reason) Nan could ask God for it in her morning despatches. She had a habit of dropping to her knees at important moments to whisper noisily at the Heavenly Father. Confirmed agnostic though he is, Dad, on at least one occasion, knelt down with us rather than be a spoil-sport. Nan was right. He is a 'good scout.'

He started doing the dishes after we girls left home and the feminist revolution hit the household. Doing the dishes was as far as he ever got. He has always lived in a five-star hotel which my mother runs to cater for his every whim.

One day around 1974, as I dried the dishes with him and he was giving me his strongly held opinion of dole bludgers, I asked him about the time he was on the dole, in Switzerland after he escaped from Italy. I said, 'There you were lounging round the shores of Lake Geneva, on the dole, while the war in Europe raged all around you. What was it like, Dad?' He didn't even stop scrubbing. 'Oh . . . the tucker wasn't very good.'

He often calls me by my sister's name. He's quite lazy in his relationships. He never says he's sorry. When he was younger, if you gave him a cup of tea, he wouldn't say thank you. He'd say, 'Sugar?' He'd be happy if I got a steady job that didn't involve all this obsessional behaviour and leaping on planes all the time. But he's always been there and available. Steady as a rock.

He saved telling me he loved me until very recently. It had just never come up. He was eighty at the time. I was forty-four. When a major relationship in my life was breaking up, he drove into town on his own to visit me. He said, 'Never mind love, I love you.'

I was glad he'd saved it till then.

✦ ✦

GAYLENE PRESTON's extensive catalogue of independently made films grew out of her work as an art therapist in the United Kingdom where she made her first film as part of a drama therapy project with institutionalised patients at Fulbourn Hospital, Cambridge. Twenty years later she is one of New Zealand's best known film-makers, with an extensive and varied filmography which includes documentaries, short dramas, two feature films and numerous television commercials.

'My films always embody serious concerns under a humorous light surface. The more serious the underlying themes, the more entertaining the experience must be for the audience. I try to make my films have resonance so that after the audience leaves the cinema, they will be thinking about the serious side, hopefully still smiling.'

Mr Wrong, Preston's first feature film (1985), tells the story of a young woman who buys a haunted car. In the guise of a comedy/thriller the film explores the Cinderella syndrome and contemporary realities of sexual violence towards women. *Mr Wrong* gained eight nominations in the 1986 New Zealand film industry awards and has screened in ninety-three territories around the world.

With *Ruby and Rata* Preston switched genres and produced a character-based comedy/drama. After a successful release in its home territory (*Ruby and Rata* was No. 1 at the New Zealand box office in the first week of release), this film was screened at several international festivals including Montreal, Toronto, London, Hawaii and Los Angeles' Women in Film. *Ruby and Rata* received nine nominations in the 1990 New Zealand Film and Television Awards, including Best Music, Best Actor, Best Editing and Best Soundtrack.

Her short films and documentaries have won awards in Australia, Canada, France and Switzerland. Preston's most recent documentary (1987) was on Booker prize-winning author Keri Hulme for Thames Television (UK). In 1986 Preston's Telecom television commercial won two silver plaques at the Chicago Film Festival. She has directed for a wide range of agencies including Colenso, Saatchi and Saatchi, Ted Bates, and MDA McKay King.

Gaylene Preston has served on the Executive of the Independent Producers and Directors Guild and is a past member of the New Zealand Film Commission.

Carroll du Chateau

• •

They fuck you up, your mum and dad.
They may not mean to, but they do.
They fill you with the faults they had
And add some extra, just for you.

PHILIP LARKIN, *THIS BE THE VERSE*

*T*his poem expresses a certain basic truth about my relationship with my parents — especially my father. Over the
forty-five years I knew him, Len buffeted me with his rage,
bullying and tantrums. And on his good days he taught me about
love, kindness and compassion. It was a rough mix and it was
dished out when Dad felt like it, so that a timid child like me was
confused, if not terrified, most of the time. My inner be-
wilderment shows in our early black-and-white family photos.
There I stand, a skinny little six-year-old with mosquito bites on
my legs, big dark eyes and a sad, sad face.

My father, on the other hand, was at the peak of his powers.
One of my earliest memories comes from when I was about four.
In the morning my sister Robyn and I would creep into our
parents' big bed, where our mother lay sleeping — or pretending
to — and wait for Dad. And, at around 6.10, accompanied by
much whistling through his teeth, he would arrive. Dad always
looked the same. His grey hair was always brushed sternly off
his face; his back, which had been injured in a rugby accident,
ramrod straight. Always he wore the same boot-style slippers
with soles like slabs of thick brown marshmallow, the same thin
green-striped dressing gown and carried the same big tray

'The mixture of emotion, love and fear Len spooned out is, no doubt, the way heroes are built. I was terribly proud of him.'
Len du Chateau.

holding four cups, a full pint bottle of milk (it had to be full — he liked his tea weak and milky and the cat needed a saucerful too), Mum's flowery sugar bowl, a plate of toast cut into thin strips and kept warm in the oven until the butter bubbled, and the stainless steel teapot.

But one morning there was something extra — something moist and snuffling peering blindly over the top of his dressing-gown pocket. 'Here Carroll,' he said. 'One for you. And one for Robyn.' Our springer spaniel, Twin, had had puppies in the night and now Dad was bringing the pups up for us to cuddle in bed. Even though Mum complained about them wetting her sheets (and they did) the pups were such a great hit that Dad made the puppies-in-the-pocket part of our family tradition. His delight in animals and nature was the most appealing side of my father's personality. But the same man who would painstakingly feed an abandoned goldfinch chick with a mixture of sieved hard-boiled egg yolk mixed with crushed wine biscuit could turn into a tyrant who could terrify me speechless. As my sister said at his funeral, 'I think that being the youngest is a great blessing, in that I had the least time being Len's daughter. Living with Len was like swimming in the seas off Raumati on a choppy day when the waves slapped and pulled you around. That was what it was like being Len's daughter — exciting, unpredictable, passionate, and full of energy . . . Len never protected me from himself. I have heard about all his loves, his anguishes, his anxiety, his deep anger. I got all of him.'

For me, the most difficult thing about Len was his un-predictability — his sudden rages over gates that weren't shut properly, brass taps that weren't polished, friends who called over when he wanted to work on the farm, me slipping a sliver of garlic into the roast hogget — even potatoes that weren't mashed with enough butter. His temper was legendary.

By the time I was born my father was in his late thirties and nearing the peak of his career in advertising. I was the middle daughter of three. The oldest child was my brother Peter, who had the toughest time of all of us. Mavis, my mother, for all her fun and warmth, was a great believer in the 'wait till your father gets home' school of child rearing. When we were really naughty we would wait upstairs until the green Chevrolet crunched into the drive, the low muttering in the kitchen ceased, and Dad would walk slowly up the stairs. Looking back it must have been tough for him but as he told us, 'spare the rod and spoil the child' and he would smack us hard — once each, on the hand. Looking back, it wasn't the pain that upset us so much, but the waiting, and the fear.

Mavis, bless her, taught us that men were the enemy. And Dad made a formidable foe. We would, Mum included, whoop with joy when we heard Dad was going away on a business trip for a couple of days. It was like a holiday — fish and chips out of the paper on the lounge floor, no housework, friends around to play. And, best of all, no arguments between my parents late at night while I lay in bed with my fingers stuffed in my ears trying to get to sleep. To this day I have a tendency to treat men as the enemy — to be outsmarted and avoided whenever possible — while women are trustworthy allies.

The mixture of emotion, love and fear Len spooned out is, no doubt, the way heroes are built. I was terribly proud of him. Having a father in advertising was great in the fifties. Dad brought home samples of new Hudsons biscuits and Cadburys chocolate well before the other kids could get them in the shops. At Christmas time the Sanitarium Health Food company would send us huge boxes of elaborate dried fruit — plump glacé apricots, fleshy muscatels, 'healthy' sweets made of coconut and nougat — which we would gorge on when our parents were out. For a while Len was the president of the Advertising Agencies Association and he and my mother used to go to conferences of the Three As and the Newspaper Proprietors Association at Wairakei every year while Robyn and I were left with a series of horrible housekeepers. We made up for it when Dad's advertising jingles like 'Clean burning Europa' crackled over the radio. 'My father wrote that,' we'd tell our incredulous school friends.

Music was a vital part of my parents' life. They were of the generation who met at dancing school — Len and Mavis were exhibition dancers in their day — and spent hours clustered round the piano singing songs like *Drifting And Dreaming* and *The Red Red Robin*. By the time I was born they were too sophisticated for sing-a-longs but still we used to sing in the car when Dad taught us how to harmonise and hold a note, often with tears glistening in his eyes at the emotion of it all. One of his favourites was *Oh My Papa*. In 1956 we were sent to board for two terms at Chilton St James school in Lower Hutt while our parents steamed to England on the *Himalaya* and I remember my father writing letters to me in rhyming couplets and me replying, painstakingly, the same way. It was my first attempt at creative writing and Dad was so pleased with my clumsy attempts I began submitting poems to the children's pages competitions of the *Weekly News* and even winning the odd book token.

As my sister said, Len never protected us from himself. He took great delight in the peculiar invented words which we made up as children — a practice which caused me terrible anguish when, after many years of putting some pretend reins and an old sack on the dog kennel and sitting there day after day, pretending to ride, Dad bought me my first pony.

'What will you call her, Carroll?'

'Tinkerbell,' I said firmly. Dad recoiled in horror.

'Tinkerbell?' he spat. 'What a repulsive mawkish name for a horse! No, you can't have her at all if you don't call her Piki Ponni.' (That was my invented name for the dog kennel.)

It wasn't until I'd endured years of shame, trotting around the ring at pony club amid dozens of other Tinkerbells and Peter Pans, that I realised Dad was right — Piki Ponni was a much more exciting name for a horse.

About the same time, when I was about seven, I remember trying to convince Dad, who was an agnostic, that there was a God. He smiled nastily. 'Well, when I went up in the plane last week I looked around and there wasn't a Heaven,' he said.

Len also introduced me to words, especially poetry. He read us *Alice's Adventures in Wonderland* and *Through The Looking Glass*, *Mowgli*, Hans Christian Andersen, the brothers Grimm, and so much more. By this time Len was an established writer himself. His output was prodigious. His was the first short story ever published in the *Listener*, 'The Law Of The Tribe', way back in the forties or fifties. He had had poems in the Australian *Bulletin* and *Landfall* — then considered the most prestigious publications for poetry. Later he published two books of poetry, *Let The Falcon Fly*, and *Life And Love*. When radio was at its peak, he wrote a nightly serial — I think it was called *Lillian And Her Lovers* — which, Mum later told us, he would write by hand at the kitchen table after dinner, totally oblivious, while we kids played around him.

My mother, much more than we children, was the centre of his life. When he was about sixty, he wrote a poem about her:

The Wife
Reflection says 'this girl is your young bride
Wife of your choosing and the good strong link
Which holds the pattern all together.' But fast
The question looms, what do I really know
Of this small woman so securely cast at the
Dead-centre of my life. I've seen her grow
Mature: adopt the poses of her peers.
But a girl she has remained, her glow
Sweetens my world, keeps me young, gives me ideas.
She's seen a lot of men, none chosen; her goal?
Family matters, her methods sharp and sane.
Nurse, mistress, wife and mother, played each role with zest.
Ran kids and I on a loose rein
and kept intact her everlasting soul.
What goes on in her mind, I guess in vain.

By the time I started to notice, my father wasn't a handsome man. Maybe it says something about his own inner turmoil that the golden curls of his youth had turned silver when he was in his twenties. But he still had the kind of features that he himself admired. He was tall with the straight back you could pick from 100 yards, straight legs, straight eyes, a firm handshake and impeccable grooming. There wasn't an ounce of fat on his body. Although he loathed and detested cosmetics for men, he always

'Living with Len was like swimming in the seas off Raumati on a choppy day when the waves slapped and pulled you around.'
Back, left to right: Len, Carroll's sister Jill. *Middle:* her mother Mavis holding Robyn. *Front:* Carroll.

smelled deliciously clean of Palmolive soap.

Len's ego was just too big to be around all the time with any degree of comfort — especially if you were the sensitive type. He could be terribly cruel about the shortcomings, especially the physical shortcomings, of other people. He had a thing about fat people, bandy people, knock-kneed people, wall-eyed people, people with big noses and women with 'strainer post legs' and 'mutton thighs' and had a great line in cruelly funny, sniggering criticism. A sturdy girl who was unlucky enough to grow solid and big-breasted in adolescence, I was an insult to the family image perpetuated by my mother with the trim ankles and slender waist Len openly admired. 'Take your fat sister out on to the tennis court and run some of the weight off her,' he would instruct my nimble sister. And down I would lumber. Then there was Len's form of positive reinforcement: from the time I turned sixteen he took me to Kirkcaldie & Staines each birthday to buy me a beautiful straw hat for the spring races at Trentham.

One of the problems about being a parent is that you have no idea of the monstrous effect your thoughtless criticism has on your offspring, even if they do shout and answer back (and I didn't). Thanks to Dad I had a complex about being fat until well after the hats he gave me were shapeless wrecks. And yet for him the criticism about my body had probably been largely academic — because his advertising agency handled the Berlei corsetry business and Canterbury clothing account, he was constantly comparing me to the models in the ads. But at the time I struggled valiantly to please, squashing the 'ample New Zealand thighs' he detested so much, into the arrow-narrow skirts he wrote about in his advertising copy. I'm certain he never knew of the effect his cutting remarks had on me and I never really told him — by the time I had worked up the courage he was an old man and it was simply too late. To this day nothing makes me rage more than men making remarks, however innocent, about women's bodies. Even if a man rakes his eyes up and down me in the street I want to hit him. Thanks, Dad.

Looking back, one of the problems with my father was that he adored women, and he did so in a very sexual way that didn't

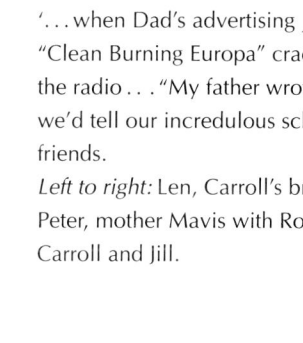

'...when Dad's advertising jingles like "Clean Burning Europa" crackled over the radio... "My father wrote that," we'd tell our incredulous school friends.

Left to right: Len, Carroll's brother, Peter, mother Mavis with Robyn, Carroll and Jill.

mix well with establishing relationships with his daughters. From the time I can remember we were never even allowed down the bathroom end of the house while my father was in the toilet and I never saw him naked. Once, when I opened my parents' bedroom door in the early morning without knocking, I was almost thrown off my feet by his shout of outrage. Although I know he was a sensual man who read and wrote about sex a great deal, we were never allowed to mention it. I remember once pointing out a ram mounting a ewe in the tupping season and getting my head bitten off in reply. Which is probably why I have trouble with public demonstrations of sex to this day.

Len was actually more comfortable treating us like boys. While Mum would mutter darkly that it was 'a man's world', Dad did all in his power to make me one of the boys. Early on he taught me how to hammer a nail straight ('Follow through, follow through!'), fire a shotgun ('Hold it firm against your shoulder so it doesn't kick too hard'), plant a row of silver beet ('Gentle but firm'), ram in a waratah standard, strain a boundary fence, dig a vegetable garden, even dag the sheep with the hand snips. I never did learn how to cook scones. Len would tolerate no 'girlie' behaviour. We were forced to eat everything from tripe and tongue to chukka and quail; the latter riddled with shotgun pellets, after he'd shot them in the wild tussock of Alexandra. And this was after we'd plucked and gutted the tiny birds. By a mixture of example and sneering at people who were timid, he taught me to be adventurous. Later, he insisted that I came and watched him cut the throat of the dog tucker sheep. I only went once.

Once he bought the farm we were all expected to work on it, chopping and spraying gorse, helping with shearing and lambing, driving the tractor. Len hated 'loafers' and anyone who was found sitting down during the day was a loafer. Sometimes I would sneak away and lie under my bed reading by torchlight until I heard him roaring at us to get back to work. Even now I'm uncomfortable reading during the day. I was also entrusted with training Dad's precious dogs — especially Stormy (who was actually only half sheep dog and not aided by instinct). Every day I would spend hours after school teaching Stormy to 'sit', 'stay', and fetch a dummy duck made out of a piece of wood nailed to the wing of some luckless bird he'd shot the season before. In a way I think Dad liked his dogs more than me. They could be, as he put it, 'bested'. They did what they were told:

> *Gypsy*
> Such a gallant little lady
> With her friendly tawny eye!
> Was the true runt of the litter
> But had the biggest heart . . .
> She worked for me because she
> Was in love and it was mutual.
> I taught her that in tussock there
> Are always some sitters after the
> First covey rises before the dogs.

From his vantage point in advertising, Len could see feminism coming. I can remember, when I was eighteen and went to work for him as a copywriter, he was keen to start an all-woman agency to handle fashion, corsetry and food accounts. However, when I became engaged to, horror of horrors, an advertising man ('Don't ever get involved with anyone in the office; advertising people are shockers'), he changed his mind immediately. Without exception Dad hated all our boyfriends. They were 'lounge lizards' and 'Johnny-come-latelys' who were 'full of bunkum'. They had clammy handshakes or bad breath and Len competed with them and hated them to a man.

The day I got married Dad was at his worst. It was all fine on the outside — marquee, food and champagne for 250 people. But for us on the inside watching Dad railing — against the nuptial mass, all that ridiculous kneeling on his bony knees, the cost, my fiancé — it was terrible. When the time came for us to drive off on our honeymoon Dad was nowhere to be found. Then, as we reached the woolshed, he stepped out of the shadows and kissed me, smiling through his tears.

Two years after we were married and I was staying with my parents for a few days, my husband came out for dinner. 'Good Lord,' said Dad, peering out the kitchen window. 'I do believe it's that young Michael Wall come to call on Carroll.' I'd like to think that this meant he loved me best — more than the others — but I know that's not true. He simply refused to acknowledge another man in his life. And he had believed he had more control over me than my more fiery sisters.

By the time I was twenty-eight, with children of my own, Len had relinquished his hold on me. He delighted in small children, and unlike other men of his generation who left it all to the women, he loved feeding and cuddling babies and giving the toddlers rides on the back of the tractor. As always, he especially liked the girls.

Jessica
She looked a picture with
Her straw-blonde hair
Gently blow-waved off her face
Every fingernail gleaming scarlet and
Her young skin radiant
Through the light powder.

'Mother,' she said. 'When I called
Margaret this morning I said
I'd wear the red chiffon
To the party. But I've decided now
To wear the long pale blue taffeta
As it is an evening affair.'
My daughter tells me Jessica
Is very social, has many friends
And attends many functions.
She is very pretty
Very assured and exactly
Eight years old today.

At the age of fifty-five Len retired from advertising and went farming full-time. As with everything else he did he threw himself into the task. Not for Len to limp along with a few motley sheep and a couple of cattle. No. We had the first architect-designed woolshed. The men from Massey University were employed to help Dad get together an elite flock of Perendales — the then-new breed of lean-meat sheep. Within five years the Perendales and Cheviots from my parents' stud, Te Tawaka, were winning prizes at A & P shows around the region. The same fierce energy that Dad had once poured into trout fishing in the Ruamahanga river, was now channeled into his sheep. Len would make me stand in the mucky sheep yards for hours on end discussing the hocks of one ram versus the wool crimp of another. And in the end, by a mixture of talent, browbeating the authorities and sheer determination, he won the coveted purple satin ribbon of supreme champion. I have the ribbon and the photo of 'Bluey', our champion ram, on my dressing table still.

People who tell me I'm competitive didn't know my father. Len took competition to an art form. He would compete with everyone — employees, his daughters (he'd sulk for hours if we beat him at tennis), my mother, other writers, stud breeders — even his grandchildren whom he would challenge to races up and down the swimming pool. He tackled everything with mighty zest. In our garden at Akatarawa he planted over 250 different rhododendrons, nestled among the manuka and native bush, and he knew each one by name. But his favourite was always Grande. This poem was published in the *Listener* in 1981:

Grande 1929
In Sampson's gown shop on Lambton Quay
I saw a black velvet ball-dress, stark
Simple, draped from an antique chair,
The waltz-length skirt stretched lazily on
The floor. At hem centre, a genius
Had placed a glowing flower. Big, white,
Jewelled with orange-scarlet stamen
Tips, from the thirty lucent bells that
Made the clustered whole. I lost breath and
Shyness before the glory of the
Contrast; could the tall dark lady tell
Me the name of the flower in her
Lovely window display? She could, it
was Grande; was it not exquisite?
Exquisite? It changed my life. Ever since
I have been a slave to rhododendrons
To the stark, simple black velvet dress
To graceful, kind and beautiful women.

When, at sixty or so, Len decided to fulfil his lifetime ambition and move to a big high country farm outside Hunterville, I wasn't surprised. Even at that age he seemed so vital — so energetic as he mowed the hay, planted (and made us eat) the swedes for winter feed, drove the tractor with its wheels lifting precariously into the air up the steep bully tracks. The only thing he didn't try to do was ride a horse. 'My haunches are too bony,' he'd complain, and I was invited to come and stay when they needed to muster for shearing or docking.

When I started back at work in 1980 and found my niche at *Metro*, Len was thrilled. I've filed away the letters he wrote me from his third farm — this one in Fielding's 'Ram Alley' — with their mixture of highly informed criticism and comment on my work. His advice was to 'keep on polishing' my copy, the way he polished his poems — sometimes feverishly screwing up half a pad as he wrote draft after draft. Ten years later, Len's energy was still prodigious. He wouldn't, couldn't, lie down. After my mother died he was like an old dog looking for its master. He'd run up to one woman after another, wagging his tail furiously, trying frantically to find another Mavis. As we knew, and he must have known deep down, he never could. But he didn't stop trying. He asked at least three women to marry him over those last, frantic, four years.

After the buffer zone of my mother was removed, my relationship with my father changed completely. For the first time he needed me and my sisters and brother. My sister Jill, the eldest daughter, took over Mum's role. Jill wasn't as submissive as Mum — more like Dad himself — and she 'bested' him the way he'd taught us to 'best' our dogs and ponies. And many fights later a new Len emerged — a smiling sweet old man whose watery eyes lit up when we came into the room.

But I still didn't know him the way others did — crushed as I'd been by his personality, drive and ego. During his funeral my cousin Michael read a tribute from Hugh Spencer, who worked for him at Carlton Carruthers du Chateau back in the fifties when it was a great agency. 'Leonard Leopold du Chateau was the finest advertising man I ever knew,' Hugh wrote. 'The finest not simply for the mastery of the craft of our business, but for what he did for me. Bless his heart, he took me under his wing and with grace, immense style and a wicked sense of humour, taught me how to write. He taught me the joy of good, clever words assembled with grace and style and humour. And in teaching me, induced a lifelong passion for the business. He was a good and gracious and caring man.'

Even now he's dead, I carry Len strutting around in my head. Only now that he's gone and I have near-grown children of my own, with their very own set of faults I've bequeathed to them, I understand what he was up against. But, consciously or subconsciously, I'm still trying to please him. Still trying to remember which rhodo to plant where; not to eat that gleaming cream doughnut for fear of developing 'strainer post' legs;

making sure that 'shockers' are not ripping me off at every turn; never trusting a man with a moustache.

✦ ✦

CARROLL DU CHATEAU was born in Wellington on 7 October, 1944, the third child in a family of four, and was educated at Chilton St James school in Lower Hutt, and later as a boarder at Sacré Coeur convent in Island Bay. The nuns never considered her to have any talent and she stumbled into copywriting at her father's advertising agency while she was waiting to start physiotherapy training in Dunedin.

In 1969 she became Women's Editor of the *Dominion* but her real career in journalism began with *Metro* in 1981. She has won the Jubilee Award for investigative journalism (1986), the Beattie Award for feature writing (1988), the Qantas Award for best feature story of the year (1986 and 1987), and the supreme Beattie award for journalism in 1989, the last time the Beattie Awards were held.

She now has three children: Oliver (21) currently studying art in Florence, Jessica (20), embarking on a BA at Canterbury University, and Ben (11), whom 'I'm valiantly trying to bring up complex-free.' In 1986 she separated from Michael Wall, their father and her husband for twenty years, and reverted to her maiden name, which pleased her competitive father enormously. She now lives on Birkenhead Point with her partner, Stephen Stratford, Ben, and their animals — Abby the springer spaniel and Patrick the cat.

'His delight in animals and nature was the most appealing side of my father's personality.'
Back, from left: Carroll, Jill.
Front: Peter, Robyn. The dogs are Flicker and Twin.

A Christmas Story

Rock-a-bye baby in the tree top
When the wind blows the cradle will rock
When the bough breaks the cradle will fall
Down will come baby, cradle and all.

SHERIDAN KEITH

This piece is taken from Sheridan Keith's first collection of short stories, *Shallow are the Smiles at the Supermarket*, published in 1991 by New Women's Press.

Wellington is a blasted place. The houses cling tenaciously to steep, bushy hillsides and their garages quiver on long rickety wooden legs. At the summit of Mount Victoria twin radio masts are buffeted by the southerly gales that sweep up from the South Pole.

The house overlooks Evans Bay. (Flying boats take off and land there, weather permitting.) The two girls are asleep in their bedroom at the top of the house. The ngaio tree scrapes against the weatherboards and scratches on the glass window panes, but these are familiar noises, they do not interrupt the sleep of the children.

What is unfamiliar, and unnerving and floats about on the surface of Sarah's dream is the knowledge that her mother's bedroom is empty. Her door, usually tight shut, is open. There is no need for her, tonight, to seal off from the adjoining bedroom where the children's father sleeps the excruciating snores that crash like waves on a seashore.

The mother's room is full of art, her paintings, her clay sculptures, her books, her journals. 'Damn fool art,' says her husband. But it is empty of her.

The father's room contains two single beds, one in which he sleeps and snores, the other heaped high with clothes: shirts, business suits, waistcoats, raincoats, overcoats, scarves, trousers, work-shorts, socks, dinner jackets, more socks. You wouldn't believe the heap of clothes he sets down there. Because she refuses to hang his things up.

And between the two beds sits the important black telephone, paid for by the Railways, because their father is high up. His job means he must be on call at any time of the day or night.

The children's mother lies in a hospital bed on the other side of the city, recovering from an operation that has removed her left breast. It is three days now since she came out of the anaesthetic and, alone, moved her hand over her chest to discover the breast was no longer there. She must have cancer, she reasons, otherwise why would they have removed it?

She is in a private room, where Christ on his cross hangs from the wall. This is a Roman Catholic hospital. The nuns still wear fanciful medieval head-dresses reminiscent of the table napkins folded, ready for flight, in exclusive hotel dining rooms.

Because it is Christmas Eve there has been carol singing at the hospital. Because it is Christmas Eve the father has taken the two girls late-night shopping in the city, at the DIC and Kirkcaldies, and for the first time that the girls can remember, he has bought them all Christmas presents.

At the hospital, the Monseigneur, leading the flock of fluttering, worshipping, singing nuns, has offered his ring for the mother, lying in bed swathed in the bandages of surgery, to kiss. And she has refused, saying, quite loudly, loud enough to send an astonished quiver through the feathers of the nuns . . . 'I won't kiss any man's hand, and I don't believe in your God.'

The Monseigneur, detecting a challenge, and something out of the ordinary, says, 'I would like to come and speak with you privately.' But she replies, 'Don't waste your time.'

Is it imagination, or do the nurses take less care when they rebandage her chest? She finds it hard to settle for the night, hard to find a position affording any comfort. The light from the corridor outside shines into her room, illuminating the coloured print of the bleeding heart. She wonders why the images of this religion are so immersed in pain and suffering.

At Kirkcaldies the father has bought the mother a silver brooch with a topaz, in the shape of a Scottish thistle. (The father fainted when the surgeon phoned him to say he had removed the breast. He fell over, a tree toppled.) He has bought his two little daughters identical necklaces, blue windmills painted on china teardrops, slung from thin metal chains.

Sarah wants to cry all the time. She wants to cry at the thought of her father buying her mother a Christmas present. She thinks of all those years her mother had to plead with him before he would agree even to a Christmas tree, set up in a bucket by the fireplace. It is as if she has had to have had a breast removed before he has noticed her.

Sarah thinks it is horrible going late-night shopping with her father. She's never been late-night shopping. They should be in bed. Their father doesn't know how to look after children. He shouts at them to keep up, and then strides off down the street without even looking around to see if they're still there.

He goes from counter to counter in the DIC. It is hard to keep him in sight in the crush of the other last-minute Christmas shoppers. And then, not finding what he wants, he is off, out the swing doors and over the dark road to Kirkcaldies.

Then, when he has chosen it, he asks them if they think their mother will like the brooch he has picked. It is very expensive and he has to get his cheque book out to pay for it. Sarah isn't sure. She knows her mother likes bold, modern things, and this brooch is delicate and fussy. She doesn't think her mother will like it. She wants her mother to be nice to her father, instead of always battering against him, as if her identity depended on beating herself into shape against him.

They wait in the cold wind for the trolley bus to take them home. Then they walk up the zig-zag in the dark, up the side of Mount Victoria. They are so tired they can hardly put their nighties on. They fall into bed, exhausted.

Now they are asleep in the twin beds in the room where their mother and father used to sleep when they were first married. Their father is asleep, and he is snoring. In the hospital on the other side of the city their mother is awake. The wind is whistling through the radio masts on the top of the hill.

In the darkness the important black telephone begins to ring.

It rings and rings and rings, and the two girls dream about bells ringing, and fire engines and earthquakes. Finally the phone rings right through and into the snoring head of the father, and he begins to fumble in the dark to lift the receiver.

Now the children are being shaken awake, roughly, with urgency and fear.

'Get your dressing-gowns on.' Their father seems terribly cross, impatient. 'Bring your pillows, you've got to spend the rest of the night at the Billings.'

The girls are deeply asleep but they do their best.

'You have to stay with the Billings tonight. I have to go into the office. There's been a disaster, the train's gone into the river.'

'Has anyone been killed?' asks Sarah always determined to get the facts.

'Yes, I don't know, it could be a large number . . .'

In the cold, dark, blustery night the two small girls struggle up the gravel path with their father, up on to the road where the southerly winds rush to meet them, flinging their hair back into their faces, and blowing their dressing-gowns apart. They hold on to their pillows as best they can, and push themselves along the road against the wind, and over, on to the other side, right to the corner where the Billings live. Their house is up above the road, up a pathway with steep concrete steps and a thin, cold, metal handrail.

Their father is wondering if the train driver was drunk. After all, it is Christmas Eve.

Mrs Billing puts them into bed when they arrive. The beds are cold, and the sheets slippery nylon. The pink eiderdowns keep falling off on to the floor. Mrs Billing takes her pillows away, and has the girls use their own. Perhaps she thinks they have nits. Their father hurries off into the night.

It is Christmas morning.

Sarah still feels like crying. They have breakfast with the Billings, and their girl Kate, whom they loathe. She is a smug girl who does her piano practice when she is told and belongs to Brownies. She has many Brownie badges neatly embroidered up the sleeve of her uniform.

She unwraps her Christmas presents. A walkie-talkie doll, with a pram for her to sleep in. Lots of other things too: a pretty pink cardigan, a string of artificial pearls, a toy set of pots and pans, a money box in the shape of a big plastic penny, and an ornament from her godmother that she has to put away carefully. It is a ballet dancer and Sarah knows her mother would think it was hideous.

Mrs Billing says they are going to their holiday house at Waikanae, and there won't be enough room for the girls, so she is going to ring around the neighbourhood and find someone who'll have them. Christmas Day!

The O'Neils will. The girls are pleased. Mary O'Neil is their friend, although she is a Catholic and they aren't.

It is fun at the O'Neils'. Everyone is coming to their place for Christmas lunch. Aunts, uncles, cousins, brothers, sisters, and people who are not relations at all, like Susan, the middle-aged lady who has been very ill and has no relatives in the world, and Fred, the liftman at the building where Mr O'Neil works, who has one leg shorter than the other and has to wear a built-up boot.

Mrs O'Neil is a big lady who used to be an opera singer. She even finds a small present each for Sarah and her sister. The two girls, along with Mary, are given the task of setting the tables. There are three tables, so that everyone will be able to sit down and have some roast turkey. First the thick felt mat called the silencer goes on, then the beautiful damask linen cloth, starched and ironed, and over the top a clear plastic sheet to stop the cloth getting spilt on. And in the middle of each table is a plastic bubble filled with water that magnifies one magnificent rose, just beginning to open. The rose is Peace, picked from the garden.

It is hard to fill the round plastic container without trapping a bubble of air that floats to the top and spoils the effect. You have to be careful, and fill the ball absolutely full, and tip it over quickly with the bottom screwed on tight. Then the air bubble will be small and hardly noticeable.

Everyone is arriving and talking and taking off their coats and saying isn't it a terrible disaster, and how awful it is for it to happen at Christmas. The radio is turned on to hear the latest news. The girls huddle up on the floor near the radio to listen.

The announcer is reading a list of names of those people who are missing. The list seems to go on and on. Many of the people were travelling in order to see their loved ones for Christmas. Sarah wants to cry again.

Then Queen Elizabeth gives a speech in a high-up tinkling voice that sounds like glasses being tapped. It is so sad, and formal. Sarah remembers struggling along the road in the dark of night, and thinks about the people who were drowning in the river with the strange Maori name, Tangiwai.

They help dry the dishes, and there are so many of them they seem to be drying forever. Then there is a knock on the door. It is their father, wearing his 'polite to the neighbours' face, but looking worried at the same time. He thanks the O'Neils for having the girls for Christmas dinner. He is going to take them to visit their mother in hospital.

She is propped up in the hospital bed with many cushions behind her back, looking much better. She tells a story of her latest battle with the nuns. They didn't want her to go out onto her balcony and sit in the sun, but she did so anyway. She took a chair, and sat out there with one of the blankets off her bed around her shoulders. Now they are hardly speaking to her.

Sarah looks out the window, past the balcony railings, down into the green gardens. Her father is giving her mother the Christmas present.

He says, 'You couldn't have picked a worse time to be in hospital.'

She doesn't like the brooch. 'I've never liked orange topazes,' she says, 'perhaps I can change it.' Down in the green gardens there are statues of Mary, the mother of God, with the baby Jesus in her arms. Sarah looks at the flower beds, so beautifully cared for, and the peaceful green lawn, trimmed to perfection.

They leave the hospital and walk through the gardens, back to the car. Sarah would like to go right up to the statues and touch them. If she could touch them she knows the cool stillness of the folds of the plaster robe worn by the Virgin Mary would make her feel happy, and if she stood directly under the baby Jesus it might seem as if the Virgin's loving smile was directed towards her as well. But, Sarah reads, she is not permitted to walk on the grass.

✦ ✦

SHERIDAN KEITH was born in Wellington in 1942, and lived in the same house on Mount Victoria for her first twenty-two years. She lived in London for the next ten, where she married and had two sons. She now lives in Auckland, writing full-time.

'In *A Christmas Story* I wanted to put some of my feelings about disaster, both personal and national, into the supposedly Christian environment of Christmas. The girl is feeling especially vulnerable, her mother is seriously ill, her father distracted by other difficulties, which are soon enormously compounded. The hospital presents images of a religion in which suffering is glorified. God is "our Father" and yet his son hangs in agony on the cross. Similarly, the girl's father is out of touch with his children, and the comforts religion might have afforded are seen as circumscribed.'

S u s a n   D e v o y

◆ ◆

When I was young, my father was never home. If he wasn't working or having the customary few pints after work, then he was attending an endless stream of PTA meetings, coaching rugby teams, or, for nearly twenty years, calling Housie for the local school every Thursday night. My father had a real conscience. He was a giver in the community. So I didn't see him that often as I was growing up, and I was under the impression that my mother ruled the roost, and that was a fairly formidable task, considering I had six older brothers. Although I can remember Dad giving us the odd clip across the ears if we went 'beyond the limit', it was generally Mum who dealt with the day-to-day chores, and she dished out the discipline.

My parents worked harder than anyone else I knew so that we kids could have the best of everything, whether it was Catholic schooling (imperative in my father's opinion) or a new cricket bat. I imagine they sacrificed a lot and throughout their lives they may have gone without, but we certainly didn't.

I got to know my father better as I developed into a potentially successful sportswoman. As I became more involved with playing squash, Dad was always there when I competed, never pushing but quietly offering advice and encouragement when needed. At the ripe old age of nine, I played my first tournament. First time up, I received an absolute thrashing. I didn't get a single point. Naturally, I was devastated and after the match, with all the world to see and hear, I burst into tears and became melodramatic. But I'd reckoned without Dad. He took me by the scruff of the neck and delivered a very stern lecture on sportsmanship. I was told in no uncertain terms that if I couldn't lose graciously, then that would be the end of my squash-playing days. On the other side of the court, my opponent was getting similar treatment from her father for not making a game of it by giving me a chance. Result — two very confused budding squash players.

When it became apparent that the only thing I really wanted to do in life was to play squash, my father persisted in trying to get me to become an academic. He wanted more than a sports bum for his only daughter. So I left school. The only problem was that I didn't tell my father. For three weeks I got dressed in my school uniform and hid under the house until he and Mum had gone to work. When I finally plucked up the courage to tell him, he accepted my decision, probably thinking I was going to fall flat on my face, and he would hang around to pick up the pieces. However, he has never had to and, if you asked him now, I know he would undoubtedly claim to be the proudest father on earth.

Of all the qualities I would like to inherit from my father it would have to be his friendliness. He is a kind, gentle man, not afraid to show his emotions, but most of all he is a jovial character who gets great pleasure from making others smile. He is a 'real charmer', and believes in the old adage, 'If you haven't got something good to say about someone, then don't say anything.'

At the local Commercial Travellers' Club in Rotorua he delights in befriending visitors, or for that matter, anyone. And if anyone has kissed the Blarney Stone, it is certainly my father. He could talk the hind leg off a donkey and generally does, if my mother lets him get a word in. I suppose his convivial character must be in his genes. Although very much a Kiwi, he was born in Ireland and emigrated here before his first birthday. As a frequent visitor to Ireland, I can definitely see parallels between the good-natured Irish and my Dad.

Beyond his smile, my Dad is a believer in the work ethic and that has probably been his greatest influence on me. He has a strong sense of duty to his family, his friends, and his community. This has certainly rubbed off on me. I have always worked harder than my peers, and have never forgotten where I came from, or where I belong and who has helped me all along the way.

One of the greatest rewards I've had from success is seeing the pleasure it gives my folks. They are very proud, and not afraid to show their pride and affection towards me for being a wonderful daughter — so they tell me — and for my success in the sports arena. But in the end, for them, my success is a bonus. It's their daughter they care about.

✦ ✦

SUSAN DEVOY grew up in Rotorua the youngest, and only girl, in a family of seven children. She left McKillop College, a Catholic school in Rotorua, early in her seventh-form year and did a variety of jobs (brickie, tea-maker, etc.) until soon after, at the age of seventeen, she was chosen for the New Zealand women's team to play in the world championships in Canada in 1981.

Since then she has played squash as a full-time professional, and is now widely recognised as one of New Zealand's sporting 'greats'. In 1985 she became New Zealand 'Sportsman' of the Year in 1986, 1987 and 1988 she was New Zealand Sportswoman of the Year. Three times she has held the Women's World Squash Championship title, and she has won both the British Open Squash Championship and the Honda New Zealand Open Championship seven times. At twenty-one she was awarded the MBE.

She is a patron of the New Zealand Muscular Dystrophy Society, for which her tireless work has included a 3000-kilometre fundraising walk throughout New Zealand from south to north, which raised more than $300,000.

'My father had a real conscience. He was a giver in the community. So I didn't see him that often as I was growing up, and I was under the impression that my mother ruled the roost...'
Susan Devoy celebrating victory with her father at the world squash championships, Sydney 1990.

Margaret Mahy

• •

THE FAMILY MAN

Sitting here in Governor's Bay so many years after his death, I think about my father. He is always a presence in my life, a domestic spirit too much a part of me to be a ghost, but on this occasion I think about him because I am contributing to a book about fathers and daughters, and have to think about what I can accurately tell.

I knew my father well, but in a specialised way. It is surprising how much there is that I don't know about him, and how much I have to rely on anecdote and guesswork to get any idea of the total man. Because I loved him so much, I have mythologised him (I am tribal to that extent). The intense affection with which I remember him is a truth so personal that it is unlikely to survive any attempt to make it part of public record, and there are other complications too, when it comes to giving a true account. Any article on father-daughter relationships artificially excludes a mother, yet I find my mother refuses to be excluded. My father was the man he was to me, partly because of the way he was to my mother, and partly because of the way she talked about him. My parents refuse to be divided. Though isolating one relationship from others can be a useful device, one must always allow for the way that the device twists truth, and my relationship with my mother was always part of my relationship with my father and vice versa.

Well, he was about forty when I was born. He was the oldest of six brothers and a sister, only two of whom were born in New Zealand. The first five children of this family, all boys, were born in Bristol in England. But the possibility of emigration smouldered for years in my grandfather's imagination, and finally burst into full flame. Indeed I was once told that my grandparents were about to emigrate to South Africa when my grandmother became pregnant with her fifth child. They postponed their emigration until after the child had been born, then tossed a coin and came to New Zealand instead.

Lucky me!

I think they saw emigration and literacy as part of what we would now call upward mobility. Not only that; my grandfather was a reader, vulnerable to the insidious suggestions of stories, during the heyday of tales which featured British boy colonists making the world their own.

The Mahys of Whakatane were a close family, though I am not sure how loving they were. They were certainly fond of each other, and extremely loyal to the idea of family. Pride was part of our view of ourselves, and it was simply and mysteriously invested in what we *were* . . . a diverse group of people with the same name, a name that apparently we pronounce differently from the way it is pronounced in Guernsey where it is quite common. I believe it may be French, not British in origin. It is quite possible we grew up pronouncing it wrongly, but it is too late to worry about that now.

My father and his brothers became tradesmen, never turning down work if they could possibly avoid it. I am the same. Working life was partly a necessary game my father's family played with the world, and, by now, I play it too. I was *taught* to play it. An aunt on my mother's side of the family says, 'The Mahys were always workaholics,' with an edge of impatience, if not scorn, in her voice. On the other hand, if one has to be addicted to something, work is not such a terrible thing to be addicted to.

At the age of forty I think my father loved being a father. I think he was prepared for it in many ways. Prepared, too, to be a good husband. His family was his fulfilment. My mother was a young teacher during the depression of the thirties. She took the first job that became available . . . in Awakeri, close to Whakatane and far from Christchurch, her home. Some criticism was made of the Mahy family by someone in the Awakeri family she boarded with: 'Say what you like about those Mahy boys, they make excellent husbands,' my mother's landlady responded.

One can't help wondering if that first comment, obviously remembered over many years, did not help to focus her attention on my father who was not the husband the more genteel and cultured Christchurch Penlingtons would have chosen for their daughter. 'The name Mahy sounded Irish,' an aunt once said to me, 'and of course we were frightened the family might be *Roman Catholic*.' Apart altogether from the papist threat, my mother's parents would have hoped for a professional husband for their daughter . . . somebody with a secondary school education at least.

My father had attended school until what would be more or less Form Three today. He was a self-taught bridge builder by trade. Well, perhaps I am exaggerating when I say 'self-taught.' Along with one of his brothers, my father had worked with a master builder on one or two small bridges, before branching out on his own. Times were hard, but my father worked strenuously, and was able, in due course, to offer support to members of my mother's family during the Depression. From my point of view this too is part of a romantic story . . . a vindication of my mother's choice, and, indirectly, of my own existence. The intellectual came to depend on the tradesman in the end. (The ways in which the tradesman depends on the intellectual are powerful too, but harder to define and not part of this essay.)

My mother, according to the custom of the time, had to give up her work as a teacher when she married. Still, my father had given her land in her own right when they were first engaged. 'It shows how he trusted me,' she said. She had various oblique ways of suggesting that she and my father had an extremely happy sex life, though it was also intensely private. Neither of them would like to think that I was sitting here recalling these things in public. But writers are essentially treacherous and I am being a writer as well as a daughter. My father is dead, my mother, due to Alzheimer's disease, cannot remember anything much, indeed rarely speaks of her astonishing marriage. It lives more in my memory now than it does in hers.

My aunt would never let me quote my parent's marriage as an example of real life, even though their happiness was every bit as real as any dissatisfaction or misery. Real life, apparently, has a statistical component. 'You can't quote your parents . . . they were an exception,' my aunt used to say to me, again with that edge of impatience, tired of my adolescent invoking of my parents' love for each other. 'Of course I love you children,' my mother once said to me, 'but it's nothing like the love I feel for your father.' So saying, she set me free to leave home and parents behind in due course, and to launch myself into the world without looking back, safe in the knowledge that father and mother had each other.

My aunt was right to caution me. What I took for the essential nature of the world when I was a child proved to be a sort of abberration. I thought all fathers must be family men (naturally!) and all husbands must be domestic (of course!). My sisters and my brother and I all agree that our parents' happiness, that great initial blessing, distorted all our expectations of what the world was like. We were shown an unusually happy relationship as if it were commonplace, and instructed by living example every day of our childish lives to expect the same thing for ourselves.

Some ferocious hope!

In a variety of ways all five of us have suffered because of our great blessing, and have sometimes imposed suffering on others through our single-minded expectations. However, discovering that family life is more fallible than we had been led to suppose, has not been able to erode the effects of the blessing. It has sometimes made us strong at times when it would have been luxury to subside into some legitimate weakness.

My father and I began our relationship sometime in 1935 when I was conceived. I have his name and a version of his nose, my nose now! Later my mother would say, 'You've got your father's tolerance.'

Is it possible to inherit this sort of thing? My cast of thought seems to me to have things in common with my father's, which may be because of the example he set me during my formative years. Yet it also seems to me that arguments emphasising the power of example cannot totally explain why some of the things my father said came to me, not as commonly received wisdom, but as the delineation of truths that had always been part of me. Once they were articulated I didn't so much learn them as recognise them. During the Second World War, though he was as anxious for our success as any patriotic New Zealander, I remember my father pointing out to me that the Germans and Japanese were not monsters, but people with approximately the same fears as ourselves, and probably as certain that God and Right were on *their* side. As he argued this, I felt an inner eye open within me . . . I felt a great ease as I embraced an attitude at variance with everything else that was being publicly said at the time.

My father was a reader. He loved good stories of all kinds and was touched by the beauty of words. He made up stories for me when I was small, and read to me as well . . . books that had been his favourites when he was a boy . . . so that, along with *Seven Little Australians* and *Anne of Green Gables* which my mother read to me, I had Ballantyne, Marryat and Rider Haggard . . . adventure stories in which heroes grappled directly with life and death, with danger and destruction. He read me the Australian balladeers, Banjo Patterson and C. J. Dennis, and was able to quote poems and pieces of narrative ballads by heart. I think he responded to a certain quality of inevitability in a well-told rhyming story.

I don't think my father read as much to younger members of the family as he did to me. His bridge-building business took more and more of his time as it expanded. He grew older and more tired in the evenings, and perhaps, though being a father was a great pleasure to him, it lost its novelty.

It is customary for my mother's family to suggest that my interest in writing was inherited as a genetic package from my maternal grandfather. He certainly wrote amusing verse and he wrote me a wonderful letter the day I was born. I have it still. It is in a drawer beside my word processor. For all I know writing is a skill that can be inherited. Yet my father's voice is the voice of story for me. Re-reading my first published book *A Lion in the Meadow*, after it had been out and about in the world for a few years, I found myself remembering something I had forgotten at the time of writing . . . the beginning of a story my father had told me repeatedly when I was three years old. 'Once upon a time there was a great big black-maned Abyssinian lion.' Once I had remembered that opening, it immediately seemed that the first story I had ever been told had lived on secretly in me to become the first book I had ever published, and that it was the same lion in both tales. I can remember watching my father as he recited *The Lay of the Nancy Belle*, by W. S. Gilbert, and being fascinated, not only by the story, but by the example of someone *containing* a story. Without books or print of any kind in front of him, he was bringing a tale out of himself, surrendering to the necessity of the story as he did so.

But three and a half years of his full attention also included punishments which could be severe. I was told, afterwards, that he had a theory that, if you beat a child for being naughty once, it would never be necessary to beat it again . . . at least not for the same offence. He also believed that if the oldest child in a family was taught to behave, the younger ones would tend to follow suit. It isn't necessarily true. I remember painful and frightening punishments on various occasions, and I remember once that he cried out passionately, 'I'd rather hit myself that hit you,' and struck himself across the arm several times. This had a profound effect on me. Once again he seemed to show me a dilemma which had no ultimate solution.

It is worth mentioning that one of my sisters says, though she loved our father, she was also rather frightened of him. I certainly feared his anger, but I was not frightened of him in himself. I suspect that being the first child gave me an advantage, and perhaps being a girl gave me an advantage too.

In due course my father was certainly vulnerable to suggestions that a single boy, brought up among a family of sisters, might become a 'sissy.' My father could be unduly hard on my brother, an essentially gentle and sensitive little boy, simply because he wanted to make a man of him. Even the happiest family life is also full of terrible dangers because members of a family are so varied, yet live so closely that they become the victims of one another's limitations. Of course we siblings still talk about the injustices that haunted our childhoods along with the pleasures that blessed them, and wonder what injustices we have inflicted in turn, on our own children as blindly as our parents inflicted them on us.

At the same time, we recognise that we children were set free from the stereotypical roles in a way we all took entirely for granted, and the edges of our controlled suburban life were eroded by all sorts of oddities.

My father worked long hours building his bridges, but after work, he would come home and take his children down to the river to go swimming, or off to play tennis, giving my mother a little time on her own, probably to get dinner ready. In the weekend, during the right season, he would help with the jam-making and the bottling. On the other hand my mother would regularly work on the accounts of my father's business, page after page of entries in her wonderfully neat clear handwriting. I cannot remember a time when my father's handwriting was not a little shaky.

Later there were times, as I grew older, when he was irritated by some of my more eccentric ways. Talking to oneself is acceptable in a small child, but when I didn't grow out of it I know he was embarrassed from time to time. He was also a little humiliated when, as an adolescent, I persisted in gathering and selling beer bottles after the dances held at Ohope at Christmas and New Year. Still on the whole he put up with the oddity of my behaviour fairly well, and even told me that it was a good thing to be different from other people. This was both good and bad advice, comforting to an eccentric aged about twelve, but tending to promote eccentric behaviour for its own sake. For the rest, my father wanted me (he wanted all his children) to be polite, thoughtful towards others, helpful around the home and to my mother in particular, and to do well at school. At one stage he offered me a shilling for every poem I wrote, but I remember feeling bemused by this offer, and I certainly did not clean up any sort of a fortune. The verses I wrote came and went in a random way, and I didn't show the commercial enterprise I think he half expected of me. I made more selling beer bottles. Still, whenever I had anything in print, my father was thrilled with me and his pleasure added to my own.

My father was nursed devotedly by my mother over the last years of his life, becoming increasingly debilitated by his illness. At last he died. He was the product of a particular family and a particular time . . . formidable, enormously loving, but, by now, mysterious too. I have contained at least part of him not only genetically, but philosophically fulfilling some of his virtues and repeating some of his mistakes.

Ridden hard by Parkinson's disease and attendant respiratory problems he was put into the ambulance on his last trip to hospital. He looked at the nurse, smiled as well as he could and said, 'I expect you're frightened to be left alone with me.' It might not be the last thing he said, but it is the last that was reported to me.

He joked to the end, and I hope I am his daughter to the extent that I do too.

'. . . arguments emphasising the power of example cannot totally explain why some of the things my father said came to me, not as commonly received wisdom, but as the delineation of truths that had always been part of me.'
Photo: Foster/Icon

✦ ✦

MARGARET MAHY is known internationally for her writing. She lives in Lyttelton, surrounded by cats, a large garden and thousands of books. She has two grown-up children and a grandchild.

Margaret Mahy has written numerous children's stories, including the classic *Lion in the Meadow,* which she mentions in this piece. She has also written collections of short stories and teenage novels which have won international awards including the Carnegie Medal in 1982 and 1984 and the prestigious Esther Glen Award four times. In 1986 she won the IBBY Honour Book Award and in 1987 the British *Observer* Teenage Fiction Award.

The First Land

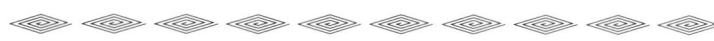

My father
built a reservoir
somewhere in the north; there
cool plump frogs and I spoke
a language that only creatures
and lonely children know.

That sacred
plot of first-owned land
was ringed with gum trees stark
skeletal white limbs clothed
in tarnished silver green ghosts
of all other trees

that have shaken before gales and
when high wind spiked branch on branch
I stood beneath and said
aloud 'if it spears me
and I die then it was meant to be.'

But when the rains came rattling
the empty water tanks
and a rime of tropical
green appeared on the cracked earth
I opened my mouth
and drank the rain.

FIONA KIDMAN

F I O N A   K I D M A N is one of New Zealand's best known writers. She has published four books of poetry: *Honey and Bitters*, *On the Tightrope*, *Going to the Chathams* and most recently, *Wakeful Nights*. Her five novels are *A Breed of Women*, *Mandarin Summer*, *Paddy's Puzzle*, *The Book of Secrets* and *True Stars*. She has also published two short story collections: *Mrs Dixon and Friend* and *Unsuitable Friends*. A non-fiction title, *Gone North*, has also been published.

'My father, Hugh Eric Eakin, died two days after the birth of my first grandchild, in the same hospital. Despite pleas to the hospital on the last afternoon of his life, he died without seeing his great-granddaughter. The events of that weekend still burden me. Yet, curiously, they stand as a kind of an epitaph — his timing was bad.

'At first I thought that his most important legacy was his water colours, painted and exhibited in the later part of his life. Lately, I have come to realise that my mannerisms, way of talking, and some of the ways I think, are a reflection of him. When he was alive, we were locked in combat for so much of the time that I couldn't see this. He seemed like a unique specimen; he had only two known relatives in the world, and I hadn't met them.

'An excerpt from Fiona Kidman's fiction piece, 'At the Lake So Blue', can be found on page 145.

'Lately, I have come to realise that my mannerisms, way of talking, and some of the ways I think are a reflection of him.'
Fiona Kidman with her father, Hugh Eakin.

Mutuwhenua The Moon Sleeps

PATRICIA GRACE

Mutuwhenua, The Moon Sleeps, the novel from which these excerpts are taken, was published in 1978 by Longman Paul, and has recently been reprinted by The Women's Press in Britain.

After my mother had grown used to the idea of my getting married she began to enjoy all the preparation and organising for my wedding. She wanted everything to be right. We bought material which I took to a dressmaker in town to make up for Lena and me. She made bookings with the photographer and florists and arrangements for the cleaning and decoration of our church and dining-hall.

My father was busy too, but I'd never seen him so quiet. It was almost as though he had hidden his real self away and left a silent stranger in his place, coming and going, eating and sleeping. It was a new mood, this quiet one, that didn't sulk or shout, cry or laugh or stamp about. One I didn't know.

'What's the matter with my Dad?' I asked one day, and he sat quiet for so long I thought he wouldn't answer me at all.

'It's all this wedding business,' he said, and was silent again.

'It's too much trouble and all that?'

'Nothing's too much trouble for my girl.'

'What then?'

'You don't know what it's like yet. To be married. Away from home.' He put his arm round me. 'It's our fault, Mum's and mine. We've kept you too close to us. You might not be ready to leave. Perhaps you and Graeme might be more different from each other than either of you can tell.'

It startled me for a moment to hear my own fear spill out into the room on my father's voice. And something made me think just then of the stone we had found, that was buried now at the bottom of a deep gully not far away. I felt a touch of stone on me, but not too coldly. Hold it a while and soon it warms, taking life and warmth from you.

'But you let us marry. You want it.'

'You'll need someone else one day. And I know he loves you very much. He's proved that to me; he has a lot of strength in him.'

I had always wanted to tell Graeme about the stone, which I call a stone to give less meaning, to simplify feeling. But I was afraid of what I might come to know about him and me, of what there could be between us, what differences. I have put many things aside over the past few years but the stone remains with me. The stone and the people do not let me forget who I am although I have wanted to many times.

'And it's your Nanny,' my father said. 'She doesn't like it. She won't come, you'll have to be prepared for that, Baby. And she blames me of course.'

Ripeka was the other name they gave me, after her.

'No doubt you are a good-looking young man,' Nanny Ripeka had said to Graeme. 'But my grand-daughter should marry a Maori.'

'But I love her,' he said. 'No one can love her more than I do.'

'You know nothing,' she replied. 'Love? Love is what you're born with and what you know. You think you know this girl but what do you know? What's wrong with a Pakeha girl for you?'

Then Nanny Ripeka had turned to me and said, 'You're as bad as that cousin of yours. Never mind the Maori; he must marry a Pakeha. Both of you just want your children to have fair skin because you think that's better. You care nothing for your own people.'

And I got angry with her, and not for the first time. I was crying, and wanting to shout, to try to make her understand; crying because there was nothing I could say that would make any difference to what Nanny believed. And I thought on the way home how glad I would be to marry Graeme and get away from Nanny Ripeka and all her cranky ideas.

'What's wrong with her?' my father asked Graeme when we arrived home.

'The old lady . . . said things,' Graeme said.

Then I sat down and told my mother and father what had happened. I was still crying. 'Well, your Nanny's old now,' my father said. 'And you can't make anything any different by being angry with her.'

'She doesn't have to say those things.' But my father didn't
answer me. 'Well, does she? I suppose you agree with her. You
think she's right.'

'I'm glad you're marrying Graeme,' my father said. 'He's a
good boy and he loves you.'

'What's wrong with you? Can't you give a straightout
answer any more?' It was as though Graeme wasn't there.

'There's some truth in what the old lady says,' my father
said. 'But you have to live a long time before you know it.'

My mother put her arms round me but I pushed her away.

'Let's go,' I said to Graeme. He had been sitting away from
us, and for the first time I disliked his quietness and calm.

'Where to?' he asked.

'Anywhere. I want to get out of here.'

I heard him say to my father, 'We'll drive round for an hour,
then I'll bring her back.' I was angered by Graeme's quiet
acceptance. 'None of you will listen,' I said as I went to the door.
'Nanny Ripeka can say anything she likes, and because she's old
you think she's right.'

We drove in silence for some time before Graeme said, 'Don't
worry, Linda. Don't worry about what she said. We're strong
enough you and I.' 'I'm not,' I said. 'I'm not strong at all.' And I
was still upset. But it was fear, I think, about what she'd said,
rather than anger. 'Then I'm strong enough for both of us,' he
said. 'Don't be unhappy. Your old man is the one who realises
the strength I have in me.'

I thought quietly for some time, wondering about what he
had said to me. And quite suddenly I felt a longing for him,
which was not by then a new feeling but only a new intensity. I
could feel my skin tight across my body and longed to be
comforted by him and to feel his strength surge through me. He
looked at me and put out an arm to draw me close to him, but we
drove homewards. His body was hard against mine.

. . .

The macrocarpa was called Papa Rakau because it was the big old
one, father of the others. And it had a long arm reaching out over

the track which was called Leaping Branch because you could tip it with your fingers if you were tall enough — if you could stretch up far enough, running and leaping the short cut home.

There was a time when I was too small to tip the over-hanging branch, and because I couldn't reach I'd yell and cry so that my cousins would have to lift me, pleading with me to be quiet because they would be in trouble with my father if they made me cry.

Then one summer day I'd reached it on my own. One day I was tall enough to very lightly touch the drooping tip; and soon I could touch it easily. Fingertips first and then the whole hand. Then both hands at once. And, later, two hands gripping even the highest part of the branch hand over hand, swinging, slipping down the bending green fronds.

It was summer too when Graeme and I first met. After the road went through — that was not long after the incident with the stone — other things began to happen as well. Before that time the place we lived in was a quiet and forgotten valley at the end of an old metalled road. Then after a short time we had shops nearby and a garage and football grounds and tennis courts. I was at the courts with Harry, Sonny and Lena when Toki arrived, bringing Graeme with him. I was nineteen.

It was not very often we had visitors to our club because in many ways we were still a forgotten valley.

We hadn't seen Toki for some months because he had been away working in the city. It was good to have him back again and I remember that I was wanting a chance to talk to him about all the things he'd done while he was away. I envied him. I thought it would be exciting to come and go the way he did, and thought, if I'd been the son my father had always hoped for, things might have been different. But being a girl and the only child . . . and Dad being Dad . . . some things I couldn't have merely for the asking, not even from my father.

'What do you want to leave here for?' my father had asked. 'You can get a good job in town, or if you like you can stay home with your mother, but there's plenty of good work in town.'

'But I want to do something different,' I'd argued vaguely. 'Be someone different.'

So I'd cried and sulked about for a few days but my father didn't give in to me in the way he usually did — and perhaps I was secretly glad, remembering the other time. Instead he'd gone into town and found office work for me, which I quite liked after all, but I had the feeling I would like to do more and know more, and I wanted to *be* different.

The office was opposite the library and I went there nearly every afternoon after work to fill in time until the bus arrived. I would get some books to take home with me. And that's about all I did after I left school. I went to work, read, played tennis or netball, and helped my mother about the house. Or I went to the pictures or a social with my cousins, wondering often if this was enough for me.

There were other things I could have done but which I had stopped doing long before, at about the time when I'd first run along the track under the branch, knowing it to be there above me and yet *not* leaping to touch it. For the first time not looking up but running with eyes down, watching the track roll back under my pounding feet.

. . .

The ti kouka is a tree with nothing hidden. It has a straight trunk, difficult to climb and with no secrets once you have levered your way up the abrasive bole. There is nowhere to hide among the upward-snaking limbs or the green tousles of heads, although long ago there had been new shoots to collect for addition to the pot, and stringy fibre with which to make nooses for the pigeon's head.

My father is a man with nothing hidden. When I introduced Graeme to him I knew he would have something to say and that whatever it was would not be said with gentleness and tact. 'You want to take my girl to the pictures,' he said.

'Yes.'

'What for?'

Graeme didn't know what to answer to such a question. 'Well . . .' he said after a long moment. 'Well, I would like to . . .'

I couldn't look at either of them. I was suffering, knowing there was worse to come.

'All right,' my father said. 'All right. But you keep your hands off. You fool around with my girl and I'll boot your head.'

'Dad!'

'Dad nothing. He might as well know.'

So I said no more although I was angry with him. I went quickly in case there was more to come.

I didn't enjoy myself that evening and could hardly speak to Graeme. I kept wondering what he thought of us, of me; it mattered a lot to me.

My father usually went to bed before ten, but when we arrived home after the pictures that night he and my mother were in the kitchen having a cup of tea. My mother got out cups for Graeme and me and I put some cake on a plate. I could tell my mother liked Graeme, and she asked us about the film and tried to make conversation, tried her best to show Graeme that he was welcome at our place. But my father went off to bed in a sulk because there was nothing he could growl about.

What my father didn't realise then was that, although I had reminded them often that I was nineteen (as though nineteen held the world), I was really very much younger than that in many ways. But when I tried to explain this to him the next morning he didn't seem to understand. 'I don't want anyone to hurt you,' he kept on saying. 'And anyway it's not you I don't trust, Baby, it's these blokes. Especially these Pakehas. You should hear them talk. They talk different from us — and they think our girls are a pushover.'

'Dad you shouldn't…they're not all the same. You don't like it when they stick labels on *us*.' He looked puzzled. 'I won't let anyone hurt you,' he said. There's only one thing they want, and once they've got it that's the last you see of them.'

· · ·

. . . Graeme got off the bus at our place and I asked him to come inside and say hallo to my mother. And there I was again, hoping the bench was tidy, hoping my mother looked all right and had her bottom plate in.

She had on a pair of old shorts and one of my father's shirts. Her bottom plate was in a glass on the window-sill and she was making pickle. When we went in she was pouring melted wax into the necks of jars to seal them, and the kitchen stank.

'I helped my mother with her pickle this morning,' Graeme said.

'What did you put in yours?' my mother asked. She was letting Graeme know he was welcome at our place. And Graeme started to tell her — beans, carrots, onions, cauliflower, tomatoes. 'Green,' he said as though he was surprised. 'Green tomatoes.' My mother said that she thought Graeme's pickle must be the same as hers. I don't know why this made me feel so glad.

We talked about the pickle for a while, then I walked back to the gate with Graeme.

'I go on Sunday,' he said. I didn't want to think about it. 'Tonight there's a film on. Will you come with me?'

'There's no bus tonight . . . ' He noticed my hesitation.

'I can have the car.' I wondered what to say. I hated my father and his stuffy ideas, and Graeme, waiting and puzzled, thinking it ended here. I knew I had to say something.

'It's him,' I said, my voice beginning to squeak. 'My father. I don't know if he'll agree . . . with you . . . in the car.' I wanted to say more to him, to explain, but my voice had gone. 'He's funny, got mad ideas,' I mumbled.

'Is that what it is?' Graeme said.

'Yes.' I was happier than I can say to see him look relieved. He kissed my cheek. 'Find out,' he said. 'I'll ring tomorrow.' He looked happy.

We were having tea that night and I was trying to make up my mind what I should say to my father when he said, 'I know that boy's old man.'

'Which boy?' — glad that I wouldn't have to break a silence to get to what I wanted to ask.

'That one you took off with the other day' — letting me know, reminding me. 'His father works with me.' All right so far.

'Not a bad sort of Pakeha.'

'Dad!' I wasn't able to let it go.

'Dad what?'

'What do you expect?'

'You can't trust them.' He was telling me again. 'Apart from one or two.'

I wanted to keep the peace and wait for the right moment, so I said no more. 'They have to prove themselves to me before I'll trust them,' he said.

He was in one of his touchy moods and I half expected him to begin on his old groans about land and about our kai being put into tins and them selling it to their brothers overseas, but he said no more. There was no doubt, however, that he was in one of his funny moods so I waited a while before I said anything.

'She's nineteen, Daddy' my mother was saying. 'Don't you see?'

But I wasn't running round anywhere in the middle of the night, in anyone's car, with anyone, according to my father. Nineteen or not. No matter how much I yelled and banged the doors.

'Never mind, Linda, we'll work on it,' was all Graeme said when I told him over the phone.

I couldn't sleep that night, being unable to get past my anger with my father and hating myself for being too old to sneak out and too young to walk out, yet still the right age for yelling and slamming doors.

There was no escape for me from the closeness of my family or from the place that had my footsteps on every stone and my touch on every tree. My shadow falling, no matter how lightly, across every path and stretch of creek bank and bed…

· · ·

After work the next day Graeme came into the library with me. Usually I took a quiet pleasure in reading the spines as I dawdled about among the neatly laid out shelves and the faded smell of books. But that day titles had become liquid and were running idiotically together. I chose two books at random and went to the desk to fill out the cards.

Graeme was sitting at a table looking through a book about cricket, and I thought that there must be hundreds of things that I didn't know about him. Cricket. Tennis. What else did he do, enjoy? Had he ever made his escape, and from what, in amongst the turning pages?

In a few more days he'd be gone.

On the way home we talked about the books we had read, and discovered much in common, so that my former mood was soon dissolved. I began to feel elated.

We sat in the car outside our gate surrounded by the words that tumbled about us. And perhaps it was the sound of Graeme and me laughing that put my father in a temper. I hadn't noticed his car turn in.

'There's your house,' he shouted, flinging his arm, revving his engine, as Graeme moved his car out of the way. But despite my father's anger I could only feel elated, and I was used to my father's tempers after all. There'd be no more shouting from me.

Graeme and I followed the cloud of dust up to the house and when we got there my father was shouting at my mother, wanting to know why she hadn't gone out and told us to come in. 'There was no harm,' she said. She was untroubled by my father's raving, and now I was too, even with Graeme there. 'Next time you know what to do,' he said to Graeme. 'I won't have her sitting round in cars or driving round anywhere with any of you blokes, so remember.'

But the only words that were important to me of those my father had said were 'next time'. 'Next time you know what to do.'

Later that evening I wanted to say something to my father. I was sorry for the way he felt and I wanted to say something — quietly — to him, but I didn't know what to say. So I put my books away and sat quietly with them both until it was time to go to bed.

. . .

'. . . Don't hit me, darling. Just kiss me sweetly like you did that time under the apple tree.'

'You liar.'

'Did you kiss him under the apple tree, Mum?'

'Don't listen; he's lying.'

'After the pictures on Saturdays I used to take her home on the bike. They lived the other direction from town, down the main road. You've seen the old place. I'd take her home on my bike, then we'd wait down at the bus stop so her father wouldn't know she hadn't come home in the bus. Then when the bus arrived we'd walk along with the others. There was an apple tree not far from her place, and I'd leave her there and go back down the road to where my bike was.

'Well, one night we got so interested in our kissing that your mother forgot to let go of me. Don't hit me, dear, you know I'm telling the truth. Then suddenly her old man was there, don't know how, but there he was. He broke my nose first, then he kicked his boot so far up that it hit my backbone. I had to lay down for an hour before I could move enough to get myself home.'

'But you went back again?'

'The next day. Your Auntie Heni and the others they all laughed at me the next morning because they guessed what had happened. And I was wild. For a while. Then I had to admit to myself that I deserved all I got. And I made up my mind I'd marry your mother.

'You know what I did then? I put on this white shirt that I'd bought for Heni and Tom's wedding, and I didn't want to wear the bow-tie so I sneaked into the old man's wardrobe and got out his black tie that he wore to funerals. I polished my shoes up and combed my hair. Then I put a cap on so my hair would stay neat and tucked my trouser legs in my socks and went off to her place on my bike.

'I roared up their road, revving as loud as I could, then I got off, took the trouser legs out of the socks, straightened the old tie, and took the cap off and patted the hairdo. Your grandfather and your mother's two brothers were in the back garden hoeing. And I knew her brothers were laughing at me but I walked, or limped, over to where the old man was . . . He was a lovely talker the old man. I wish you'd known your other grandfather, Baby. He had a quiet voice, you know, and a way of saying. Leant on his hoe and looked at me. "Back for more," he said. "And already dressed up for your own tangi I see." Your uncles were splitting their sides. "I want to marry your daughter," I said. I didn't like to say your mother's name so I said "your daughter". Well, the old man just looked at the ground and kept on hoeing, and your uncles looked as though they needed a pee. "Get him a hoe," he said to one of them. And when we'd weeded half the garden he said, "What for? What have you been up to with my girl?"

'"Only what you saw," I said. So we kept on with the weeding. He was hoeing fast and it wasn't easy keeping up with him because of my sore back and my nose almost covering one eye. "Give me a good reason," he said. Your uncles were hoeing fast too so they could keep listening, to see what else there was to laugh at.

'At first I was going to say, "because I love her", like they do in the pictures, but I thought he would laugh at that. I kept weeding along the rows thinking of a good reason. Trying to sort out my reasons. And all I could think of was her and me the night before under the apple tree kissing and forgetting to stop, and her forgetting to let go of me. Then I said, "Because I want to get along a bit better than what you saw" — thinking what other reason could there be; if he's going to hit me he'll hit me now. Your uncles stopped work and waited for the excitement. The old man stopped hoeing and looked at me for a while. Then he said, "It's more than a bike you've got between your legs then."'

My father stopped talking and was quiet. After a while he said again, 'I wish you'd known him, Baby. I've never felt prouder than when he said that. He was letting me know he thought I had guts — balls you might well say. Your uncles thought he was telling me I was randy and they were waiting for the connection — his fist, my face. But I understood. We always understood each other your grandfather and I.

'When he finished the hoeing we went inside. Your Mum and your grandmother were cooking a feed. And when we were all sitting down at the table he nodded his head towards me and said, "This one wants to marry our girl." Your mother wouldn't look at me and no one spoke for a long time. Then your grandmother said, "There's nothing against it, and she's old enough."

'Your grandfather asked Mum if she wanted to marry me. You know what she said? She said, "I suppose so."'

'Well, I thought it would stop him pinching things off me and being a nuisance, and I could give him a hiding whenever I wanted to.'

'"You bring your old man and old lady over one day soon and we'll talk," he said. That's how it was done in those days.'

There was a question that I wanted to ask my father but he went on. 'When I told your Grandpa and Nanny they talked about it together and said they would visit your mother's place. They said there was nothing against it. And your Mum and I were married not long after that.'

'And we'll get divorced in a minute if you don't get away from the table. They'll be here in carloads soon. This isn't an ordinary week-end you know.'

'And only one little girl to show for it. Had to wait ten years . . . for our girl.'

'Easter. All your relations will be here any minute . . .'

'Your Mum, she's been growling ever since. I don't know why I married your Mum. . .'

'Any minute. Yelling the place down . . .'

'I knew I should've married that beauty queen.'

'You should've too.'

'Plenty of money that girl.'

I was pleased to hear them bickering at each other even though there was a question I wanted to ask my father. 'This boy Graeme, he'll be coming to see you. Well, I don't mind; things are different these days. As long as he's good to you, that's all.'
Easter passed the way it usually did at our house, with people calling in, passing through, or staying. That Friday it rained and a bladed wind cut through the gully in long swipes, yet it was warm enough. I was warm.

Auntie Pare and Uncle Hemi were the first to arrive, shaking off drops of rain, stamping away the cold, and complaining that the weather wasn't too good, brother, sis, for the time of year.

But warm inside with the walls and ceilings beginning to sound and the pots on to simmer, huffing steam as Auntie Pare lifted the lids to pry. 'Fruit-cake, Linda. I say, your Mum's fruit-cake. I know the right time to come.' And in the deep-freeze. 'I say, I knew you'd have eel and water-cress frozen, and fish-heads and paua and corn. We brought some crayfish with us, six big ones, fresh cooked yesterday in our big pot. Put a couple in here in your deep-freeze, and put the rest on the table for when those others come. I say, you know what Lena told me in her letter?'

'Yes, I know, Auntie. He'll be here later.' For you to look at, I thought, pry at — I sa-ay.

'It's true what our niece wrote to me then? That's what I came for. And to see all of you of course, and help with the digging of course. But it's true, ay? I say, what does your Dad...'

'He hasn't given him a black eye yet. Hasn't turned him out.'

'I sa-ay. But your Daddy's not looking so well; he better keep his hands down now, Linda. He's a bit skinny you think. And quiet.'

'He hasn't done much yelling lately. Nor have I.'

'You? You're a young woman now. And a boy-friend, I sa-ay. I didn't think he'd ever let you have any boy-friend let alone a... Oh I sa-ay, I bet you old Ripeka don't know.'

'She knows but I think I'll keep out of her way for a while.'

'That's right; you keep out of her way. They don't understand, these old ones. It was hard enough in our day to know who. And to know there was nothing against . . . Unless you knew all the old things, then there was no way for you . . . until the old people got their tongues going and told you everything. And sometimes it was too late by then and they blamed you. My sister who was brought up by an old auntie on our mother's side, she married a second cousin and didn't even know they were related. They don't like that, the old ones; then they blame you.'

'Nanny Ripeka and Dad, they do tell us the old things, every chance they get.'

'Yes, they're fussy about those things. That's why I thought Lena's letter...Oh I sa-ay . . . But who else? Who else is there?'

It was the question I had wanted an answer to, and Aunt Pare was nodding her head, 'Yes, oh I sa-ay, I sa-ay.'

But there were others arriving by now, stamping and shaking the rain off and bringing in armloads of things. 'Not so good this weather for digging.'

'But should clear; the moon will see to it.'

'Sunday is . . .'

'Rakaunui.'

I remembered the other time.

Graeme came in the afternoon. For them all to look at and watch, talk to, wonder at, and find out about. At any moment I thought my aunties would begin to poke him to find out what he was made of, to see whether or not he would crumble to a touch.

I was proud of Graeme's quiet friendliness towards my family, and pleased that my family — my aunts and cousins especially — were doing all they could to include him in whatever we did, to make him feel at home.

Sunday was a day as crisp as the new mushrooms that had suddenly appeared, their cauls as yet unsplit. I decided not to go to Nanny Ripeka's to help gather up her kumara. There were enough people to help for the few rows and, as my mother said, you don't tread on an old woman's bunion just to hear her yell.

And it is good to be alone at last with the one you love and who loves you, and who you begin to know and love more and more all the time. We picked the mushrooms and I showed him the trees: Papa Rakau rocking slightly against the new blue wash of sky, and the Leaping Branch, still warm, still smooth, from the touch of stretching fingers, the grasp of fingers clawing, gripping, and hand over hand. Though there was no one now to play there, leaping, stretching, swinging, sliding the long bending fronds.

The ti kouka flowers that had split out in streamers of white at the head of summer had now dried into dark ragged tufts. The round bundles of leaves, which at the tops of the reaching limbs made the tree many-headed, were yellowy and split, and many-eyed from the brown-ridged holes that had formed.

There in my own tree, which is a quiet tree, we sat on my

own branch, still smooth and warm, and talked about the thousands of things, but not the one thing. But I did tell him about the tree and its name. Told him the new name and the old name, and told him the new name which I had chosen for myself because it had seemed important when I was younger to try to be different from the person I was.

The next day we all went to Uncle Rawhiti's to help with his kumara crop so Graeme and I had little more chance to be alone together.

And soon he was gone again. My life became one long wait between letters and week-ends, and holidays when he would get work at the timber yards with Toki. All this time my father was quiet, even friendly towards him, and beginning to treat him like a member of the family. I began to suspect after a while that my father was saving jobs for the week-ends when he knew Graeme and Toki would be there. One week-end it was the roof that needed painting, on another the shed needed repairing or there was weeding or digging to be done. My father was quiet, and different. He seemed tired, so I was glad that Toki and Graeme were there to be the sons he had never had.

And all this time I avoided Nanny Ripeka as much as possible, even though there was something I wanted to say to her, something I wanted to find out.

Then one day my father said to Graeme, 'You love my girl, don't you? You really love her?'

'Yes,' he said. 'I really do.'

'I want you two to get married then.'

◆ ◆

PATRICIA GRACE was born in Wellington in 1937 of Ngati Raukawa, Ngati Toa and Te Ati Awa descent, and is affiliated to Ngati Porou by marriage.

She has taught in primary and secondary schools in the King Country, Northland and Porirua. *Waiariki,* her first collection of short stories published in 1975, was the first published collection of stories by a Maori woman writer. Her short story collections since then have included *The*

Dream Sleepers (1980), *Electric City and Other Stories* (1987) and *Selected Stories* (1991). A novel, *Potiki*, published in 1986 won the fiction section of the New Zealand Book Awards in that year.

With illustrator Robin Kahukiwa she has written children's books, including *The Kuia and the Spider*, which won the Children's Picture Book of the Year award in 1982. In 1985 she was Writing Fellow at Victoria University, Wellington. She is married with seven children.

Photo: Jane Ussher

Joanna   Paul

♦ ♦

FATHER

I was named after my father. It was hoped I would be Joseph II, and I've always sensed a little disappointment that they got a girl instead of a boy. I got fed up with reminders that I couldn't be their only son. I tried hard to 'do' things with my father — golfing, fishing, eating kina, scuba diving, even attending a tangi when my sisters weren't allowed to go — all those things I sometimes hated, and yet endured for the sake of an impossible dream. However, it did mean that unvoiced though my feelings were I've always felt closer to this untouchable parent, sharing experiences my sisters couldn't, learning from him my deep appreciation of Aotearoa's great outdoors.

But I got tired of always trying to be something I was not...a son...a boy...Whatever I did was never going to be good enough. Since then, I've rebelled against the tomboy image...and I revel in exactly what I am . . . first a female . . . a girl . . . and now a woman.

Father never talked much. He was by no means mute, but limited his communication with us to grunting a greeting, dispensing the punishment, or explaining the line of a good golf shot. His most articulate moments occurred after a drinking session, when he could wax lyrical about any given subject, from the cultural genocide of the Maori race, including his own memories as a Maori boy growing up in rural New Zealand and not being allowed to speak his own language, to the significance of poetry in all our lives. His most lively moments came when he was sloshed and singing, or out on the water when the big one was being hauled up, accompanied by a bit of booze.

The alcohol made it difficult to know which 'father' I could talk to: the happy and contented drunk, or a far more serious and solitary figure. I never really felt he had much to say to me personally, and I think that hurt me for years. It certainly tainted the way I saw men, for a long time. Strong, silent people coming alive in a wondrous and scary way after a few drinks. It's taken me a long time to discover something different.

My father is a deep cocoa brown, and I am the darkest of his three daughters. My sisters could always get away with looking European, but, like my father, I was unmistakably Maori, growing up in a time when it was not fashionable to be Maori. He and I shared that nebulous space on earth — a foot in both worlds. He seemed to be a proud, and regrettably, silent Maori. I grew up hearing how hard it was for my father, being Maori in a country that was desperately trying to forget one race and assimilate another. He was instructed to forget his language, because it would be of little use to him in the future. I've felt sadness for him and for his family in that respect.

He is the eldest of twenty-one children and with that goes enormous responsibilities. I often felt him burdened by this and unsure of what was best for us all: to be brought up Pakeha or Maori? How do you get the best of both? I saw my father alienated from both worlds. The working-class man with three kids and a Holden, living in suburbia, a man without a marae; and still a proud Maori man. This was a slow realisation for me. It began with a burst of pride, then anger, frustration, pain because I hadn't been exposed to my Maori side, and then a period of intense learning. Now my wairua has been woken and I am forever Maori in Aotearoa. I'm reminded of it with simple things I still share with him, like the waiata and kai at Grandma's at Christmas. I still believe my father has one of the sweetest voices I've ever heard.

I always knew what was right and wrong, and would cop a hand across the backside from my father if I deviated. I don't think he

'The working-class man with three kids and a Holden, living in suburbia, a man without a marae; and still a proud Maori man.' Joseph Paul, father of Joanna.

liked meting out the punishment much, as he was sullen for the rest of the day.

I can't remember any chit-chat, and praise was a rare thing indeed. I'd try hard to get straight A's in all my school exams, be the best little actress on stage, the brightest little dancer. I wanted to excel at everything I did. Nothing was ever good enough so I'd strive harder for a bit of appreciation. These habits of mine haven't changed much. My parents' lack of praise has been replaced by my own worst critic — me. This part of me tells myself that if I am to do a job, then it must be one of the best, or I move on. Without it, I might never have made it this far. Its origins certainly go back home. And it makes enjoying any kind of success difficult.

I didn't see my father for a few years. I went my own way, and dutifully dropped him a line with a new address every few months. Now I see him every couple of months, as we cosy into reversed roles. I've become more like a concerned parent, and Father . . . is just Father. He actually said I made him proud the other day, and I nearly cried.

✦ ✦

JOANNA PAUL's broadcasting career has spanned ten years, both here and overseas, a career that includes being a film-maker, producer/director, radio producer and actor. She has been TV3's news anchor for prime news and for *Nightline*. Currently she is anchoring *Frontline* for TVNZ. With an increasing public profile comes a number of charitable appearances and her favourites are speaking to large Maori and Polynesian groups. Her other professional interests include encouraging and developing Maori film-making aspirations. She has no feeling of having reached the end or even the pinnacle of her career, and expects to go on and tell more of her people's stories on television and the big screen.

She spends her spare time outdoors, enjoying water and snow skiing, tramping, camping and travelling.

'. . . if I am to do a job, then it must be one of the best, or I move on.'

Johnny Come Dancing

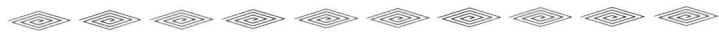

to Long John Montgomery

1
On Douglas Bridge*
On Douglas Bridge
They were dancing! Dancing!
And he seventeen swinging home
Through the twilight
A day's work done
And not a care in his head
Stopping in wonder
What dancing! Dancing!
Their black curls bouncing
And their red shoes flashing
Five little girls — dancing! Dancing!
With their dark eyes gleaming
And their green dresses shining
Saying — Dance Johnny! Dance!
And we'll give you a shilling!
And he danced and he danced
And he danced till the dawning
Then they were gone
with the grey of the morning
And Johnny limped home
Clutching a shilling
And his mother cried out
And covered her head

*Pronounced 'Dooglies'

Oh! Johnny my darling
You were not in your bed
And the fairies were out
On Douglas Bridge
Did you dance with them Johnny?
Did they give you a penny?
When he showed her the shilling
She kissed him goodbye
Then she wrapped him a loaf
And a coat for the weather
And that was the last
They were ever together.

2
He wept and he cursed
And he called to his mother
But the five little girls
Dragged him down to the river
Then he begged and he pleaded
That they take back their shilling
But they shook their dark heads
— It's no good your crying
You danced for our shilling
Now you'll dance till you're dying
You'll dance down the road
And you'll dance to the sea
And you'll dance till you reach
The last country
But it won't all be sorrow
Though you'll always be lonely
And you'll weep when you hear
The wild north wind calling
Then they jumped in the river

And when he looked over
There was only a swirl
And the sound of their laughter.

3
So he walked to Lough Foyle
And he met a sea captain
One man short
To sail for New Zealand
Where's that? asked Johnny
Is it far far away?
It's further than that
And we sail in the morning
I'll come then said Johnny
There's nothing to stop me
If I turn back now
The wee folk will get me
And I'll drown in the river
Below Douglas Bridge
And I'll always be cold
And I'll never be resting
For the five little girls
Will be dancing and leaping
And my dear dear mother
By the bridge there weeping.

4
So he sailed for New Zealand
On the outgoing tide
And it wasn't all pain
And it wasn't all grieving
Just so long
As he kept on dancing

And the new land was almost
As green as Ireland
And he married a girl
With her black hair waving
And she led him a dance
And she sneered at his pining
For a two-roomed cottage
With a rammed earth floor
And nothing to keep
The wolf from the door
And she scoffed at his stories
Of little girls dancing
With their black curls bouncing
And their red shoes flashing
But she stopped when she saw
His quick feet flying
For where had she ever
Seen such dancing! Dancing!
With his long legs weaving
And his blue eyes sparkling.

5
So he danced through the years
Through the love and the hating
Through the birth of his children
And her final betrayal
And he danced to his death
One mild spring evening
And he called out her name
As he fell to the floor
And the five little girls
Came through the door
And as he lay dying

He saw so clearly
They all had her face
And her black hair waving
With their dark eyes gleaming
And their green dresses shining
And the very last thing
That he ever saw
Was her dancing . . . dancing . . .
. . . dancing.

BUB BRIDGER

L i n d s e y   D a w s o n

••

*T*here was once a time when I reckoned my parents loved my brother better than me. Silly, huh? The thing was, Richard slept at the back of the house then. My room was closer to the living room. Every night, at tucking-in time, Mum and Dad would troop past my door, barely glancing in at me (or so I grumpily thought), to go to my brother's room first. Only then would they return to kiss me goodnight. My anxious little heart got really knotted about this. Why was he always first? Why wasn't it ever my turn? Finally, one night my jealousy spilled over and I whined pathetically about how they didn't love me. I remember how appalled they looked. Poor parents. They'd just fallen into a habit. A routine. They hadn't meant to hurt. Parents never mean to hurt. I'm amazed that forty years later, I still remember this small nonsensical pain.

It's such a silly little thing to remember, for it's outweighed so heavily by other bedtime memories that are so much sweeter. My earliest memory is of standing in my cot in the glassed-in sunporch at the back of our house, looking out over the garden where later I would make fairy houses of moss and tiny sticks, and where I'd be scared by the big weta in the pepper tree. I remember hanging on to the cot railing at chest height, so I must have been only about two years old. I remember pointing to the early morning mist outside and watching the birds. My father was there beside the cot. Today, aged eighty, he still recalls the way I babbled on. I have no other memories from so early in my life, just that sense of clinging to the railing in my long night-gown exclaiming to him about the wonders of the world outside.

We lived in an ordinary weatherboard house at the lower end of Upland Road in Remuera, Auckland. These days, it's a pretty smart sort of address. Back then, it was a very average sort of place. New Zealand was an average sort of place all around. My father, Joseph Peter Buddle, was a public accountant. His friends call him Bud. He'd rather have been a carpenter, my mother used to tell me, but his father was an accountant and his before him. The dutiful son was expected to join, and later take over, the family firm. So he did.

He worked very hard. He'd leave in the mornings in the trusty family Austin, wearing his three-piece suit and his felt hat. Fathers wore hats to work then. And often he wouldn't be home until seven. My mother didn't have a car. Mothers didn't, then. She stayed home and looked after us and we'd walk down to the Benson Road shops to see Mr McSweeney the butcher, and Mr Puttick the greengrocer, and Mr and Mrs Galley who sold cigarettes and magazines.

Mum was a very good fifties wife. She always waited for her husband to come home so they could eat together. And she always 'put on her face' and her high heels so she'd be nice for him to come home to. Sometimes, at night, they'd foxtrot slowly on the bisonia squares in the living room, holding each other close, crooning in each other's ear. My mother was a romantic woman. I think there were probably many times when she wished she could still be a painter instead of someone who peeled vegetables and bottled fruit and soothed bee stings with blue-bag. But back then, that's what wives did. There wasn't the money or the time to keep on being an artist — or even an expectation that it might have been possible. She was a good wife. My father was a good husband.

By the time he got home at night I'd often be in bed. He'd come in, still in his suit, and kneel beside my bed in his shiny shoes. His thick dark hair would be combed into place with Brylcreem. He'd ask about my day at school. And sometimes he'd say his favourite little prayer for me, the Nunc Dimittis. His face would glow with pleasure, lit by a quiet contented little half smile. Arms folded on the edge of the bed, he'd softly run

'Rich and I would curl up on the back seat under a blanket while Dad drove back to our bach on the dark and dusty country roads...'
Lindsey Dawson with her brother Richard.

97

through the words he'd been taught sometime back in his boyhood. And I'd lie there, cuddled into my pillow, and listen. And listen.

I remember rare times when they'd be going somewhere grand, like a ball; Dad handsome in a black dinner jacket, Mum in something long and swishy. I can still see her coming in to tuck me in one night looking gorgeous in a strapless white satin number, its big, full skirt splashed with lavender flowers. She'd made the dress herself. I thought she looked like a princess.

Party nights were best, when they'd have the neighbours round. You could lie in bed and listen and sometimes peek along the corridor to see what was going on. There'd be home-brew and smoke (everybody smoked Capstan and Craven A) and gusts of laughter. Dad was a dab hand on the ukelele. He'd sing 'Five foot two, eyes of blue, coochy-coochy-coochy-coo, has anybody seen my gal . . .' His other party piece was to play his Swannee whistle — warbling out swoopy tunes on the cylindrical black pipe that looked like a smooth-sided recorder. It had a little silver handle coming out the end that you could pull up and down to alter the notes. I've never seen or heard one anywhere else.

But parties didn't happen all that often. Usually it would be a quiet Saturday night and Dad would go off down the road for the *8 o'Clock* sports edition and maybe bring home some chocolate. The next morning I'd go off to Sunday School with a sixpence in my purse for the plate. There'd be a roast for lunch and at night we'd have cheese and Marmite toasties and sit around the fire. Mum and Dad would listen to 'Take It From Here' on the radio and laugh. It didn't seem very funny to me. I liked 'Biggles' better. We didn't have telly until I was about fourteen and even then it only ran for about an hour a night. You made your own fun.

Sometimes my parents went out. There must have been sitters but I don't remember. But there was one night they had a friend in and then they both drove him into town, thinking we were safely asleep. But I wasn't. And the house went deathly still. And dark. Things creaked. And the time inched by as I lay staring into the blackness. I heard a siren in the distance. A police car? A fire engine? An ambulance! They'd had an accident! That was it! They were *never coming home*! I was tear streaked and shaking when they did come back. They'd probably only been away half an hour. It had seemed like forever. Silly child.

There was another night I woke up with an earache. Oh it hurt. And it went on hurting. I waited for it to go away. It got worse. I started sobbing. And there was a parental rush of concern and loving whispers and lights going on. In the middle of the night my mother cuddled and calmed me while my father went off somewhere to get ear-drops or medicine or something that would help. Then I knew they loved me, oh yes. I was awash with it.

Years later, when I was well and truly grown up, that rush of love still had the power to soothe me. I'm going back twenty years now. I was newly wed then to an airforce pilot and working hard as a newspaper reporter. I must have been under some strain or other; the cause escapes me now. But I was miserable for some reason. And I can clearly recall sitting in my Fiat Bambina at a Stop sign on the perimeter of the Whenuapai airfield and suddenly remembering the love I'd been given the night of the earache and the way Dad got up and got dressed and drove off without a word of complaint to find something to ease my pain. Why the memory flooded back then, I don't know. But it brought with it a surge of gratitude that I'd been so cherished as a child.

The memories aren't all night-time ones. Daddies were home on weekends, of course. If I was really good, I could go to the office with him if he had to go in on an errand. It was just a few rooms in a small concrete building on Shortland Street. I loved it. You went up in a slow old lift with concertina black metal doors that clashed shut. You could see through the mesh and watch the walls and the doors on the other floors sliding sedately past as you rose up to J. F. Buddle & Co.

Today there's a glass-walled tower on the same site and his old firm has been swallowed up by a multinational company with a string of surnames that does not include my father's any more. But back then, in the fifties, his office had brown wooden walls and a brown lino floor and brown wooden desks with clacky old typewriters which always had their covers primly pulled down the way nice ladies tugged at their skirts. You could slide in an old bit of paper and press the white silver-rimmed keys and waggle the lever that made the letters go red or black, whatever took your fancy.

In Dad's office there was a huge brown leather-buttoned chair with a curving back. His father, Fred, then retired, used to take a leisurely lunch at the Auckland Club over the road and then meander into his old office and take an afternoon nap in the chair. A little girl like me could curl up in it with loads of room to spare, but its horsehair stuffing was hard and uncomfortable so it was more fun just to slide down its concave back into the seat.

Fred's chair was to cause a small flurry in the family years later. My father, fed up with its lack of comfort, and no doubt remembering with little joy the irritation of having his father snoring gently in it day after day while *he* was trying to work, decided to sell it. My brother heard about the sale at the last minute and rescued the chair, determined to keep it in the family. Now upholstered in velvet, and only marginally more comfortable, it graces his study. I'm glad he's got it. I can pat it occasionally, with fondness.

The most thrilling part of my father's office was the strong-room, a big walk-in safe where documents and valuables were kept, its concrete walls and door a good six inches thick. You had to heave on the door to make it open ponderously. Inside, the air was thick with the musty smell of old paper and stale air, and it was deliciously frightening to think how awful and scary it would be to be locked inside. I would scamper out quickly, back to the delights of the red half of the typewriter ribbon and the fun to be had with blue carbons sandwiched between sheets of white paper.

There were other special weekend times. There are certain smells that bring them back to me now. The sea-salt fishy smell of oysters. And the smell of malt and hops and enamel paint.

My parents were partial to home-brew. Most Kiwis were in the fifties, except for the 'wowsers' who disapproved of strong drink. Spirits were expensive and nobody drank wine at all. Or hardly ever. So people made their own beer, and at bottling time, I delighted in marking the tops of the shiny metal caps so that Mum and Dad would know which brew was which. I'd use one of Mum's long, slender oil-painting brushes. I'd have a little pot of paint and I'd carefully dab a colour spot on the top of each little crimped cap. A small sea of yellow or red or blue dots would spread before me, atop the ranks of bright brown bottles. I loved the colours. I didn't like the taste of the beer.

And then there was oyster opening. Dad loved oysters. We'd sit together in the basement on wooden crates for the ceremony. It was too pongy a job for the kitchen. Dad, in old shirt and shorts, would have a damp and sandy sack of rock oysters between his knees. He'd reach into the bulging sack and, one by one, he'd open up the grey and crusty shells with his special oyster-opening knife. I was mystified by how he knew just where to insert the knife to prise them open. They just looked like smelly rocks to me. And then he'd carefully pass each opened treasure to me, grey flesh and swimmy juice a-tremble in each ragged-lipped shiny, white saucer, and I'd scoop out the oyster for him to eat later with Lea and Perrins sauce. Sometimes though, he'd eat an especially succulent one right then and there. I'd watch, fascinated, as the slippery lump would slide into his mouth. I couldn't bring myself to try one. I still can't.

Holidays were special times, too. We'd rent a bach somewhere on a lake or a beach. I learnt to row on Lake Rotoiti and drifted dreamily on still mornings gazing down through the crystal water at the weeds and the stones on the bottom down below.

One blue and sunny day I thought my brother was drowning. I heard him scream, I *knew* it was him, and I heard the spluttering and I panicked and pelted up the path from the boatshed. 'Daddy! Daddy!' I shrieked. 'Richard's drowning!' And my father's face tightened with shock and dread and he ripped off his shirt and pounded down to the lake and I raced

'I remember rare times when they'd
be going somewhere grand,
like a ball...'
Here Lindsey dances with her
father at her deb ball, 1961.

after him, a great lump of horror and fright filling my chest and
my throat. And Richard was sitting quietly on the shore with a
'what's-up?' expression, mildly puzzled at the fuss. The shocking
noise had come from the boy next door playing silly games in the
water, hidden behind an overhanging willow. My father's face
was still saggy with shock, jittery with adrenalin rush. I was sick
with relief and happy all at once, and so grateful that he'd been
there when I screamed for him — and grateful that he didn't
growl at me for scaring him so.

The good night-times abounded on holiday. Lots of ukelele
playing and sausages on the barbecue. Evenings spent rowdily
with other families when the grown-ups gossiped inside over a
few gins and us kids whooped on the lawn or played ping-pong
in the garden shed. And on the way home, late at night, Rich and
I would curl up on the back seat under a blanket while Dad
drove back to our bach on the dark and dusty country roads, and
he and Mum would sing in soft harmony, 'You're just a flower
from an...old bouquet, I've waited patiently for you, each
day...'

Some of my teenage years were tough ones for my father.
His business partner got cancer of the spine and slowly shrank
and died while Dad coped with a double workload. He became,
necessarily, even more of a night-time and weekend Dad. No

102

doubt I gave him sleepless nights, too. I remember 'pashing' on the sofa and hearing him get up to move about in the kitchen, carefully making just enough noise to alert teenagers to the fact that *someone* was up and listening to the heavy silence that falls when people are kissing.

Later, after I'd left home, I had the feeling things weren't so very easy between my parents. My mother often seemed frustrated, and had cause to be, for she had a succession of elderly relatives to look after and little time to fulfil her own needs. She was volatile in those years — sometimes her old laughing and vivacious self and other times stressed and depressed. We were soon to find out why. She had lung cancer. Treatment was agonising. Useless. She died six months later, at the age of fifty-eight. Another night-time memory. Dad was staying with me and my little daughter. I was pregnant again with a baby Mum knew she would not live to see. The hospital called. We went. She had already gone. We sat helplessly. I didn't know what to say. I couldn't cry. It was too terrible for tears.

That was eighteen years ago. My father was sixty-four, and if anyone had told me then that he would marry twice more, I wouldn't have believed it. But he was lonely. His second wife Beverly, whom he also loved dearly, died of cancer too, in Brisbane, where they lived in a retirement village. I flew to join him immediately and arrived in the middle of the night. It was damp and foggy, the blue gums wreathed with grey mist. Beginnings and endings. Always at night.

Then in 1990, in my father's eightieth year, we flew to Australia again for his third wedding. Pat, my lovely new stepmum, had also been widowed twice before. They are content and spend time on both sides of the Tasman. He has been welcomed into his new family. At the wedding, they said such nice things about him. I felt so proud.

Some people tend to giggle a little when I tell them about how Dad got married again. And then they think about it a bit more and say, 'Gee, isn't that terrific — there's hope for me yet!' I think it's wonderful. So many people turn up their toes mentally and emotionally before they've even hit seventy. My

'Lord, now lettest thou thy servant depart in peace ...'
Lindsey on her wedding day in October 1966 with her father.

father's vitality gives me hope that I'll live to be a hale and hearty octogenarian too. Hell, if he's anything to go by, my life's only half over. I've got nearly forty years yet to turn myself into a lively and interesting old person. If he can do it, so can I.

I rang him the other day to tell him I'd been invited to write this piece and to ask whether he minded. And I had a question.

'Dad, I want to put in something about that prayer you always used to say to me at night, when I was little. You remember? The Nunc Dimittis. It's one of my best childhood memories. And now I haven't a clue how it goes.'

'Oh yes,' he said. 'I remember. It's a beautiful piece of writing.' Without pause, then, out it came again. And thirty years on, I was suddenly back in my small bedroom, snug and safe, as the words rolled over me.

'Lord, now lettest thou thy servant depart in peace, according to thy word: for mine eyes have seen thy salvation, which thou hast prepared before the face of all the people, a light to lighten the Gentiles and the glory of thy people Israel.'

✦ ✦

LINDSEY DAWSON has been editing magazines in New Zealand since 1983, when she was founding editor of *More* magazine. She started her journalism career as a cadet reporter for the *Auckland Star* at the age of seventeen and tried television, public relations and talkback radio before returning to print journalism in her early thirties, after a seven-year period spent mainly at home looking after young children.

Her interests include reading books voraciously, travelling, wall-papering her home (it never ends), and writing a novel (which also never seems to end). In 1991 she became founding editor of a new magazine, *Next*, and was appointed to the Broadcasting Standards Authority.

Sandra Edge

◆ ◆

As I write this I have by my side a cup of coffee. What's a hot drink without a slab or two or three or four of chocolate to go with it? I shouldn't develop such bad habits, but it's Dad's fault: I've inherited his love of chocolate, battered oysters and chips, meat pies (of good quality!), ice cream, and other foods that don't appear on the bottom three layers of the healthy food pyramid. As children we loved being surprised with yummy things to eat. For this, we relied on Dad. Mum was the fruit and veg department. What's more, if Dad had been a foot taller, and longer-limbed, instead of being a true-blue mesomorph, I may have been able to eat more of the above list of food and get away with it. I could also have continued playing my favourite position of goal keeper instead of being moved to centre for no other reason than my height.

Originally I thought it would be difficult to write about Dad without Mum because I can only picture them as a team, a very successful team. I've been part of successful teams in the netball world, and the thought of singling out members always seems unfair, when everyone contributes so much. However, teams are made up of individuals and each person has their own special qualities, unique to them. For this reason it is an honour to acknowledge someone who has played one of the two major roles in me being me: my Dad, Tom Edge.

My father began well by loving my mother, for I believe the greatest thing a father can do for his children is to love their

105

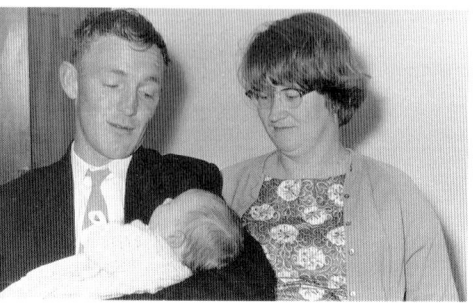

'Originally I thought it would
be difficult to write about Dad
without Mum because I can only
picture them as a team.'
Sandra held by her father, Tom,
watched by her mother.

mother. After that, the best lessons I learnt in my life I learnt from my father:

+ Lesson number one: you are what you are, so be happy and be the best person you can be.

Followed by:

+ There is so much beauty in the world — the sea, the sky, the mountains, the rivers, the lakes, the flat plains, the seasons, animals, even people. Take time to enjoy what they offer, but be cautious and respect them always for they, like people, can turn nasty and dangerous at times.

+ Try not to judge a book by its cover, for it's not until you look deeper into the pages that you start to understand the full story.

+ Treat others as you would wish to be treated. Everyone is special.

+ The most wonderful things in life cannot be bought. Some things can. That's why Dad taught us all to be hard workers. But alongside that was the certainty that nothing is quite as special as being part of a family, the knowledge that you belong somewhere and are loved by someone. Family and friends are the greatest treasures of all.

+ Be honest and true and stand up for what you believe in, but consider the feelings of others — no-one likes to be hurt.

And there were times I hurt — learning other lessons with the help of a brown one-inch leather belt.

'Don't go out the gate, Sandra.' The road was one metre from the gate, the sea 50 metres away.

'Did you belt up the next door neighbour and push her in the drain?' Physical violence is not the answer if you are frustrated and angry.

'Did you steal a lollie from the shop?' Stealing is a crime.

'Were you nasty and rude to your mother?' I forgot, or at least didn't realise, she was Dad's best mate. She was my mum, that's how I saw her then.

At times I thought Dad didn't like me much, and after a couple of lashings with the strap, he wasn't exactly top of the pops with me. He was tough, and issues were black and white; there were never any in-betweens. As a child I thought he didn't understand.

He guided me, determined that when the time came, I would have the courage and confidence to survive on my own. He encouraged me to enjoy the good times that life has to offer. Make the most of them, he'd say. But more importantly, he made me understand that there will always be hard, tough times, when I need to be strong, accept what happens, cope and get on with life.

＋ ＋

SANDRA EDGE was born in Te Puia Springs on 26 August, 1962. Her parents, Thomas, then a shopkeeper, and Alison, an ex-school dental nurse, lived in Tokomaru Bay on the East Coast. It was at this special place that Sandra, with younger sisters Margaret and Carolyn and younger brother Thomas spent their childhood.

At twelve Sandra was sent to Iona College in Havelock North for her secondary education. After four years there and a final year at Lytton High School in Gisborne, she chose a career in school dental nursing.

For seven years she worked in the Wellington and Hamilton areas. Since resigning in September 1987 she has worked as a Postbank officer, a netball co-ordinator, a Telecom storeperson and a netball promoter, until obtaining her present position at St Cuthbert's College in Auckland.

Sport has always been the greatest source of enjoyment in Sandra's life. Until she was seventeen she participated in all sports with equal enthusiasm but, after leaving school, netball became the dominant sport. In a netball career extending from 1979 to 1991 Sandra represented the Poverty Bay, Wellington, Waikato and Southland provinces. She played for New Zealand under-twenty-ones in 1982 and represented New Zealand from 1985 to 1991.

'I've inherited his love of chocolate, battered oysters and chips, meat pies (of good quality!) ice cream...' Sandra on her father's knee with her sister Margaret on her mother's knee.

Sylvia Rands

❖ ❖

'Echo Valley' was no ordinary bach. Built by my father on the back lawn in sections, it was then transported to the Wade River, Whangaparoa, and bolted together. As a child this humble structure and the land it stood on contained for me a world of magic. The creak of my top bunk, its sacking base alive at every turn; the pale blue of the plastic tub we washed in; the sturdiness of the old brass bilge pump which pumped the water from the underground tank (complete with wriggling mosquito larvae) into the cracked porcelain basin — all these memories are etched indelibly into my consciousness.

Particularly rich were the smells of the day and the sounds of the night. As Dad's homemade lampshades lit up their fiery painted Chinese dragons, the gentle strains of the wireless wound around me in my bunk next door. Interspersed only with the chuckles of glee from my Scrabble-playing father, I was lulled into a luxurious dreamworld. Living at 'The Wade' was simple and everyone played their part. My mother fed and nurtured us, as always, but the textures of this world I remember as those of my father.

On arrival from the city, a delicious primeval odour welled up to greet you. It was the smell of the country — fresh air, pine, manuka, clay — and it permeated the woodwork. By the time I came to know them, eight years after their assembly, the creosoted pine walls of 'The Wade' had become one with the dry clay hillside they backed on to. The land continually tried to reassert itself against this imposed strucure, and for many years my father met the challenge, taming and shaping the forces of the wild while still honouring their beauty. For the nine months of the year during which our visits were rare, Nature had her way. Glorious cobwebs were a permanent feature. Grey and dense, they stuck to the rough pine walls creating a sense of antiquity I loved. Tufts of green grass sprang up between the large square concrete slabs that were the bedroom floor and insect life flourished. In its prime the bach was a feast of idiosyncratic design features which intrigued and delighted me. One of my favourites was the outrageous wallpaper Dad used to line the ceiling. It was covered in stones. Grey, painted stones of varying sizes lent a certain weight and much texture to the room. This wallpaper tickled my sense of the ridiculous and many were the times I lay in my favourite 'invisible' place (the top bunk in my parent's corner) and studied the intricacies of this upside-down riverbed.

This top bunk had a 'secret' feature all its own. A plank in the wall, immediately next to the mattress, pulled up by a leather strap to reveal the outdoors. Separated only by a mosquito-preventing sheet of fine wire mesh, one could relay spy signals to pals on the bank outside and even arrange whispered assignations. This bunk was, in fact, my father's but I have no memory of him in it. Always an early riser, he was as 'non-stop a doer' here on so-called holiday as in his garden and workshop in Glendowie, the house of my youth.

The son of a Methodist minister, my father was thrust into a position of responsibility at a tender age. His father, the Padre with the New Zealand Expeditionary Force stationed in occupied Germany, contracted influenza in the epidemic that swept Europe in 1919 and died. At the age of six my father became 'man of the house' to his mother and younger sister. On his marriage to my mother, he maintained close contact with his mother, Dorothy, who eventually followed her family to Auckland and lived close by right up until her death at the age of ninety-one.

Graduating from Victoria University with an MSc in

Top: '"The Wade", Echo Valley was no ordinary bach.'

Below: '... a touchstone...' Sylvia at sea.

'Everyone played their part. My mother fed and nurtured us, as always, but the textures of this world I remember as those of my father.'
Sylvia, seated, and the family on holiday.

chemistry, my father's first professional job was with the DSIR as an analytical chemist. It was there he met my mother, the laboratory's new typist. After a certain amount of wooing among the test tubes, Maxwell Barrett Rands married Amy Constance Gunn, aged twenty-six, on 16 March 1940. Their first child, Susannah Murray, was born in August of the following year.

In 1942, in response to call-up, he appealed as a conscientious objector on religious grounds. He was turned down and shortly before Christmas that year, when Sue was fifteen months old, he was imprisoned in Strathmore, then moved to Whitanui Detention camp for the duration of the war, a further three years.

On his release in 1945 he was manpowered by the government to work for the Wellington Gas Company. A job as chemist in an Auckland cosmetics factory, Morro & Company, freed him from the government's hold and the family moved to Auckland. They settled in Te Papa where my brother David and sisters Mary and Margaret were born. Next was a spell at Westfield Freezing Works and then in 1948 Father joined Auckland Farmers Freezing Company (AFFCO) as an industrial chemist and remained there for thirty-one years until his retirement.

By the time I arrived in 1958, the youngest of five, the Rands household had become a well-oiled machine. The efficiency of our domestic structure I attribute to my father's passion for order, his belief in daily rituals, and his ability to maintain the discipline necessary to enable seven people to co-exist in a small house. By then my father was chief chemist at AFFCO and was involved in breakthroughs in the processing and preservation of skins. Of my one visit to his workplace, apart from the friendliness of the staff, I remember only the smell — the nausea-inducing sweet sickliness of indefinable animal substances — and the desire to escape it.

With my father I shared the love of open spaces — the smell of salt waves and pine needles. The intimacy I now feel with the sea and bush was formed during the hours of my childhood spent at 'The Wade' and on board our boat, the *Susannah*. Like our bach, the *Susannah* was no ordinary boat. Reputedly the first trimaran in Auckland, she started life as a small launch built in the garage of our Glendowie home, in the suburbs of Auckland. Floats were added and bingo! — a multihull! In following summers she grew bow and stern and received new floats; longer and sturdier with hatches to allow for extra sleeping quarters. Flat, wide decks linking the floats to the main hull were her most luxurious feature. Thirty feet when finally complete and without a keel (leeboards gave direction) she sat low in the water. The return to the mooring when sailing into the wind always meant a good dousing for the thrillseekers on the deck. For me this was the way to travel, meeting the elements head-on.

In terms of design, *Susannah* was definitely in a class of her own. Wherever we moored, some curious yachtie would appear in his dinghy to take a closer look at this 'Max-made' phenomenon. The essence of my father, which was captured in his persistent ever-optimistic relationship with his boat, also inspired 'Echo Valley', a three-wheeler car made out of a motorbike and a sidecar and numerous other inventions. His resourcefulness, sense of humour, creativity, on top of competent building skills, combined to stamp a certain eccentricity of style on most of his creations.

Down through the bush of the back section of 'The Wade' he had crafted a winding path which led to a clearing at the bottom boundary. Here was the fallen pine — an irresistible, safe climb even for a youngster. One could perch just below the top branches, sticky with sap, overlooking the valley dense with pine and patches of bush. A little further afield at the bottom of the neighbouring spare section, my father had told of a spring. The spring itself turned out to be barely visible and rather anti-climactic but the journey to it yielded a moment of joy. Having pushed through scratchy manuka for some time we entered a magical grove of pine trees complete with a thick dry carpet of orange pine needles. I was amazed that this majestic place — like some throne-room of the forest spirits — could be so near to my usual haunts and have remained undiscovered. These humble pines seemed to be empowered by their grouping and always had a special draw for me after that day. The trees on *our* land were

'The efficiency of our domestic structure I attribute to my father's passion for order, his belief in daily rituals, and his ability to maintain the discipline necessary to enable seven people to coexist in a small house.'
Sylvia with her father, Maxwell Barrett Rands.

an odd mixture: a few kauri, a few pine, a beautiful redwood and father's 100 gums planted for firewood and shelter.

Like all of us, my father has his flaws, his unrealistic expectations, and like many men of his generation, he is unskilled in intimate communication with his children. However, as one of the latter, if I have inherited and can put to use even a small part of my father's ingenuity, resilience, creativity and faith, I will be richer for it.

The textures he has given to my life are part of me and provide me with a touchstone when I need to feel that the aliveness of my youth was not just a thing of the past, that this aliveness can and will surface again for me.

To this day, my father has never lost the ability to see with the eyes of a child. His vision is truly his own and in his retirement he has turned again to the painting of his youth. Vivid surrealist fantasies and comments on our world cover his walls, and recently he exhibited for the first time in his life at the age of seventy-seven. It is all of him I love and cherish, but it is the spark in his eyes when describing his latest painting that speaks most of his undying spirit. This is the indefinable essence of Max which is his gift to me, his daughter.

❖ ❖

SYLVIA RANDS is Auckland-born and grew up by the sea in Glendowie. She gained a BA at Auckland University in 1978 whilst becoming immersed in the theatre, and began her professional acting career a year later. She trained at Theatre Corporate and after a couple of years left to work at the Fortune Theatre in Dunedin, where she met John Gibson. They married a year later and their son Theo was born in 1982, an event filmed for a Parent's Centre training film.

Since her return to an Auckland base in 1983, Sylvia has appeared in many roles on stage and screen. *Hanlon*, *Hotshotz*, and *Gloss* are the most well known of her screen roles while her favourites on stage have been the Marquise de Merteuil in Christopher Hampton's *Les Liaisons Dangereuses* and Katherine Mansfield in *Jones and Jones* by Vincent O'Sullivan — both at Downstage — and Portia in Mercury Theatre's

Merchant of Venice.

In 1986, on her return from a study trip to the USA, Sylvia began teaching 'The Natural Voice' — an holistically based approach to voice training. Her renewed passion for Shakespeare dated from this time also; after studying voice with Kristin Linklater within the context of a course run by members of the Boston-based Shakespeare and Co. This passion has resulted over the last few years in the creation of her solo show *Such Sweet Thunder* which deals with the theme of 'woman emerging' and this show has toured twice in the North Island to much acclaim.

Now separated, Sylvia's recent directions include a more metaphysical approach to her teaching, a novice's fascination with writing, plans for another show based on poetry, and an increasing commitment to a saner lifestyle.

Marilyn Duckworth

✦ ✦

My father was an unusual person — idealistic, peace-loving, an original thinker. He was also a rather shy and private man, I think — not easy to know. He had grown up in rural New Zealand, milking a number of cows before walking to school — as he would remind my sister when we were reluctant to get out of bed on cold English mornings. He was a believer in hard work and inquiring minds, cold water and raw rolled oats. During my childhood years I was influenced by his ideas but he himself was often away from home, of necessity, working on the Air Raid Patrol and studying. When he came home on Sundays my mother used his presence as an excuse to make me eat my spinach, which I was glad to do in order to impress him.

For me he was a holiday person, someone who cheerfully took us camping in an old car and an army tent, in a disused chalk pit, or a farmer's field. When he returned to New Zealand the camping trips continued but now in regular campsites — Wanganui, Taihape, Waitomo. Our tents and cars were always of a more patched and peculiar variety than any of the others in the camp which gave me, conversely, a feeling of superiority. In 1949 he and a university colleague built a boatshed in Paremata out of car cases — I seem to remember my father doing most of the work. I spent one summer holiday in overalls helping him paint the inside of the boatshed and creosoting the outside — I still have a faint creosote burn on my wrists to remind me of that time. He sang tunelessly as he worked and swore in Esperanto, a companionable presence, while I wrote poems in my head.

When or if I write about camping holidays perhaps I will

114

draw on my father in my writing. So far I have not. Father figures are either totally missing from my novels, or are total inventions as in the piece that follows.

In 1987 my father and I were each awarded an OBE for our different fields of work. His award was three-pronged — for his contribution as a psychologist, and also for the part he played in the Workers' Educational Association and in Esperanto. We looked forward to receiving these awards together. Sadly, he died before the investiture.

'My father was an unusual person — idealistic, peace-loving, an original thinker.'
Marilyn Duckworth with a photograph of her father as a young man.

Moving Parts

MARILYN DUCKWORTH

This fiction extract is from a novel
in progress.

*T*he next day Parker calls into Bundle's office with a packet of wedding photographs. Bun is glad to have these delivered by her father but not ready to examine them in his company, especially not now.

'I'm very busy just now, Par. Can I hold on to them and look later?'

'They're your copies. I had two copies done. Biggies.'

'Oh. That was thoughtful of you.'

'I do think of you Bun.' He lays his fingers over hers on the packet of photographs. *I couldn't remember one moment of gentle tenderness . . .*

'Don't judge me, Bun, for wanting a life.' His eyes beseech her.

'You had a life. *We* had a life.'

'You know what I mean. You're not stupid. I want you to be happy as well. And there wasn't much chance while you were stuck with your old father.'

'Well thanks. But really I am busy, Par. I've got to go.' Meaning — you've got to go. Go now. She has no intention of looking at the photographs in her lunch break or in the camera room or in the privacy of a lavatory cubicle for that matter. Perhaps in the privacy of her own living room? They pursue her for the rest of the day, these images of a large lime-green jelly bride and Parker looking faintly green too, hollow-cheeked as if Marge has sucked the air from him. Flowergirls in waxy skirts like upside down tulips, screaming happily after the ceremony, on the stairs, sliding and giggling and asking to be tickled. And Cherry watching from under her dark brows, pushing her mouth about unattractively. Where in all this is Bundle? Has she let herself be trapped in the middle of this farce? Why doesn't she remember the camera? Who was it? Which one of the guests?

'What's the matter?'

'Cheer up, it may never happen.'

'Are you all right, Bundle?'

She catches the Wadestown bus without thinking. The mistake pleases her. It is her first pleasurable moment in a long time. She grins at her fellow passengers and some of them smile back. They are so familiar. She hasn't realised till now how well she has become acquainted with these fellow passengers who have never introduced themselves.

She is going home. Well, why not? At least to the gate. She has the right to walk along the street as far as the gate. Parker is in the habit of saying — 'when we sold Wadestown' — as if they had signed away the whole suburb, but of course this isn't so. If there is no one home she can creep into one of her garden dens — there she will feel safe to open the packet from her father, examine the prints so long as it is still light enough to see.

There is no one at home. This is easy to divine because there is no children's chatter, no barking dog, no car in the parking space. The house broods in the secretive way that she remembers. How could she have forgotten the silence of the trees — where has the wind gone? She has forgotten too that the gate creaked this way — or perhaps it is a new creak, objecting to new ownership, the swinging feet of Bata Bullets. She treads cautiously past the windows, noting new shrubs in the beds, akeake, hoheria. Below the house she feels safe, protected, and follows familiar paths, ducking under the rhododendron branches. At the big tree she stops. Someone has built rough wooden steps against the trunk, and a few narrow feet up — lucky Bundle is so small — a platform and the four walls of a tree house, cobbled from car cases. Bun has always wanted a tree house. In the walls there are slotted narrow slits, like the arrow loopholes in a castle. There is a pleasant smell of saw-dust and pine. She puts her eye to a slit and there it is spread out beneath, her world, pretending nothing has changed since she was eleven years old.

The sun is off the hillside and soon the light will go. Okay, let's have a look at these wedding photos. Just a quick look and then she can throw them away if necessary. Before she can do this there are voices on the path, children, a barking mongrel, a mother calling to a child to go back and collect a dropped skate. The disturbance moves closer to Bundle then cuts out. The family is inside the house, her house, unaware of her. She discovers she is trembling violently with shock. Supposing that little boy had climbed the ladder? She'd have looked pretty silly. But after all it is tea-time, bed-time soon for a child. Well, she can't leave yet and be seen from the windows. So.

The photographs.

Here they are. Not half as threatening in actuality. The photographer whoever he was — must have been a friend, not a professional — has moved about taking snaps rather than posed shots. There are only two capturing the bridal party lined up in the living room before the minister. Bun recalls the flash now — she must have thought it was her own anger flashing electricity at the time. What a farce. Parker doesn't look too happy either. If her gift doesn't desert her now she might expect to hear Parker say it again — 'Sorry?' Inclining his ear comically towards the camera. Sorry! She laughs with pleasure at the aptness of this word. Then the tears threaten again, but before they can fall —

She is there, zooming, panning, fast-forwarding the scene, dizzy with the speed of frame changes. Until now — what is this? Parker and the grandchildren on the stairs. 'Chase me! Chase me. Me! Me! No, me.' He has caught Kirsty in her tulip skirt and set her on his lap while he rests on the stairs to catch his breath. The champagne is pink in his face now. He is stroking the child's leg, casually, almost absent-mindedly. The camera locks onto his hand in this position. Freeze frame. Bundle stares, and then the scene begins to unreel backwards, flying rewind, dizzily rocking Bun's senses so that it feels as if the tree house will leave its moorings.

The rocking continues and now there is another sound accompanying it, a buried humming rumble. Through an arrow slit she sees the house lurch sideways and the vegetable plot crack like a large dropped chocolate cake crumbling apart. The tree house has slipped forward so that she is gazing past the brick incinerator at a close patch of angled earth. Somewhere she can hear other sounds, shrill screaming. Her own? The little boys in the house? Is this it? The big one? The disaster. To her left there is a high clay bank where a moment ago there was only a gentle grassy slope, and over this sharp bank the shiny bonnet of a big black car dangles its front wheels. Parker's longed for Daimler? The mud-coloured answer-phone has sicked itself up out of the ground, out of the cracked chocolate cake which was the vegetable garden for two survivors. Bundle tracks a sob of laughter vomiting up out of her throat but when it arrives the sound is like the yowl of a dying cat.

When she comes to some time later she is collapsed with her hand out of the loop-hole window, like Alice in Wonderland. Where is the white rabbit, or better still, Lewis Carroll to get her out of here? She panics and searches for the ladder opening. She could be trapped. A cold sensation she locates as the memory of that old refrigerator. But she slithers sideways and down and the next moment she is free. It is dark now. There are no sounds from the house, no lights. Well, that makes sense, a safety precaution — turn off the power, don't use the phone. The moon is not part of these restrictions and tonight it is full enough. If someone glances out of the window they will see Bundle collapsed in a heap. Or is the house empty, the family departed to the nearest civil defence depot — the library, was it, or the school — taking personal papers and warm clothes? She feels unable to move. Her bones have simply turned to rubber and her knickers are wet.

Earthquake. Her fault perhaps. She feels she has willed it. She pats the ground about her, searching for her belongings — her bag, the photographs. She can still scarcely believe. It's no good, she will have to take another look and make sure. She drags herself up onto the sofa which for some reason is sitting outside on the lawn, and lays out the photographs again in the moonlight. A cat comes and bumps against her hand but she pushes it roughly away.

Which photo was it? Does it matter which? She leafs through, peering short-sightedly, until she reaches one of Parker and Marge.

The premonitory sensations of her trance are the expected

ones — that indescribable smell of singeing cloth, the reeling, dizzying movement of the flickering images. But this time something is different. On this occasion she travels further forward in time than now. She has never been able to travel beyond now — it isn't logical. Some would say her gift isn't logical at all, but for Bundle it has seemed so. This evening in the ravaged garden she witnesses the ravages of a different kind of disaster.

Parker is crying. She has seen him cry before — at the tramways museum — seen him put his head down on his sleeve and shake, his chest creaking embarrassingly. She remembers how when he raised his head a string of saliva had still attached his mouth to his sleeve. But this is worse. It is worse than anything Bun has ever seen on TV, worse than pustules and gangrene and rats running over live bodies. She has never seen a person so possessed by grief, disgust, whatever it is. Self disgust. He is pressing his fingers on his forehead so hard Bun is sure she sees the bone bend like a new baby's fontanelle. And Marge, the doting Mother Christmas Marge, gift-wrapped now in an ugly Shevelva dressing gown, is chucking words at him from her mouth, along with sparkles of spit. She is leaving him, 'As soon as I can get myself together! I must have been mad, or blind!' And Bundle knows why. Kirsty. Or who? Some other child? Some other child who might have needed comforting after being shut in the refrigerator?

The revulsion Bundle feels for what her father might — must have done coils in her gut making her nauseous. But it isn't as simple as that. He is Parker. He is her Dad. Her fellow television conspirator. Her fellow survivor. She is programmed to forgive him. Across the gap which is time she calls out to him silently.

As he lies on the bed, his lips snarled back in grief, in shame, Bun can see little shadowy particles of food lodged in his teeth. She finds this as revolting as the rest of it, but at the same time a great tenderness shakes her, the first overpoweringly strong feeling she has ever had, perhaps the last. She knows the way her life will go from now. She isn't sure she wants her father's burden, his depression, his self-hatred, well enough earned, not to mention his domestic mess, the ring around the bath tub. She has complained of this in the past. But she is needed. He needs her. No one else would give him absolution. The only other candidate is in the cemetery — Eileen, perhaps another conspirator of sorts, condoning his serious misdeeds, exacting her own payment? Misdeeds that Marge apparently is unable to condone. Could it be — Bundle flinches at this possibility — could it be that Marge, the new wife, is less corrupt, less greedy and frivolous than the dainty Eileen, mother of Bun, fluttering her skirts and eyelashes? Eileen, who nevertheless taught Bundle to sit tidily so as not to display her school knickers? Could Bundle's mother possibly have known? Never mind that. Eileen is out of the picture. Marge is out of the picture. It is up to Bundle. She can't ride away from this one on any white horse. She has been sentenced. *Jeg har kopper.* Smallpox. She looks down at the backs of her hands to see if her sentence is writing itself there. Not yet.

Not yet. And wait a bit! This scene is in the future — must be in the future, beyond *now*. There is something she can do to prevent it once she is released from her trance. Someone she must tell about her father's stroking hands. Or will she? Perhaps when she is recovered she won't believe, or perhaps she will forget what she has seen — forgetting isn't so difficult after all.

A drop of blood has fallen out of her nose onto the back of her hand. The moonlight studies her bitter satisfaction.

✦ ✦

MARILYN DUCKWORTH was born in Auckland in 1935, but spent a wartime childhood in England before the family returned to settle in Wellington. She has raised her own family of four daughters and three step-children here, written novels, poems, short stories.

She was awarded a Scholarship in Letters in 1961 and 1972, and gained an award for achievement in 1963 and the New Zealand Book Award for fiction in 1985 for her novel, *Disorderly Conduct*. She received an OBE in 1987.

In 1989 she was the Australia-New Zealand Exchange Fellow and in

Photo: Robert Cross

1990 held the Writer's Fellowship at Victoria University, Wellington.

Her nine novels include *A Gap in the Spectrum*, *The Matchbox House*, *Pulling Faces*, *Married Alive*, and most recently *A Message from Harpo*. A short story collection, *Explosions in the Sun*, appeared in 1989. She has also written a book of poems, *Other Lovers' Children*. A new novel, Unlawful Entry, will appear later this year.

Today she lives in Wellington with her husband John Batstone, and writes full-time. She is the sister of Fleur Adcock, whose poems also appear here.

S a n d r a   C o n e y

✦ ✦

'ANOTHER BLOODY GIRL': DAUGHTER OF A KIWI SPORTING HERO

*T*his is not just a portrait of my father, nor one of my family; neither is it just an essay about growing up. Although it is all of those things, it is also about male culture in New Zealand, viewed from the perspective of someone who is now a feminist.

Tom Pearce, my father, was larger than life; he took male values to an extreme. He exaggerated masculinity, making its component parts easier to see. As his daughter I was in an ideal position to examine it.

· · ·

My father went to Kowhai Junior High School and won a Junior National Scholarship to Mt Albert Grammar School, where he played rugby in the 1st XV. He also boxed and swam, and held a wrestling 'school' in the playground every lunchtime. Sport and politics were the two most important things in my father's life, with sport coming a clear first. A career, or making money, was never a priority, although my family was always comfortably off. He made his mark in the sporting world as a wrestler first, but rugby, then surf life-saving and later diving were the great loves of his life. He used his skill at wrestling to good effect on the rugby field with some crushing tackles.

He went to university, where he studied law while working in the Public Trust Office to earn a living. In those days you had to pass every paper to progress on to the next year; when he failed some exams he gave up his ambitions for a legal career. He might well have made a devastating court room lawyer. He had a quick mind, and was an eloquent speaker with an overwhelming manner in argument. As teenagers, my sister and I were

'Another Bloody Girl', written by Sandra Coney, has been edited for length and, as printed here, is slightly more than half the extent of the original, which came from *Out of the Frying Pan* (Penguin 1990). The editor and publishers are appreciative that permission was given for such an extensive reduction to meet the space limitations of the present collection.

123

subjected to gruelling cross-examinations about our activities. Our tea table was frequently a battleground.

Our father's constant accusation to us was that we had been 'up to no good', which was often true. I particularly remember one incident, heard from the comparative safety of my bedroom. My sister, then at university, came home a little late and said she had been to a movie in town. My father, who suspected she had been 'up to no good', proceeded to grill her about the content of the movie which he, as an inveterate movie goer, had of course seen. At first she gamely defended herself against the barrage, coming up with the right answers. But he didn't believe her, insisting that someone else could have coached her in the correct responses. Finally he produced the coup de grâce: 'What colour horse did Gregory Peck ride?' he shouted. Helen said dark brown. He said black. As far as he was concerned, this proved she had not seen the picture. No dire consequences followed this 'defeat'. My father was simply pleased to have been proved right. Helen actually had taken the precaution of seeing the alibi movie during the daytime, but had faltered under his questioning.

He was also a master of bluff. He once accused me of a secret assignation with a lover: 'I know he's been here,' he said, 'I saw him broken down on the side of the road up the hill.' I confessed, forgetting that he had never clapped eyes on the man in question, let alone his car.

At twenty-four my father was selected for the All Black squad to play against the 1937 Springboks, but he never actually took the field. To what must have been his intense disappointment, he was a reserve for every test.

Rugby commentators expected him to play. 'With brawny limbs and arms akimbo,' said one newspaper, 'he will be "the goods" when "tough men will be required against the boys from Africa."' 'Pearce impresses,' said another, 'as one of the liveliest forwards seen during the week. He was in the thick of it all the time. The harder the play the better he appeared to like it. And he is at home whether on top of the ground or in the mud. Full of aggression, he is just the type to oppose South Africa.'

But he sat on the sideline for all three tests, much to the pleasure of the Springboks if newspaper reports are to be believed. They had met him when they played Auckland and he had felled Boy Louw with what a newspaper called a 'sensational diving tackle'. The Springboks called him 'fierce Pearce'.

My father was not a tall man. He was about five foot nine, but he made up for his lack of height in brute strength. Once he stopped playing rugby, he never weighed under seventeen stone. He used to get me to spar with him and when I punched his stomach it was like a rock. If he put me in a headlock and told me to try and escape, I would feel as if my head was going to crack. He had strong legs and arms, a big back and a hard head. A newspaper in 1934 wrote: 'With his sleeves and shorts rolled up just as far as he can get them, Pearce looks quite a picturesque figure on the field, and this, combined with his caveman antics, seem to make him a very popular player with the crowd.'

· · ·

My father was greatly admired for his speech-making ability and his picturesque use of language. He loved words and what he could do with them. A newspaper report of a speech to rugby coaches describes his 'slick turn of phrase' and 'biting delivery': '[When] Tom Pearce goes into verbal action, he makes his presence felt . . . His listeners may be shocked (they are meant to be), they may feel they should disagree, but they will certainly sit up and take notice.' On this occasion he chastised the current pack of Auckland forwards, who, instead of attacking 'scratch like a lot of hens in a fowl-yard looking for grit that isn't there.'

The use of metaphor was typical of his style. He never talked in vague generalities, but frequently reinforced his arguments by using images and analogies which related to everyday life. He would quote (not always accurately) from Shakespeare, Byron and Tennyson. These great poets were drawn on, not to illustrate some highflown point, but, by association, to dignify New Zealand's natural assets: its hardy people, its natural beauty, and its national pastime — sport.

· · ·

Surf life-saving was described in a newspaper profile of my father

'Surf life-saving, with its combination of physical challenge, sporting competition and the company of men, offered irresistible attractions to my father.' Sandra at Piha with her father and mother.

as a 'hobby'. It was just as consuming of the summer months as rugby was of the winter. If anything he was more passionate about it. He once called rugby 'a pleasant way of seeing dreary winters through'. But he called summer 'my season'.

Both my sister's and my births were planned not to interfere with his surfing arrangements. Helen was born on 11 October; I was planned for the same date but, serving notice from the beginning that I would not do what was expected of me, I arrived late, right on Labour Day, the start of the surf season. My father told my mother she'd 'mucked up' his 'bloody weekend', and took one look at me and dashed out to Piha.

Piha was more home to us than Point Chevalier where we grew up. The wildness and the rugged grandeur of the place attracted my father to it. Whenever my father went overseas he'd make straight for the beaches and he always reported that nothing compared with Piha. When I finally went overseas I discovered he was right.

The Piha Surf Club was founded in 1934 and five years later, in the first subdivision of the beach by the Piha Tramway Company, my parents bought a seven-acre block of land, which they paid off from their wages at a few shillings a week.

Surf life-saving, with its combination of physical challenge, sporting competition and the company of men, offered irresistible attractions to my father. He joined up and began a lifetime involvement with it.

. . .

One of my father's favourite quotes was the lines from Tennyson's *Ulysses*: 'To strive, to seek, to find, but not to yield'. Giving in, collapsing, 'dropping your bundle', or even showing hesitation were demonstrations of such terrible weakness it was unlikely you could recover from them. No one was sneered at more than the person who was 'all talk and no do'. The accepted style was modest understatement. You did not talk about it, you did it. The greatest value was put on action, on physical prowess beyond the normal.

. . .

My father met my mother while both were working at the Public Trust Office. They had a long courtship, during which time they both saved; for, according to the policies of the day, marriage would spell the end of her public service career. My father was only twenty-two when he and my mother began courting. Although she was only eighteen months older than him, my father never stopped joking about this older, more worldly woman (his description) having snapped him up. He seemed never to come to terms with it.

My mother's background was respectable, even straight-laced. Her parents never entirely approved of my hot-headed and undomesticated father. Her Scottish mother, Helen Robertson, had been a nurse in Ballarat, where she met and married Benjamin Morgan, a carpenter by trade. He was devoutly Welsh, with red hair, which came out in my younger son Morgan. Grandpa Morgan worked in a joinery firm which made school desks. He was a mild man, whose sole vices were smoking a pipe, cribbage and following the races. He led a very home-based life, keeping ducks and tending his vegetable garden. Most of the furniture in the house was made by him. My mother always wished that our father had wanted the same kind of home-centred life her father had led.

My father had hoped for a boy for his firstborn, but Helen arrived, a girl. He was soon entranced by his daughter so that when I was expected he announced that he wouldn't mind another little girl if she was like her. This may have been merely brave talk, an insurance against the worst happening, for when I was born my father arrived out at Piha with a crate of beer under each arm and said, 'I've had another bloody daughter.'

In his world families full of girls were seen as somehow deficient and incomplete. There was an unspoken suspicion that the father of daughters wasn't virile enough to produce the right genes. When my sister and I gave birth to nothing but sons, my father appeared almost to resent it. It seemed to affront him that other men could do what he could not, especially men to whom he considered himself superior.

As we grew older, my father, on his off days, would moan about being forced to live in a house with 'a pack of women on his back'. This would always be said to himself, rather than to us, as if he accepted the irreversibility of the situation. All he could do was rail against it. I would occasionally feel some vague guilt and sense of failure at having contributed to this defective ménage. At other times it occurred to me that he couldn't blame us, he'd done it. It really served him right. There was a kind of poetic justice about it — our sex was the one thing that was beyond his control.

We were also periodically reminded by his friends that he could have destroyed a son. 'Just imagine if your father had had a son who wanted to be a ballet dancer!', they would say. A failed son would obviously have been a tragedy of truly Homeric proportions. It was hard to imagine a daughter being a failure of the same magnitude. I felt directly responsible for having saved this poor unborn boy from his lifetime of martyrdom.

He was a proud father but took little part in our actual care. My mother had many stories of his ineptness. On one rare occasion when he was left in charge, Helen dirtied her nappy. He removed it, but unable to put a fresh one on, simply spread the clean one underneath her.

When I was about four, I was left in my father's care while my mother took Helen out. He fell asleep on the sofa. My mother returned to find that right under his nose I had carefully removed all the snap-shots from the family photo albums.

. . .

People liked being with my father, for he was dedicated to having a good time. He was like a honey pot around which the bees clustered. He never lacked companions. Enjoying life enormously, he threw himself into everything. Relatively mundane activities became events and adventures. Things happened around him.

From his daughters' point of view, he was the ultimate fun father. He took us to the swimming baths, for rides on his surf ski or out in the boat. Under his leadership, a project as ordinary as laying concrete was transformed into an epic endeavour. The floor of the garage at Piha has carved into it the names of its builders:

Tom
Doris
Tiger [my father's friend]
Helen
September 1944

Helen was only three at the time, but there were still things she could do. My father liked having a team around him to whom he could issue instructions. He did not exclude us because of our sex or age. He would give us useful jobs to do, such as fetching and carrying, or holding boards while they were being nailed.

When we were little he would carry us around sitting on his shoulders, clinging to the bristles on the top of his head. This was a privileged position and he was suitably outraged when, on a visit to the zoo, Helen peed down the back of his Auckland representative blazer when she saw the seals splashing in the water.

Together we had great adventures, like the time he and I set off from the foot of our section at Pt Chevalier and swam across the harbour to Pollen Island. We sat on the beach on the other side in the sun, then swam back. I felt a huge sense of achievement.

Until we were teenagers, he made no concessions to our sex. We were simply treated as surrogate sons. I never heard the

129

words 'Girls don't . . .' or 'Girls can't . . .' throughout my childhood. Whatever we were capable of, we did. Although we were girls, we were his daughters, reflections of his ego, and we had to do well. He constantly extended us.

He did not encourage us to be or look 'feminine'. When I told my mother I wanted only one chop for tea, he would butt in. 'A growing girl needs more than that,' he would say. 'She needs two.' So two I would get. We were not allowed to be 'scrawny' — his disparaging description of women who conformed to the feminine stereotype.

Conventions about suitable female behaviour later came as a shock. When I started going out with a man from the local tennis club, I ended up in the finals of the club championship mixed doubles playing against my boyfriend. My mother cautioned that my boyfriend would be unhappy if my partner and I won, because 'men don't like being beaten'. I was incredulous, and all the more determined to win. I was so unaware of conventional male attitudes that, if I cared at all, I thought he must like me better for being good at what I did. My diary of the time records that he asked me out the same night, and I turned him down. I probably liked him less for having lost.

In the absence of sons, the toys my sister and I were given as children were those usually given to boys. Flippers, cricket bats, fencing foils, bows and arrows and Hornby trains were usually found in our Christmas pillows, along with chocolates and books. But despite this, nearly every photograph of me taken over my childhood shows me clutching a doll or a teddy. I had a good many of them and took them all to bed at night. I had to lie flat on my back to sleep so they wouldn't be squashed. I remember coming home from school one day when I was about fourteen to find my mother burning a badly moth-eaten koala in the incinerator. I burst into tears.

My father did not find this feminine preoccupation objectionable, presumably because it co-existed comfortably with my more vigorous interests. My second doll came back with him from a rugby trip to Wellington — a plump baby doll wearing the palest blue, flower-sprigged organza frock. She was called

Rosalie, the name he gave her.

. . .

Once we were teenagers, our relationship with our father became more problematic. We were beginning to slip out of his control and make decisions about our own lives. He liked being in charge in all parts of his life; he did not like the troops mutinying. Consequently, his attempts to maintain his power became more extreme.

When I tried to leave home after one fight, he threatened to 'slap a writ' on me to prevent it. When my sister went to training college in Christchurch, he said he would cut her out of his will, and forbade her from ever entering the family home again. He was distraught, cried inconsolably and said she would no longer be his daughter.

On top of this, the whole business of sex was looming large and he found it enormously difficult. He sensed, quite rightly as it turned out, that it was the one thing that might be completely beyond his control. Until this time he had had our undivided attention and affection, now he might have to share it with another man. He did not like it. He had not devoted so much effort to us to have us squander ourselves on some other, less worthy, man. Although our mother was expected to wait on him hand and foot, he hated the idea that his daughters would do this for some other man.

My father's role changed from fun father to guardian of our virginity. This did not spring from any moral prescription against premarital sexual experience; it was purely pragmatic. He wanted us to have educational qualifications and careers, to be equipped to support ourselves. He saw our reproductive potential as a threat to our ability to control our lives. As a man he believed women should submerge their lives in those of their menfolk; but as our father he tried to protect us from that fate.

His attitude to sex was far from prudish; he thought every-one wanted to do it all the time. His job was to see that his daughters went without, a daunting mission, as even he realised. 'I don't know where they are,' he would moan to our mother. 'With all this bush around, they could be up to anything.'

131

I had some trouble in my romantic life because young men recoiled when they heard who my father was. They were terrified of him. 'Do you know who her father is?' someone would say to warn off an interested potential beau.

The only official date, as opposed to sneaking out with boys, I can remember having when I was at school was with the halfback of the Mt Albert Grammar School rugby team, who invited me to his school ball. When he came to collect me, he arrived with reinforcements in the form of other members of his old school team. My father ushered them into the sitting room and shut the door. There was nothing for me to do but wait in the kitchen in my ballgown.

My father gave them all sorts of rugby memorabilia, including All Black badges. They were overwhelmed by this attention from the great Tom Pearce. My father judged the young halfback eminently suitable for me. I, however, did not, having accepted the invitation solely because I wanted to go to the ball. I treated him rather shabbily. My father even told me off for bolting in through the back door without lingering for a good-night kiss. The path to the back door took us past my parents' bedroom window and my father was aware of the speed with which I had accomplished the journey.

My father did not enjoy the entry into our lives of a series of young men. He was as erratic in his reactions to them as he had been in his disciplining of us. He could be benign or ferocious. Meeting an ex-boyfriend of mine years later, my father was reminded that he had ordered him off the property when he was quite properly escorting me to the front door.

When I was at university, my father could not cope with my active love life. At one stage, when I was going out with four young men, he ordered me to choose one; he was 'bloody sick,' he said, 'of answering the phone and getting a different boyfriend every time.' When I retaliated that I was 'sowing my wild oats', he was outraged. This was something young men did, not his daughter.

My father had many tales to tell of the exploits of his touring rugby teams and their sexual peccadillos. They expected women to be available wherever they went. However, there were separate standards for male and female behaviour, as I found out in the following way.

After my school ball in my sixth-form year it was arranged that I would take a taxi to the function for the visiting French rugby team, which was held under the grandstand at Eden Park. I was delighted to try out my schoolgirl French on the Frenchmen and they were by this time in a very jolly mood. I took the precaution of positioning myself as far away from my father as possible, also taking advantage of a number of pillars in the room.

I got on very well with the French halfback, and when he asked me to go outside I was quite agreeable. 'Outside' was the main rugby field, a hardly romantic location for a dalliance. We climbed up the back of the Number 1 grandstand and sat down. I inadvertently said something in my blundering French to try and slow him down which actually had the effect of galvanising him into action. I later learned it was a very explicit invitation, a glowing testimonial to the sexual delights that awaited him.

Suddenly a bellow like a wounded bear was heard from the direction of the rugby field. We peered down through the darkness and there, far below in the distant floodlight, was my father bawling my name. I had thought him well preoccupied with his cronies at the other end of the room, but he had actually been keeping an eagle eye on me. 'Where's your daughter?' he had suddenly said to my mother, and charged off after me.

I was sent home in disgrace. So was my mother. In his version of the double standard, she was also responsible for her daughter's behaviour. He expected his players to philander when they toured, would actually boast of it, but he did not expect his own daughter to entertain visiting sides. My mother pointed this out to him, which made him as sour as a boil.

. . .

At the age of twenty-one, despite all my father's efforts to prevent such an eventuality, my sister married a surf club boy. A few months later I also married. Helen had at least finished her degree; I had a mere two units towards mine.

By the age of eighteen I was married and a mother. Everything about our upbringing should have deterred me from marriage. I had had continually stressed to me the importance of education, of having qualifications, of a secure job, of not getting 'tied down' to a man to scrape his pots, and I had been warned against having children too young. My father would actually begin his harangues on what I should aim for in life with the words, 'You don't want to end up like your mother . . .' My sister and I had not been groomed for domesticity; we had had it held up to us as something to avoid. Our father thought we had more important things to do and our mother thought we were a nuisance in the kitchen. My father conceded that I might marry, but I should work as well; the plan for my sister was that she would become headmistress of a girls' high school. But powerful as my father was, he could not triumph over the sexual conditioning I underwent as a girl in the fifties.

As a child growing up I had never envied my mother's role, her sole responsibility for arduous domestic work — the fact that my father was out acting on the world, in the public eye, well thought of and achieving, while her role was private, unrewarded, and lacking in status. I could see all this. Yet, like a lemming, I leapt towards it.

Despite the messages I had learned during my childhood about striving for excellence, about competitiveness, individualism, ambition and going against the crowd, I believed being in love was the most important thing in the world. Every time I fell in love, I thought about getting married. It was the only authentic grown-up state I could think of for a woman.

I had no role models of women combining marriage with a career. I had been educated at a school where the articulate, able, and brilliantly educated women teachers were almost invariably single. We pitied these middle-aged women for their unmarried state. The measure of success was not the honours board, the illustrious old girls of whom I now know there were many, the elevated degrees, or the breadth of knowledge; it was simply being married, and at this they had failed. We told stories about their imagined pasts, inventing fiancés tragically killed in the

First World War to explain their single state; the possibility of active choice never occurred to us.

My father was a very powerful figure. He had status, public success and was widely admired. Many of the men he brought into our lives were similarly exalted. My autograph book of the fifties contains the signatures of Fred Allen, Winston McCarthy, Danie Craven, the 1956 Springboks, and the All Blacks year after year. There were no equivalent women in my world. The only powerful woman I knew was my headmistress. There was no doubting her ability to manage her school, to speak eloquently and to be a force in the community. But she had never married and had no children. To be powerful as a woman, it seemed, was to be sexually disqualified, to be doomed to spinsterhood and childlessness, to be relegated to the margins of life.

To have a man was the only social role that really counted. This was the touchstone of success, the symbol of having made it as a woman. And despite the drawbacks of the role my mother played, she had my father, the most exciting man in my world. Nothing my father offered as alternatives could compete. His ambivalence about his daughters as females also undermined his ability to train us. There was a flaw at the heart of his aspirations for us. His own personal preference was clearly for women to play the traditional role, to adore and support men, to look after them and have their children. He would not have admired as women, the kind of women he wanted us to be.

From primary school age, he had us learn elocution so that we might cope competently with any future public role. But we heard him disparage as women the few women he encountered in his public life, for they did not meet with his approval as a man. We could see that he made an exception for us, but he was our father, destined to be part of our pasts, not our futures. The women he wanted us to be would not please other men. There were inbuilt contradictions in his ambitions for us.

Ours was an unusual household in some respects, but in others it was very conventional and did not challenge the sexual politics of the time. It was a male-dominated household; there was no model of equal power between the sexes in our domestic life. Our father controlled the family punishment and reward system; his approval was necessary. It was not hard to slip from this system into the one which made the rest of the world go round, where once again men were central. Other men might offer approval for different (stereotypic and feminine) qualities, but there was a consistent pattern of male hegemony inside and outside my family.

He also set limits, determined by our sex, on what he offered. School teaching was the route he offered to independence and the better life. The 'freedom' he offered was circumscribed by sexual stereotyping. Medical school, the law, accountancy, an academic career, his carrying business, or any of the options that would have been available to brothers had we had them were never offered, and indeed, the pursuit of them would have been fraught with obstacles at the time.

One of his final acts of dominance in my life was his insistence, against my wishes, that I train to be a primary school teacher. My wish had been to be a librarian and there had been a vacancy for a trainee at the university library. Typically, it was my father who went for the initial job interview, not me. When he came home he said I could not apply for the job. The chief librarian, it transpired, had a couch in his office, and 'no daughter of mine is going to work for a man like that!'

I hated training college with its boring, conventional image and conformist people. It was not very different from school and I had long ago had enough of that. On section, I found the classrooms dull and the staffrooms, stale with chalk dust, cigarette smoke and banana skins and peopled by the most unexciting of men, unutterably boring. Marriage, when it was offered, seemed infinitely exciting.

In my tenth year of marriage, I was Hostess of the Week in the *Auckland Star*. This was the high point, or low point, of my ultimate immersion in the stereotypic female role — the successful suburbanite. Six, I said, was the ideal number for a dinner party. 'Any more than that and I find the conversation breaks up into men talking together and the women likewise.'

This was punishment indeed, as I was one of those women who found talking to men much more interesting than talking to women.

I described my ideal menu: raw fish or a cold soup to start; duck with orange sauce, baked potatoes and spinach cooked with fennel seeds and cream; and for dessert, pears baked in red wine. By this stage I had learned to say dessert not pudding, sweet dishes not coupes and table napkins not serviettes. I had been so undomesticated that when my mother-in-law came to stay for the first time I asked her if she had brought her sheets with her.

Shortly after being Hostess of the Week the scales fell from my eyes. A guest at my dinner table asked me to come to a meeting about women's liberation to be held in the Ellen Melville Hall. I said I would, not because I needed it myself, I had such a kind husband, but because I felt sorry for other women who did not and wanted to help them.

What happened after that is another story.

One of the first things I did when I became involved in women's liberation was write to the *New Zealand Herald* about the women at the Whakatu freezing works being refused work on the viscera tables. I wrote saying that washing nappies was every bit as disgusting as working with sheep's innards.

My father saw the letter and rang me. 'Why do you want to get yourself mixed up with that bunch of women?' he said.

'I thought you would have been pleased,' I said, nonplussed. 'You sent us to university and made sure we had a good education.'

'You've got biology against you,' he said, and for once in my life I was truly speechless.

✦ ✦

SANDRA CONEY was a founder and editor for fourteen years of the feminist magazine *Broadsheet*. Her special interest has always been in the area of women's health.

In 1986 she wrote a history of the YWCA, *Every Girl: A Social History of Women and the YWCA*. From this and her continued research she has built up an unequalled knowledge of the history of the women of

Auckland and the role they played in its development.

In 1987 her article 'The Unfortunate Experiment', co-written for *Metro* magazine with Phillida Bunkle, caused a controversy that was to have a profound impact upon the medical care of women in New Zealand. In 1988 her book bearing the same name was published. Her selected articles were published in *Out of the Frying Pan* by Penguin in 1990.

Her latest book, *The Menopause Industry* (Penguin), provides a guide for mid-life women, examining the risks and benefits of interventions such as hormone replacement therapy, mammography and cervical screening.

Alison Holst

✦ ✦

LEGACY TO A LITTLE GIRL

*M*y father was a quiet, scholarly, rather serious man. A rather lonely, only child, he came from an orderly family who lived unobtrusively and neatly in a little house in a small country town. Having three loud, large and lively daughters must have been a real shock to his system!

My mother, outgoing, and people-orientated, was one of seven children raised in the sunshine and open spaces of a Canterbury farm, where friends and strangers were welcomed by her warm-hearted mother and her MP father, who was blessed with 'the gift of the gab', rather than farming skills, by the sound of the stories I enjoyed. She thrived on, and probably initiated much of the rush and bustle, laughter, noise and disorganisation that surrounded our father, and filled our small suburban Dunedin house, as we grew up.

I have never been able to decide whether my father was at heart a scientist, or whether his interests leaned towards the arts. Perhaps he was a bit of both. He graduated with a First Class Honours Degree in Geology, and I always got the impression that he would have really enjoyed an academic life completely within university confines. The Depression had left its mark on him, however, and he worried a great deal about security. Like several of the enthusiastic young men who joined the staff of the Teachers' College in Dunedin, when it opened its doors soon after he graduated, he lectured there until he retired, adding part-time work in the Geography Department at the university to his other work.

I was lucky to be the oldest child in our family, and my

'I was lucky to be the oldest
child in our family, and my
father spent a lot of time with me
when I was a small girl.'
Alison with her father, Arthur Payne
and her mother, Margaret,
holding Patricia.

father spent a lot of time with me when I was a small girl. Did he do this from choice, I wonder, or because he was asked to keep me occupied? I'll never know, but I'm grateful for his attention in those early days, and I'm sure that his influence on me was considerable.

What was a story? I knew. It was not read from a book. It was something that came out of my father's head. My earliest memories are of wriggling into bed beside him, insisting that I had been awake for ever, and *needed* a story. His stories were wonderful, and left books for dead. I can remember few details, just the feeling of excitement they gave me, as suspense built up. George Cat and Percy Seagull are the characters I remember most clearly. As I got older, I used to interfere with the plots. 'No, that's not what happened. He did this . . . ' and obediently my interruption would be noted, and the story would take another direction! Even as a very little girl, I could sense the pleasure he got from the sound of his favourite groups of words, as they rolled off his tongue.

These stories were never written down, but they were often illustrated. My father had a talent for drawing cartoons. His lines were sure, definite, and flowing. A few strokes and squiggles, and the hero of the story jumped up from the paper. I always admired this skill, and did my best to copy it. Occasionally, the drawer of the desk in our living room would be unlocked, and I would turn the pages of his artist's pad to admire the indian ink cartoons, done some years earlier. Sometimes, I would be taken into the deserted, echo-filled college at the weekend. We would draw together, with coloured chalk, on the blackboard in his lecture room, and I would ask him, for the umpteenth time, if, one day, he would let me hide in the knee-space under his desk, and listen to him teaching students. My drawings would be erased before we left, but his blackboard work, the quality of which was much admired, would be left, ready for use on Monday.

College was a magic place. After the war, children's books were hard to come by, but the college library had a seemingly endless supply, and new books would be brought home several times a week, extracted from the briefcase instantly, and immediately devoured by me, while my father greeted the rest of the family.

Another treat, brought home for the night, about once a year, was a prism. It never lost its fascination for me. Until it was too dark to see, I would look at my world with new eyes, marvelling at the way it gave rainbow edges to everyday items.

I 'helped' my father with a number of his chores. The coal was piled in bags outside our cellar, by the large, smudged, scary, and never-to-be-spoken-to coalman. We would drag the heavy bags inside the low door, tip them into the bins, and admire the shiny smooth surfaces of the 'fast' coal. Occasionally we would find fossilised markings on the coal 'faces,' and even though I could never recognise all the features he described, I shared his geologist's excitement with these rare and special finds.

My father and I walked long distances in the weekends, when I was young. We took picnics to a reservoir, miles away; we visited the museum where I needed to be quiet and restrained, and where I always detoured to admire the large bluestone crystal that my father had made himself. We talked to my father's friends, staff members in the bowels of the museum building, where 'ordinary' people were not allowed to go. These naturalists showed us their lizards, frogs, and recuperating penguins, rescued from the peninsula.

I was glad that there were never-to-be-broken rules about the things that men never did. They never wore aprons, and they never wheeled prams or pushchairs. Otherwise, we might have been forced to take a baby sister with us, and this would have completely spoilt our outings and conversations. It must have been my father who taught me to notice all the plants we passed, as we walked. I can still remember, nearly fifty years later, the appearance and names of the plants that grew in every garden I passed on my way to school. Dad was a keen gardener, growing flowers for pleasure, and vegetables for economy. I regarded gardening as boring because I was not allowed to make any of the decisions involved, although I tried hard to impose my will on different garden projects. However, I *was* allowed to help plant seeds in rows in prepared ground, and occasionally I planted radishes in the form of my initials, and I thought that this was pretty good. I took full credit for the plants that pushed up through the soil, and I rationed them to the cook, with a sense of power.

We had no car, the nearby corner store sold only a limited range of foods, and my mother was completely housebound, with babies, so my father went shopping after work. He brought home all our meat, and cases of produce from the city market, on the tram. He enjoyed deciding what we would have, and choosing the meat, and I would share his excitement as he unwrapped the brown-paper parcels that emerged from his leather briefcase. He would show me the rainbow-like membrane on the surface of the chunks of shin beef, and would explain to my mother that he had found such beautiful sweetbreads that he could not resist them. Perhaps we could have them, in parsley sauce, for breakfast, the next morning. Sure enough, amid the usual morning rush, with school lunches being cut at the last minute, and shirt collars being ironed, they would appear as one of my mother's many and varied delicious breakfast treats.

Sometimes there was half a pig's head in the leather briefcase. It would be scaringly recognisable. We would make the cuts for crackling, rub salt into them, and put the head in to roast immediately. By mid-evening the house would be filled with its wonderful smell. We would all gather round.

Could we have just a *little* taste of the bubbly brown crackling, straight away? Sometimes the whole thing would be demolished, as an evening snack, so there was none left for sandwiches in the morning. We felt guilty, greedy, but happy.

My father's enjoyment of the food he brought home was infectious. It was said that he could not cook, I suppose because he never baked or served a structured meal, and because this would have been moving into my mother's domain, but he certainly loved dealing with food. 'Do you want to help me take the top off this box, and see what's inside?' We would pull out the nails, lift off the lid, fold back the wad of shredded paper, and stroke, smell and admire the peaches or apricots, especially excited if they were the first of the season.

Rabbits came from a butcher at the bottom of the hill. To get them my father caught a different tram, then climbed the half mile, steep road, up the hill, home. The little rabbit bodies were recognisable. Sometimes, horror of horrors, fragments of fur remained. I watched as the carcases were dismembered, the pieces wrapped in bacon, and packed into a pot. How orderly and satisfying! I knew how good they would taste, later on.

The packages from the fish shop were especially interesting. In those days, crayfish were cheap enough to be used for sandwich fillings. I learned the finer points of dismembering them, and begged for the legs, to break in exactly the right place, and suck. Sole fillets, the only fish we ate, were remarkable only if they had large pieces of roe to admire. The big brown paper bags of oysters in the shell were best of all. The kitchen was filled with a briny smell. My father rolled up his sleeves and went to work. In between the oysters there might be a starfish, or a crab. I watched as the oyster knife was forced between the shells. We admired each oyster together, as it was opened. Wasn't it fat, and wasn't the shell iridescent? Wasn't it the biggest, and best oyster he had *ever* seen?

These early memories are so clear that I can smell the oysters, feel the shiny coal, and see the rainbows on the prism.

When and why did my father and I move apart, and lose this very special one-to-one relationship?

Did I suddenly get big enough to help my mother, so I no longer needed to be entertained by my father? Did he need to spend more time with those little sisters?

Was this the time that he started to study again, so that extramural lectures and exams filled his spare time?

Or was it just that my own world was expanding, and I developed other interests?

Was my mother surfacing again, after being buried in babies? Was it time that I started to learn girls' skills from her?

Whatever the reasons, my father moved back into the shadows, and, sadly, I associate him more with worries than

'My father's enjoyment of the food he brought home was infectious.' Alison beside her father, with her mother and sister.

pleasures, after this time.

What wonderful things I learned from him, though. He treated me as a person, without any emphasis on my sex. He opened many doors for me. From my point of view, his time with me was very well spent.

Stories can be invented, not just read. Words are wonderful things, to be enjoyed and played with.

Pictures can be drawn, not just looked at.

Food is something to be searched for, found, and rejoiced in, at all stages of its preparation, whether money is short, or not.

And the world is full of all sorts of exciting things, large and small, waiting to be noticed, examined in detail, and enjoyed. They are easily found, as long as you don't pass them by too quickly.

◆ ◆

ALISON HOLST was brought up and educated in Dunedin, and graduated from the University of Otago in 1960 with a Bachelor of Home Science degree. After several years of lecturing in the Foods Department of the School of Home Science, she made her first television cooking programmes, and published the recipes in her first cookbook in 1966.

She has made television programmes at intervals ever since, has published more than thirty successful cookbooks, as well as doing regular work on radio, in newspapers, and in live 'cooking shows' around the country. She has travelled widely, both in New Zealand and overseas, sampling international cuisine, and in particular promoting New Zealand lamb and beef.

Alison's particular interest is everyday family cooking. When she's not cooking, Alison can be found walking, gardening, dressmaking and embroidering, reading, taking photographs and taking a lively interest in assorted craft activities.

In 1983 she received the Queen's Service Medal for services to the community as a result of her fundraising cooking demonstrations, and in 1987 she received a CBE for her services to Home Science.

At the Lake So Blue

. . . My father was a patriotic man. The war was like yesterday to him. He admired valour. When he talked of brave deeds he got a strange high catch in his voice as if it would break with sorrow at any moment. I wished he wouldn't be like that; now I hear my own voice at times, just the same, though from different causes. It is to do with being swept with emotion.

He was, he said when we arrived that afternoon, about to play some records. I introduced him to my unsuitable friends. He cast an eye over them and decided to make the best of things. He played all of *My Fair Lady*. Linda and Miles went outside and smoked, even though it was raining quite hard by then.

My father sang a few snatches of the 'Ascot Gavotte'.

When the record was finished, I called out brightly, 'Rain stopped out there?'

'It's still going, can't you hear it, duffer,' my father said. 'Now listen to this.' And his eyes were shining and his voice caught, and I remember this with love, though I hated him for it then.

He played both sides of the dramatisation of Paul Gallico's novel *The Snow Goose* while I looked at my feet, and stole glances at the others; they were pulling faces at each other. At the end of side one Miles said politely, 'D'you mind if I use the phone, sir?'

I knew he was organising an alibi for them to get away.

'No phone,' said my father triumphantly.

'There's a wait with the Post Office,' I said in quiet desperation. We had been living there for four years.

'Who says?' roared my father. 'I don't believe in 'em.'

'It's not actually raining any more,' said Smitty, and everyone stood up at once.

'D'you have to go?' said my father. 'We've had such a nice time.'. . .

FIONA KIDMAN

'I wrote "At the Lake So Blue" in 1986. Set in Rotorua, it's about the summer of 1958, when I was eighteen. Like a number of my stories, it is an experiment with my own altered realities. The central character is me but things happened that I largely imagined. In this story, however, the reality extended to a number of other characters who were identifiably themselves. My father is one of them.'
This is an extract from the short story 'At the Lake So Blue', which was published by Century Hutchinson in *Unsuitable Friends* in 1987.

Susan Lojkine

. . . .

MY FATHER AND I

'We're going to New Zealand,' said my father. 'There they have fields of ponies by the sea, and you can ride on one.' So we went, and so, over the years, the wooden horse on wheels which I pushed around the tiny garden of our terrace house in England was succeeded, first by the garden gate in Plimmerton by the sea, on which I galloped many determined miles, then by the long hard black stems of flax flowers, sturdy hobby-horses to carry me all over the green hills and swamps behind Plimmerton during the late forties, and finally, when we moved to the Bay of Plenty in 1952, by a succession of borrowed nags, other people's unwanted cast-offs for the most part, but real ponies for all that.

My father was a town boy, a working-class boy, a night-school educated young man, with no advantages in life but those he made for himself. He was brought up in 'Paradise Place', eleven cottages flanking a narrow yard, in a small Lincolnshire town. There were two cold water taps and five privies for the eleven families, and a noisome midden for their other household refuse. Yet it was not an unhappy childhood. Throughout my life I enjoyed hearing over and again Dad's reminiscences of his boyhood. The lads played homely versions of cricket and football in the streets and back-alleys, and on the Council recreation ground, 'the Levellings'. There were the traditional seasonal games: whipping tops and bowling hoops in the spring, clay marbles all the dusty summer, conkers in the autumn, and ice-slides and tobogganing as winter came on. Another favourite game was 'Relievo', which my father later wrote about in his memoirs:

146

Then as the autumn gloom began to descend on us and gradually to deepen and turn cold the local lamplighter would walk round earlier with his long rod, poke it through the aperture at the base of the street lamp on its tall cast-iron lamp post, and a tiny segment of the street would be lit up. Lots of dark or shadowy corners abounded so that for the ensuing weeks, until frosts and then snow put an end to such outside activities, we played a game called 'Relievo', an elaborate form of hide and seek. Two opposing groups, chosen by leaders who took it in turns to nominate who they wanted in their teams, operated within a given area; the one group melting into the shadows behind trees, bushes, sheds, or in doorways, garden entrances etc, the others stealthily approaching to capture them by a touch.

For many years after we came to New Zealand, my father retained his English habits and cast of mind — playing and coaching soccer, gardening allotment-style, dogged devotion to self-betterment. But he was captivated by the free and easy New Zealand lifestyle, delighted to be part of it, responding with warmth and modesty to the ready acceptance of himself and his differences by the locals. And I and my sisters were, for him and my mother, to be the very embodiment of this new life of engrossing opportunities.

I was to ride ponies — my parents could not afford to buy me one, so they tracked down one after another that could be lent to me, found grazing, bought the 'gear', went to Pony Club rallies and camps. I, unlike them, was to be musical — they coached me through piano lessons, brought me back a cello from one of their later visits to England. I, unlike them, was to be a swimmer — they drove me over the winding dusty road from Te Puke to the Rotorua Blue Baths, for special swimming lessons. Above all, I was to be academically successful.

'Ask me questions, Dad,' I would beg. And he would go on and on with a general knowledge quiz, until he ran out of steam. I read his books: *The Iliad* and *The Odyssey*, Shakespeare, the English poets, and turned them into living parts of my life. We played 'Twenty Questions' with equal gusto. He was the

coach, and I was his student. I was also his companion. Many are the games of cribbage I have had, with my father and his father, using a triangular crib-board my grandfather had made. The three of us often went to the races, too, driving over to Te Rapa in the days when the Kaimai hill road was an unsealed succession of hairpin bends. They would study the racebook and have a modest bet, and I would admire the horses from yards to birdcage to track, and dream of riding a race-horse.

Student, companion, and unwilling surrogate son. How I hated having to help my father with the annual task of sawing up the winter's supply of firewood. He had a circular saw, set in a movable wooden bench, with a long trail of extension cords leading back through a window to a point in the house. He used to buy a load of macrocarpa off-cuts from the local sawmill, cut them up and stack them under the house for the winter. My job was to hold the far end of the length of timber, keeping it steady and straight as Dad put the other end through and through the saw, so that I got nearer and nearer to the screaming blade. I hated the roughness and resin-stickiness of the bark shuddering in my hands, I hated the scream of the saw in my ears, the jolt as it jammed because I hadn't kept my end straight on and my father swore at me, I hated the dust and grime as the day wore on, and I hated the back-breaking stoop as we children carried the pieces under the house and stacked them up.

It would never have occurred to my father not to push me along. I was the daughter and the son, I could do anything, and in fact I *could* do just about most things. Perhaps that's why the relationship continued to work, in spite of the occasional sharp clash of egos. I was just too successful for my father ever to feel comfortable about really bullying me. He respected me, even though he kept wanting to improve me. In fact, Dad never stopped coaching me all his life, and all mine, as I grew up, got married, had children, got a job, worked my way up. We changed the tyres on my car together, we put up the lining in the bathroom together, we made clunky carpentry things, like the guinea-pig hutch, together. Even as he lay dying, he still worked away at me. 'You know,' he said, 'if there's one fault you've got, I think it is that you're a bit arrogant — couldn't you try to be less arrogant?'

It was a strange time, the time that my father was dying. I think he must have been satisfied with what he had made of me, for he resigned himself, and my mother for the future, into my hands. I tried my best to extract information from the hospital doctors, found a hospice for him when the hospital kicked him out as incurable, found a GP who knew how to care for the dying. The tumour in his neck collapsed the vertebrae on to the spinal cord, leaving him paralysed from the neck down for the last four months of his life. He could just raise his arms, but could not move his fingers. Yet his body was not mutilated in any way, nor did it become wasted; he looked as he had done for many years, healthy colour in his skin, clear eyes, wavy silver hair above dark eyebrows, longish face with an asymmetrical jaw-line, and a smile of singular sweetness. With visits from my out-of-town sisters to spell us, my mother spent all day with him, I took over for the evenings, and together we did for him all the things he could not do for himself. Everything that a normal person would do to take care of his body and mind, we did for him, and more besides. Because he lay so still all day, being turned only every two hours, he loved to have his limbs exercised, his joints rotated, his skin massaged.

Was that a labour of love? My anguish during that period was so great that I simply could not bear to express my feelings. Neither did he. He knew he was dying, we all knew it, but it was never mentioned. All of us simply worked away all day and evening, so that he could best continue to live, while dying. He received his visitors, my mother wheeled him about the hospice gardens, I read to him, he continued the work of tidying up his life. One of his last conscious acts was to dictate to me a very thoughtful letter to a friend from the bowls club, about the best way to dispose of his set of bowls.

At length my father's hospice bed became his death bed. He developed pneumonia, and it was clear the end was not far off. My sister Alison came down from Wellington and one or two of the senior hospice staff came in to see him, so there was a small group at his bedside. Dad did not seem to be distressed. He was morphine-confused, but still intent on observing the social niceties. He mistook some remark for a joke, laughed politely, and capped it with an incomprehensible rejoinder. I will never forget the thrill of pity and horror I felt as, slowly and painfully, he raised a trembling hand to his mouth, and I realised he was not trying to suppress a moan of agony, but even in extremis was still covering his mouth as he coughed. Finally he said: 'I have to go now; you understand, don't you? I have to go. Goodnight Alison, goodnight Hugo, goodnight.'

'Dad', I thought, 'Please say goodbye to me, please recognise that I'm here, that I've been here all this time. Please don't go without a word to me.' But he said nothing to me. After a short time alone with my mother, he went to sleep, and died after three days in a coma.

✦ ✦

SUSAN LOJKINE was born in Gainsborough, England, in 1942, eldest daughter of Walter and Edna Turtle. Early in 1948 the family emigrated to New Zealand and soon recognised they had found a place to settle for good.

The first five years were spent in Plimmerton, on the coast just north of Wellington. During this time, Walter completed his BA at Victoria University and his teacher training — a hand-to-mouth existence for his family, but the children led a wild and carefree life. After a second equally happy five years in Te Puke, the family finally settled in Christchurch, where both parents taught for many years.

Susan studied science and maths at high school, but switched to English, French and Russian at Canterbury University. She married her Russian lecturer in 1965 (separated in 1985 and later divorced), and had two daughters. After completing a PhD in Russian, she found it offered no job opportunities, so she did a BCom ACA while working for a major accounting firm.

She became a partner in Peat Marwick in 1979 and resigned in 1987 to co-found the tax specialist practice of McLeod Lojkine, which was bought out by Arthur Andersen two years later. Her most stimulating job over this latter period was as deputy chairman of the Bank of New Zealand. Since 1989 Susan has been chairman of the Commerce Commission.

My Father

When I got up that morning I had no father.
I know that now. I didn't suspect it then.
They drove me through the tangle of Manchester
to the station, and I pointed to a sign:

'Hulme' it said — though all I saw was a rubbled
wasteland, a walled-off dereliction. 'Hulme —
that's where they lived' I said, 'my father's people.
It's nowhere now.' I coughed in the traffic fumes.

Hulme and Medlock. A quarter of a mile
to nowhere, to the names of some nothing streets
beatified in my family history file,
addresses on birth and marriage certificates:

Back Clarence Street, Hulme; King Street (but which one?);
One-in-Four Court, Chorlton-upon-Medlock.
Meanwhile at home on my answering machine
a message from New Zealand; please ring back.

In his day it was factory smoke, not petrol,
that choked the air and wouldn't let him eat
until, the first day out from Liverpool,
sea air and toast unlocked his appetite.

He took up eating then, at the age of ten —
too late to cancel out the malnutrition
of years of generations. A small man,
though a tough one. He'll have needed a small coffin.
I didn't see it; he went to it so suddenly,
too soon, with both his daughters so far away:
a box of ashes in Karori Cemetery,

a waft of smoke in the clean Wellington sky.
Even from here it catches in my throat
as I puzzle over the Manchester street-plan,
checking the index, magnifying the net
of close-meshed streets in M2 and M1.

Not all the city's motorways and high-rise.
There must be roads that I can walk along
and know they walked there, even if their houses
have vanished like the cobble-stones — that throng

of Adcocks, Eggingtons, Joynsons, Lamberts, Listers.
I'll go to look for where they were born and bred.
I'll go next month; we'll both go, I and my sister.
We'll tell him about it, when he stops being dead.

FLEUR ADCOCK

♦ ♦

FLEUR ADCOCK was born in New Zealand in 1934, went to England
with her family in 1939 and spent the war years moving about from place
to place and school to school (a total of eleven schools). In 1947 she
returned to New Zealand and lived in Wellington and Dunedin until
1963, when she settled in London where she has lived ever since. Until
1979 she worked as a librarian. Now she is a freelance writer. She has
two sons and three grandchildren.

Her books include *Selected Poems* (1983), *The Incident Book* (1986),
and *Time-Zones* (1991), all published by Oxford University Press. She has
also published a volume of translations from medieval Latin poetry (*The
Virgin and the Nightingale*, Bloodaxe Books, 1983, reprinted 1988) and
translations of two Romanian poets, Grete Tartler (*Orient Express*, OUP,
1989) and Daniela Crasnaru (*Letters from Darkness*, OUP, 1991). She
edited *The Oxford Book of Contemporary New Zealand Poetry* (1982)
and *The Faber Book of Twentieth Century Women's Poetry* (1987).

Her sister Marilyn Duckworth is also featured in this book.

Dame Malvina Major

•••

I only ever saw Dad angry twice in his life and I don't remember what it was over, I just remember thinking something must have been terribly wrong. I grew up thinking all men were quiet and smiling, just like my father. He hated arguments, and if he saw one coming, he'd disappear into his workshop to string tennis raquets, clean a gun or two, or mend someone's fishing rod.

I was the seventh of eight children; four boys and four girls. My mother said I was the only one he ever nursed — if you call a ride on Dad's foot a nurse. I always knew that if I asked my Dad for anything he would give it to me if he possibly could.

Dad always had a short cut when he drove Mum and me to concerts in country district halls around the Waikato. Mum and I would despair — we knew we would be late. Dad's short cuts always took longer, and often we got lost.

There was no short cut on a regular holiday drive to our bach at Whangamata, a lovely beach once you got there. The road over was winding and unsealed. Dad always had a roll-your-own cigarette butt in his mouth. It was usually out, but it had a putrid smell and that smell stayed for hours in my nostrils. I'd always be car sick, the windows would be wound down and the cigarette smell would seem to get stronger. Mum would nag him to put out his cigarette, out would come a little pair of scissors, he'd cut the end off the cigarette and both cigarette butt and scissors would go back into the pocket. Some time later the butt would be relit and finished. It was the only thing I couldn't stand about my Dad. I'm sure the awful fumes from his cigarettes, rolled with such dexterity, killed off the budgerigar whose cage sat right above his chair.

At Whangamata Dad's flair for inventions flourished. He made a kontiki fishing raft. In fact, I have always believed he invented them. We'd all go down to the wharf and Dad would throw his line out there. The kontiki would be taken up to the main beach, set in the breakers and be allowed to sail out to sea as far as it could go. By some magic trick, the little white sail would collapse and we'd sit on the beach, building sandcastles or drawing pictures while we waited. Dad never took his shoes off. He wore sandals and long shorts on his very white legs. He hated getting his feet wet or dirty. Or his hands. It was Mum and I who would dig for pipis because Dad hated getting his hands dirty.

People of all sorts flocked around my Dad. I never questioned his popularity, I just accepted it. But one poor young fellow was very persistent. He came to our Te Kowhai home every week and always brought a gun for Dad to clean. I realise now he could easily have cleaned it himself. His nickname became 'Pullthrough'. One day Mum rushed out to the shed and told Dad to get rid of him. It was years before I realised Pullthrough was coming to see me, not Dad. Dad was just an excuse and Mum was having none of it.

When my mother died in 1967, Dad was completely lost. All their lives, my mother had run after him. Not till then did he learn how to boil water and wash dishes. He never learnt to cook properly. As a result, I always insisted that my husband learn to cook and have the baby sit properly on his knee.

Now I realise I took my Dad for granted because he never made demands upon me. Instead he gave me peace and happiness. He died in 1976 aged almost seventy-five and I miss him sadly.

'He hated getting his feet
wet or dirty.'
Dame Malvina Major with her Dad.

♦ ♦

DAME MALVINA MAJOR was born in Hamilton, January, 1943, the seventh child of Eva and Vincent Major. She started singing country music with her brothers and sisters when aged two. She played the

ukelele and later the piano accordian, and piano. She studied singing at Ngaruawahia Convent, and went on to study for four years at the age of seventeen with Sister Mary Leo in Auckland. She won the 1963 Mobil Song Quest, and the 1964 Sun Aria Contest. In 1965 she went to London to study under James Robertson. Later Madame Ruth Packer was her singing teacher at the Royal College of Music. She won the Kathleen Ferrier Award in 1967 and sang in the Camden Town Festival in London. She was Matilda in *Elizabeth Regina,* which opened the door to Europe and Salzburg, and Rosina in *The Barber of Seville* with Claudio Abbado, Conductor, and Gernando Correra, Luigi Alva, Paulo Montaserto, Herman Prey. In 1968 and 1969 her summer seasons were spent in Salzburg.

Concert work in London and England ended when she returned to New Zealand to raise a family, one boy and two girls. While working with her husband on their farm in Opunake she continued singing for radio, television and the New Zealand Symphony Orchestra. She also sang in operas — *La Bohème, Madam Butterfly*, and *The Merry Widow.*

In 1985 she returned to Europe and was asked to join the Brussels opera company, the Théâtre Royal de la Morraie Bruxelles. Since 1986 she has sung in Brussels, Vienna, Salzburg, Amsterdam, Antwerp, New York, Covent Garden, Sweden, Australia, USA and New Zealand.

The 1992–1993 season is already booked and return visits to Salzburg, Australia and the USA are included. An operatic recording and a recording of light songs have been released with Kiwi Pacific and the NZSO.

'Malvina Major aged three, the seventh of eight children, stands in front of her father for this family photograph.

Gillian Walker

●·●

*T*wo o'clock. Still Dad had not come from the boat for lunch. Mum and I sat down to eat. We could see his dinghy was no longer hitched to the yacht, so we presumed that he must have rowed ashore. The storm that had prompted him to go down and check on the boat was beginning to stir. We ate our sandwiches. Still he'd not come. We went down to the bay. Dad's boat was nowhere to be seen, nor were there any signs that he had been there. Panic, fear, and dread knitted our nerves together. With abhorrence, Mum dialled 111 to report her husband, my father, missing.

From then it was as though we were up above looking down on ourselves, playing out this horror story. People rushed around, desperate to find Dad to relieve our aching hearts. The minutes became hours, and now the news, sickening — a boat, smashed, had been found and a man sighted bobbing lifelessly in the water not far from the swamped dinghy. I can remember feeling hot and clammy. The pain seemed to consume me.

The next days and weeks were a blur of people, coming and going, searching and not finding, sympathising and not knowing how best to soothe the pain. Each night we thought, 'Maybe they'll find him tomorrow.' I couldn't allow myself to believe that my Dad, part of me, had been taken away. They never did find him, just an oar, some boat keys and the remains of the wrecked dinghy.

Now whenever I think of Dad, I don't think of those last moments. I think back to the years of my early childhood, and to

'... we appeared the epitome of the "perfect" family unit — content and happy in our love for each other.' Gillian, just born, with her father and brother.

a Dad who was my best playmate. I picture that bronzed figure in his bathing suit, fit and strong, driving our waterski boat, and playing with us on the sand. We spent so many happy summers staying with my grandparents on the Whangaparaoa Peninsula. My favourite thing was to sit on his crossed knee; he'd hold my hands and I'd pretend I was riding a horse. My brother and I would help him cut the lawns, riding atop piles of cut grass in the wheelbarrow until he'd tip us out, burying us in grass; and of course there were the endless piggy-back rides. I can almost feel the contours of his warm skin against my body and hear the laughter ringing in my ears. He was a man who was full of fun, active, and he always had time for us. My fondest memories are of those long hot summer days, full of enjoyment, with Dad the central figure. I suppose we appeared the epitome of the 'perfect' family unit — content and happy in our love for each other. I know that that's how Dad would've liked to have thought of us. He was a perfectionist in everything that he did. Unfortunately my faltering eyesight started to chisel away at that ideal.

I contracted chronic iritis at the age of six and clearly remember being fitted with my first bifocal glasses. I sat at my grandmother's table and Dad brought the glasses to me. The first thing that I saw as I looked through those pink glasses was the definition of my grandmother's face. 'Oh Nana!' I exclaimed, 'I can see your wrinkles!' The world around me came to life, people had faces, cars had drivers, trees had leaves, seagulls had feathers and colours were brilliantly distinguishable — my world was no longer a rained-on water colour. As I remember those moments, I can still feel the anxious presence of Dad standing behind me, and the warm security of his paternal cloak extended around me.

My eyesight continued to deteriorate. From the age of nine to nineteen I had fifty admissions to hospital, having up to three operations each time. My dad used to call in at lunch-time but I knew that he found it upsetting. He was a self-made man; he'd continually striven to better himself and to provide the best that he could for his family. He'd been confronted by many obstacles during his lifetime, but this time it seemed he was beaten. Why? Why was it his daughter that had been cursed by this affliction?

What had his 'sweetheart' done to deserve this? Why couldn't he take away some of her pain and suffering? He found it hard to cope with the feeling of helplessness. It was as if life was playing some cruel game with him.

Ironically he'd always secretly feared having a blind child. Before he was married he used to travel by tram from Avondale into the city of Auckland to work. Every day he'd see two blind men tapping their canes to get on and off. It was as if that memory was haunting him and teasing him as he looked at me in my hospital bed. He never used to talk about his feelings to me, he was a very private person, but I was always aware of his frustration and bitterness. He continued to do everything that he could for me, but this sense of failure continued to eat away at him. I wished I could do something to make things different, and that I could be just like all the other kids, but it didn't worry me unduly. Unlike Dad, I had a child's natural optimism and I always believed that some miracle cure would be found.

During the course of those troubled years he changed, as did our relationship. He was as caring as before, if not more so. I'd always wanted a horse, and when I passed School Certificate that was my reward. He advertised in the paper and spent months examining prospective horses. At the same time he bought a horse for himself and rode with me every weekend until he was totally confident that I could ride safely by myself, despite the fact that he was busy and tired from building our house at that time.

He gave everything of himself to help me live through his eyes. When it was obvious that it was only a matter of time before I would lose my sight totally, he arranged trips overseas to ensure that I saw as much of the outside world as possible. He was incredibly loving, but the sense of fun had disappeared. The frustration and bitterness of this 'imperfection' in his life never waned. He became more and more engrossed in his work almost as a form of escape and as a means of proving that he wasn't inadequate after all. He climbed the corporate ladder. Consequently he became stressed and irritable, and there were inevitable emotional clashes as I struggled with the reality of

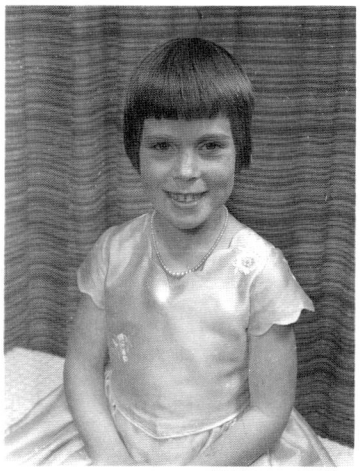

'I contracted chronic iritis at the age of six.'
Gillian Walker at age seven.

'He continued to do everything that he could for me . . .'
Gillian and her father in 1977.

159

being blind. I probably increased his feelings of helplessness by rejecting his and everyone else's help, but the only way I could cope with the situation was to be 'Miss Independence.' That's how he would've coped with it too, had he been in my position.

When I was twenty I finally lost my sight completely. As it transpired, it was my first guide dog that succeeded in allaying some of Dad's fears. He used to marvel at the rapport that I developed with Nina, and how easily I could get around with her help. The knowledge that I would be able to fend for myself in my future years seemed to relax him a little. It's comforting to me that he experienced this before he died.

He died only months later, when he was forty-nine years old. The years following his death were hard times for me. Dad had always been my security and then suddenly one day he was no longer there. For a few years I just seemed to exist. It was as if my every limb was numbed by the cruelty of his death. I went to work every day only because my dog needed the exercise and because of my mum's persistent encouragement.

I've come a long way since those black years of my early twenties. My mum is my best friend and confidante, and my dad has continued to be an inspiration throughout, despite his physical absence. I always wanted him to be proud of me. I've always tried to emulate him. I have the same energy and drive. I'm also a perfectionist, and I set very high standards for myself and for others. One of the reasons I push myself so hard, whether it be during a triathlon or in my work, is because I know that Dad would be disappointed if I didn't succeed. However, I have learnt to accept my blindness rather than fight it and search in anger for a reason for it. Dad continued to ask the question, 'Why?' My response was, 'Why not?'

Now one of my favourite runs takes me through the grounds of the Chelsea Sugar Refinery. I look out over the bay and can see the beautiful view across the harbour in my mind's eye. I'm at peace with the idea that my dad lies beneath the waves somewhere in that bay. My memories of him are always of my favourite playmate and those fun times spent in the waters lapping the Whangaparaoa Peninsula, so it seems a fitting place for him to come to rest. I know that he is still looking out for me. Contrary to his own perceptions, his paternal cloak was never torn away.

✦ ✦

Gillian Walker, winner.

GILLIAN WALKER is New Zealand's only blind triathlete and the only blind triathlete ever to compete in the world's most arduous and most prestigious triathlon, the Hawaii Ironman contest. She is renowned in her local Auckland community and amongst top-class athletes worldwide for her successful completion of the Hawaii Ironman in 1990. She qualified again to participate in the 1991 contest. Gillian has also successfully built up a business, running her own Remedial Sports Massage Clinic.

Ngahuia Te Awekotuku

• •

THEY SAID HE WAS DEAD

They said he was dead. Her father. He was dead, they said. Gone, dead, dead, dead. So she wondered, instead. It was safe, so she wondered.

I peer in the mirror, and I wonder, while steam from the bath curls around my freckly face.

Do I look like him?

I am eleven next week. They tell me I look like my mother. My real mother. I saw her once. And I do look like her. Yes, I do. But not all of me. Not the colour. Not the hair. Not the mouth. Do I look like him?

Was he dark, like my mother, too? Or freckly, just like me? Auntie Rima, she's so dark, just like my real mum. Just like Kuikui too; chocolate-scented laughter at Adams Bruce Tea Rooms with special china cups, and me, wide-eyed, watching, wondering. Too small to ask questions; and anyway, I never knew until later that she was my real auntie. She was his sister, they said. And not just my Kuikui's best friend. Tall, and dark, and rolling; huge round eyes and teeth that flashed broad across her face. She was his sister, the big one. Best friends with the girl's own kuia. Best friends who laughed all the time, they said. Laughed and laughed. His sister. Her father's sister. Her own, real, auntie. They never...they never said. That bit.

So was he tall, and big? Strong white smile and shining blue-black hair? Like Auntie Rima? Or was he freckly? Was he?

Too old, they said. He was too old. Past it. Couldn't look after the sick missus. Couldn't look after the new baby. Couldn't look after himself. But he worked, they said. He worked hard, too. In town. With a broom and shovel. Autumn leaves in the gutter. Scrape, slosh, scrape. On the streets with a broom and shovel. In town. Oh yes. He worked hard, they said. Past it. But not too old to work. And not too old to make the new baby he agreed to give away.

I find out that my father was nearly sixty when I was born. That the sisters he left me have children even older than me. We go to the same school. I know about them. They don't know about me. I am too scared to say anything. But I still wonder. Hiding myself, I search their faces secretly, looking for a sign, a link. They are wonderful, my nieces. Wonderful. Is he there, in their proud athlete's posture, and slim-line sophistication? Is he there, in their quickness that never ever sees me? Their grandfather, he was. Their koro. They might have even known him. Is he there? With them? In them? My father, living on in their sportiness and speed. In their lives, in their lines. My father, dead. Gone, dead, dead. Their koro. My father. I wonder.

Is he there? With them? And what about me?

She took the young woman's hands in hers, silky warm and soft. She smiled. He was a good man, she said. Your father, he watched out for us. He was a boxer, and he could fight, and he watched out for us girls, he did. He kept the other boys away, and he walked us home after dark. He was quiet, very quiet, but strong. And he watched out for us girls, she said. He did. Always. He watched out for us.

I hug my grand-aunt's words close to my heart, and think about the grainy, xeroxed image that my oldest, newest, half-sister, now a great-grandmother, recently gave me.

He is there. My father.

Army uniform and lemon squeezer hat.

Black painted black shapely curved eyebrows.

(Like mine!)

Smouldering dark slightly tilted eyes, inclined to sulk.
(Not quite like mine!)
Curly, considering mouth with a thinnish upper lip.
(Like mine!)
Sprinkled dots across his nose. The xerox? Or the freckles?
(Like mine, I hope. Like mine!)

He is there, my father. And that is all I know. Which is enough. To stop the wondering. He is there. And now. I don't care.

About what they said.

♦ ♦

Ngahuia Te Awekotuku.
Photo Gil Hanly

NGAHUIA TE AWEKOTUKU was born and raised in Ohinemutu, Rotorua, by an extended family of weavers, entertainers and storytellers. She has always enjoyed the patterning and magic of words, the making of stories. Currently she lectures in Art History and Women's Studies at the University of Auckland and writes fiction when she can find the time. Her collection of short stories, *Tahuri*, was published in 1989 and a selection of writings on Maori women's art, culture and politics, *Mana Wahine Maori*, in 1991.

Judith Potter

‹ ◆ ›

*S*tability is what we got, the children of the fifties. Our parents had experienced at least one world war, times had been tough, and stability was what they wanted. New Zealand was still isolated and air travel, as we know it today, didn't exist. Many families did not have a car. We walked to school and drank compulsory school milk at play-time.

During that decade I grew from the age of eight to eighteen and entered a workforce where there was virtually no un-employment. Dull, boring, almost unreal — viewed from today's perspective — but for me, a very happy time.

My father was, I believe, very much a product of that era. His father had been a man of great vision, a leader who had developed, created, expanded, experimented. But when the depression of the thirties came, my grandfather, with most others, suffered severe financial strain. So my father understood the stress on family life caused by financial difficulties. It made him very cautious, very conservative, consistent with the environment of the fifties. His conservatism would irritate and enrage me later in life, but it never changed.

He had also experienced a childhood without a mother; for his mother died young and my father, the eldest of four boys, took early responsibility in a household headed by a committed but distant father in the Victorian mould, a household run by a series of housekeepers, then a stepmother, then more house-keepers following her death. My father's responsibilities kept him single longer than many, and he was almost forty when I was

165

'My father saw the broadest horizons for his children, including, my sister and me.'
Judith turns five.

born. My mother was thirteen years his junior.

I believe it was his own childhood which made my father value his home and family so highly. Nothing was more important to him. His love for my mother and us, his three children, was infinite. He was proud of us and deeply contented in his home and his family. Not only did my father love my mother, but he respected her abilities. It would have been unusual in that era for my mother to work, and it would not have been my father's wish that she be involved in paid employment. Her abilities were typical of women of her era, and were exercised with talent and resourcefulness. She ran the household and was responsible for our care and discipline, and my father admired her for it and valued her skills.

In his business life there were women whose ability my father respected, praised and relied upon. Those women became household names — Miss Hollis, Miss Clements, Mrs Roberts and others. They were spoken of with admiration and respect. Their skills in management, book-keeping, retailing and organisation were known in our household because my father shared with us his acknowledgement of their skills.

My father, like his father, had always been interested in local body politics. My grandfather had been mayor of Mt Eden and my father, after many years on the Mt Roskill Borough Council, became its mayor and my mother became mayoress. Our household was always alive with political discussion and conversation which covered community and business matters on a national and local scale. I always saw our family and the members of our family as part of a much larger whole. While we, as children, were always encouraged to believe in our own worth, it was part of the culture in which we developed that we knew and understood that worth depended, not only on our own efforts, but on the proper and positive functioning of the society in which we lived and worked. I am grateful to my father for this broad perspective. It is much easier, I believe, if this understanding is part of a growth pattern, rather than having to be assimilated in adulthood.

My father's public profile exposed me to many other influences, which have been important in my own development. Our house was the focal point for meetings and election campaigns. The telephone, once we acquired one, was constantly busy. My father's speeches were a topic of conversation and my mother, and anyone else who felt inclined, was invited to comment and criticise on content and method of delivery. It was a standing joke in the household that my father jingled the coins in his pockets as he delivered speeches and my mother went to considerable trouble to remove the offending coins before any public appearance. My father, who had no formal training, was a good, if slightly formal, speaker. His commitment to honesty and forthrightness was evident in all his public communications. So public speaking, a public profile, an attitude of responsibility towards community matters were all part of my upbringing and are now part of me.

I also had the opportunity to witness my mother, with no training at all, take up the responsibilities of mayoress. I witnessed, without realising it, the benefit to a person in a public position of support from a partner who is loyal, intelligent and able to offer constructive criticism. My father's respect and admiration for my mother encompassed the ability she showed in her responsibilities as mayoress.

It is significant, therefore, that from my earliest days through the eyes of my father, I saw women as being competent, talented and capable of achieving whatever they set out to achieve. While my father would not have wished my mother to pursue a full career, because he perceived her obligations were to us and the family, he certainly perceived no such limits or restraints in respect of his children. Education was of prime importance and we were encouraged in every way. Education was seen in the broad perspective — not just academic learning, but sporting, other interests, and participation in the activities of school, college, university or whatever organisation we were involved with.

Common sense was forever emphasised. My father developed a reputation in our household as a total bore for his insistence on common sense above all else. Eulogies on the

'I believe it was his own childhood which made my father value his home and family so highly. Nothing was more important to him.'
Judith, left, with her sister and brother.

'Common sense was forever
emphasised.'
Judith Potter's father, once
Mayor of Mt Roskill.

virtues of what he called 'CS' were greeted with good-tempered howls of anguish by the children of the family, but I guess the admonitions on this important topic did not go unnoticed. We were encouraged to develop our potential, and were quietly assured that our potential was limitless, dependent only on our own energies and dedication. Independence and self-reliance were part of our upbringing, with the standards set by our parents infiltrating our lives.

My father saw the broadest horizons for his children, including my sister and me. There was no discrimination between sexes. The decisions we made in respect of our own lives were clearly acknowledged to be our individual responsibility. In the context of decision-making about our respective careers and lives, my father would often utter, 'Anyone can get married — even I got married. Not everyone can pass exams and be successful at sport and other things.' He was treated by us and our friends as a great joke for such statements, but the message was clear, and it was important to me. I never felt under any pressure to marry, settle down and raise a family, as was the expectation of many of my friends. I was encouraged to believe that marriage and family would happen if they were meant to happen, and that there are many other things to do in life which had equal or more importance.

When the time came for me to make a decision about a career and I mentioned the topic of law at home, the response was immediately positive. My father took the attitude that if I wanted to do law and was prepared to undertake the considerable amount of work involved, then it was an excellent thing for me to do. It was quite different for some of my peers. I remember well that others of my era, who proposed the pursuit of law or other careers, were met with opposition and comments such as, 'But what is the use of that? You'll get married and all those years of study will be wasted'; 'It takes years to do a degree like that. You'll never finish it because you'll get married'; 'Girls don't do things like that. If you want to go to university, why don't you become a teacher?'; 'Even if you got a degree, you'd never get a job. There are no positions for women in law.'

I, of course, absorbed all those comments and felt the uncertainties that came from contemplating breaking new territory. I brought them home for analysis by the family. My father's response was always positive, without being pushy or in the least bit arrogant. He simply believed that anyone who had ability, and was prepared to make the effort to use it, should be given the opportunity and success would follow. After all, he had not been afraid to stand out from the crowd himself and to take on responsibilities from which others shied, so he naturally saw no impediment or limit as far as his children were concerned.

I flourished in this atmosphere. The financial support needed in the early days of my degree was difficult for my parents, so I studied only one year full-time and then worked part-time. There were sacrifices, I know, to enable me to do it, but they were never presented to me in the form of a sacrifice my parents were making on my behalf; rather as their contribution in a joint venture.

My father loved to walk, as I do. I remember long quiet walks when no words were needed — especially the walks along the black sand beaches of Auckland's west coast, where you kicked up the sand with your toes and avoided the bluebottles, while the sea roared in the background, the gulls swooped, and the excitement of the wild coast surrounded you.

Then there were rugby games. My father was very keen on rugby and I recall endless sidelines, mud, early morning starts to put out the corner pegs on the local grounds, discussions of tactics, the thrill of a close encounter, the excitement of broadcasts of overseas matches played by the All Blacks. My father loved all sport, but rugby was a particular enthusiasm.

And music — music of all kinds, but not too classical. My father often sang around the house, and I came to know that he would sing as much when he was worried about something, as when he was full of joy. I think I have inherited that habit, too. My sister and I used to be greatly annoyed when, after a meal, my younger brother would be relieved of the chore of taking the tea-towel during dishes time, provided he was prepared to play his guitar. My father would sing as he washed the dishes at the kitchen sink; my sister and I would sing as we dried; my brother would play and my mother would sing as she went about her chores. It is impossible to realise the happiness of such occasions until you look back on them, but they are so important in a child's life.

There are delightful memories of collecting the eggs from the hens my father kept at the bottom of our long backyard, helping to pick the colourful Iceland poppies which he grew with great pride, and benefiting from the enormous quiet patience which pervaded all he did. I remember one occasion when my sister and I had jointly purchased our first car, a Mini Minor. My mother, at that stage, also had a Mini and a fibrolite carport had just been added to the garage. This was a significant expenditure in our family's terms, and I was warned by my father, as I drove into the backyard to wash my car, not to reverse it accidentally into the carport. I duly washed the car and reversed into the carport, demolishing the new fibrolite side in the process. I recall my father sitting on the back steps roaring with laughter and simply saying that Mr Ennis (the family handyman) would have to be asked to come back again to reconstruct the carport. No amount of criticism could have made more of an impact on me, the guilty teenager, than that patient laugh.

My father was slow to anger and there was little in the way of traditional parent/child battles. Rather, he would appeal to our rationality, usually successfully. But as I became more familiar with the ways of the world and, in particular, business matters, my father's arch conservatism irritated me. We would debate at length, with some heat on my part and rarely more than tolerant amusement on his, investment opportunities and business management. He was not inclined to be tempted by the ideas that I had developed as a product of a stable, and then inflationary, era. I often think that if he had lived to see the aftermath of the 1987 crash, he could not have avoided saying to so many of us, 'I told you so.'

The influences which parents bring to bear on their children occur without the parents realising it, but the extremely positive relationship I enjoyed with my father, indicates how much a parent can contribute to the ultimate direction of the child, without being aware of it. There are many times today that I wish I could call upon the comment and criticism that I know my father would offer in the most positive and kindly way. Fortunately, the memories are always there to call upon.

✦ ✦

JUDITH POTTER is the President of the New Zealand Law Society. She took office on 11 April 1991, the first woman president of the society in the 120 years of its existence.

Judith completed her law degree at Auckland University in 1964 and has been a partner in Kensington Swan, a law practice, since 1972. Today she is a senior partner specialising in corporate and commercial law.

Judith's involvement with the governing body of the legal profession started with her election to the Auckland District Law Society Council in 1977, when she was the first woman to be elected to a Law Society Council in New Zealand. Since that time she has held a wide range of positions, including Auckland President in 1988.

She is a member of the Securities Commission, to which she was appointed in 1988. She is a member of the Board of Trustees of Epsom Girls Grammar School. She enjoys sport, in particular golf, and has travelled widely, including two visits to the Himalayas on trekking expeditions.

Judith Potter, President, New Zealand Law Society.

Jane and Heaven

RACHEL McALPINE

This fiction piece is from a
novel in progress entitled *The Hum*.

*J*ane has a new frock, given to her by one of her aunties, back
from a trip to Australia. Not a hand-me-down and not a
home-made dress, but a bought dress with proper seams and a
label inside saying 'Pretty Lass Size Eight'. May and Pamela have
also got new dresses. May's is in bumpy yellow everglaze with
capped sleeves and a scalloped neckline.

The everglaze dress is very grown-up, and May is going to
wear it to the Youth Social at Uncle Harper's church. Uncle
Harper has an enormous book of games and the young people do
all sorts of things in teams: pass the orange from chin to chin,
crawl under one another's legs, run to the end of the hall and toss
a beanbag through a hoop. Nearly all the games involve running
flat out from A to B, and stopping suddenly. May is over the
moon about wearing her new dress to the Social.

Pamela loves her dress too. It's in pale blue flocked nylon
with white lace on its own built-in petticoat. She twirls around
and says she's the Fairy Bluebell. Unfortunately Jane knows
perfectly well that her own dress is the best one. It's got puff
sleeves and a real waist and a Peter Pan collar. It's made of pink
flowery spun silk, soft and cuddly to the touch. Hers is the best
frock because it will be suitable for best till it starts to look
shabby, and then she can wear it to school without looking too
dressy. The pleasures of her frock are private, intimate: the soft
touch on her skin, the little breeze she can create by suddenly
twirling around.

Jane's big problem is this. At church they have to ask
forgiveness for their sins. Jane is sinning dreadfully and she just
can't stop. On the surface she is nice to Pamela and May, but
underneath she is vain and proud, secretly gloating all the time
over her dress. She is sinning so badly there is a very strong
chance she will go to Hell. Every night she lies awake worrying
about going to Hell.

'Daddy,' asks Jane one night, after her father has told the

girls the latest episode in his made-up adventure story. May's gone back to her own room and Pamela's in the bathroom. It's just her and Daddy. 'How many people get into Heaven?'

Daddy looks at her speculatively. 'Just about everyone, I think.'

'How bad do you have to be to go to Hell?'

He looks again at Jane and he thinks about what to say. Then he tells here very emphatically: 'God is a loving God. He doesn't want people to go to Hell, because he loves us all very much. To get into Hell you have to do something really really wicked.'

'Yes, but how wicked? Like . . . being selfish and vain?'

'Dear me no! Like murder! Like killing someone on purpose and not being sorry afterwards.'

He tucks her in and kisses her cheek, and Jane gets her first good night's sleep for ages. It's such a relief! She's certainly not going to murder anyone. She's safe!

◆ ◆

RACHEL McALPINE was born in 1940, the third of six daughters born to Celia and David Taylor. Her mother was a dynamic individualist. Her father was then a country vicar who took an active part in child-rearing. Later he became a lecturer in theology, then general secretary of the National Council of Churches. David Taylor wrote many reports, and one extraordinary book, *The Oldest Manuscripts in New Zealand*.

From Rachel's first marriage (to Grant McAlpine) came four children, now adult: Geoff, Kate, Ben and Diana. A second marriage (to Michael Smither) is now at an end and Rachel is living in Wellington.

In 1975 her first book of poems was published. Six poetry volumes, three novels, various plays and much other work followed. Latest: *Maria and Mrs Kominski*, for children, and *Farewell Speech*, a novel about Kate Sheppard (New Zealand's celebrated suffragist), Ada Wells, Rachel's great grandmother, and her great-aunt, Bim Wells.

'My Dad was and is kind, affectionate, clever, honest, idealistic, hopeful, approving, forgiving, and utterly innocent. Much to his own surprise he was also a good horseman, tennis player, gardener, firefighter and washer-replacer. My experience with him has caused me to live for the past fifty-odd years a strange life based on the assumption that all men are fundamentally kind, affectionate, clever, honest, idealistic, etc. This has been at different times an awesome asset, and a profound embarrassment.'

'My Dad was — is — kind, affectionate, clever, honest idealistic, hopeful, approving, forgiving and utterly innocent.' Rachel gets some help to milk the cows from her father, David Taylor.

Megan Douglas

◆ ◆

A small child is possibly the most flexible creature this world can allow, and within a child is all the potential this world can hope for. A child, however, is vulnerable and dependent and seeks love and guidance from those closest and nearest. With some luck this will come from loving, sharing parents. I was a fortunate child whose parents gave love, knowledge and acceptance, but it is only now, as I become more and more independent of them, that I can understand our relationship.

As we emerge from our mother's body there already exists a real and immediate bond. However, fathers are outside. It would seem that the development of this 'outside' relationship creates a certain pattern in one-to-one relationships as we grow. I see this clearly in my father's interaction with me, and in my friends' relationships with their own fathers.

My father has had a dramatic effect on certain aspects of the belief structure which determines my life and career. He is always a great one for new ideas and new truths. He has a genuine explorer's nature and is at his happiest when creatively pursuing solutions to problems, new concepts and ideals. He listens, more than most people, to his intuition. All of these attributes are, thankfully, ones that I have inherited.

He and my mother gave me freedom of choice from the start and, most importantly, allowed me my own sense of destiny. They never tried to influence me unduly or coerce me to go in a particular direction, towards any career, religion or relationship. This gave a wonderful excitement to my life, and I see it as a

175

'Do you remember when
you were young?'
Megan Douglas at the beach with
her father, Roger.

continual adventure. Some people may believe this a dangerous road to allow a child to travel, but I believe this attitude gives the child, growing to adulthood, a responsibility to build his or her own truths and moral structures — often much more effectively and naturally than those forced on children.

Too often children rebel and create chaos not only for the lack of love and security in their lives, but also because they know, intuitively, that what they are being told to do or be is wrong for them.

Patterns are created early, and they are often hard to break. I have, at times in my life, found it hard to express what I want to say in relationships — to open my heart in honesty. But I am slowly finding myself much more open to personal expression. I share this difficulty with my father. This, it seems, is a common problem for fathers and daughters.

When I think of my father I appreciate his generosity, his loyalty, his passion and I acknowledge his stubborn pride, his relating timidity and I see it is all part of me. I love him for everything he has given me and shown me, but mostly I appreciate the freedom of mind invested in me to find my own beliefs, my own truths.

Do you remember when you were young
And every moment was a mountain
And every flower was a field
And you knew
You knew
That what you saw was sure and
Wonderful
Well life can be that too
When you see with
Old eyes new

MEGAN DOUGLAS is a fashion designer, stylist and creator/catalyst. She was born in New Zealand and at the age of seventeen went to Tokyo to work as a model for a year. Japanese fashion inspired her to set up her own clothing label when she returned to New Zealand. In 1986 she moved to London and set up her own women's fashion label 'Megan Douglas, London'. Her sensual designs sold fast in fashion centres worldwide.

In 1990 she was described in the British daily, *The Guardian*, as the designer and shaper of things to come. Both she and her designs have appeared in *Vogue, Elle, Harpers and Queen* and *The Face*. She has designed and styled for internationally acclaimed music artists including Annie Lennox of the Eurythmics, Julia Fordham, Yazz, Shakespeare's Sister, Seal, The Brand New Heavies, and Bomb the Bass.

Her special interest has always been in the promotion of fashion with other arts, especially music. She believes fashion to be as important a creative vehicle as music and other arts, and works to combine street/club culture and other media with fashion.

In 1990 Megan Douglas closed her London operation down and moved to Tokyo where she believes Japanese innovation and technology can play a major role in introducing a 'New Age', which will discard fashion as we know it. Instead, 'adornment' will combine natural and 'green' materials, resources, skills and other elements to create a totally new type of clothing embodying the essence of the 'New Age'.

'My father has had a dramatic effect on certain aspects of the belief structure which determines my life and career.'
Megan Douglas with her father.

Erin Baker

• •

Sitting down to write about my father, I find I have to search deeply in my mind to recall the times we shared together, what he has accomplished during my life, the sacrifices he has made for me and my sisters and brothers. Then I remember him: biking home for lunch from the freezing works, blood spattered on his white overalls; bringing party guests into our rooms to show us off (we were never asleep, just pretending); taking me, in the early morning, to age-group swimming meets; always in the kitchen at night when we returned from swimming with a tea-towel around his neck (a Baker trademark), having wiped the bench for the twentieth time that evening; eating dinner in the kitchen with me keeping him company while the others ate theirs in the lounge watching TV; tolerant of me, not punishing me, making excuses for me because he knew our moods were so similar; screaming at us to 'put more bloody clothes on' — he couldn't bear to think we might be cold.

My childhood was spent in Kaiapoi, North Canterbury, surrounded by my family — parents, six girls (with less than eight years between us) and two younger brothers. My parents have always talked about the way we quarrelled. We seemed, they said, to be worse than the families of their friends. I do remember that the eldest three, Maureen, Alison and Roseanne, fought a lot. Kathy, number four, always had her say, but my special friend when we were young was Philippa. We did nearly everything together. I, of course, being the elder, insisted on being the boss.

Dad always seemed to be working. In fact, for many years he had three jobs to support his large family and all their interests.

His main employment was at the North Canterbury Farmers' Freezing Company (NFFC) as a butcher, then boardwalker (a kind of supervisor) and then as a foreman. He always enjoyed his work and was a popular figure at the works. Alison and I liked to go and see him there sometimes, and take him his lunch.

As in most large families, life was so busy that none of us seemed to get much individual attention. Our early days revolved around kindergarten with a baby always in the background, and then off to school at St Patrick's Convent School.

Our parents both felt it was important that we participate in sport, and we all learnt either dancing or music as well. At

'Dad always seemed to be working. In fact, for many years he had three jobs to support his large family and all their interests.'
Erin sits on her father's knee in this photograph.

179

Father and daughter at the high school ball. Erin is eighteen.

different times the piano accordian, tap dancing and gymnastics were all tried. Maureen, especially, has continued to use her dancing in operatic shows and in aerobics. But the rest of us loved swimming and we all learnt to swim at the local 25-yard pool with its wonderful diving board. Every Christmas holidays, we spent hundreds of hours there.

We joined the local swimming club and revelled in the competition around the small clubs of North Canterbury. Roseanne, Kathy and Alison wanted to start some serious swimming training and so, in 1968, it all began: those early morning starts. At 5.15 in the morning Alison would get the others out of bed, Dad would take them up to the Rangiora 50-yard pool, and by 5.45 they'd be in there swimming for an hour and a half. At night the coach came down to the Kaiapoi pool for more training.

When I was nine we moved to Christchurch. I attended Sacred Heart Girls' College, starting at intermediate level and then on to secondary, until I left at the age of seventeen. We lived in a wonderful old 'house on the hill' in Gloucester Street. People never believe us when we talk about this hill, but indeed it is there. The house had five bedrooms and a big cupboard in the hall with a light in it. That was a great place for members of the family who like to read — or dodge a bit of work, and hide for a while. I don't think I was ever relaxed enough to read much. I was always on the move. We had a marvellous mulberry tree on the back lawn; a source of income for me. During one of the school holidays I picked punnets of mulberries, sold them to the local Chinese fruit shop, and bought myself my first new bike — a Raleigh low-line — very smart. I was proud of that bike.

After we shifted to Christchurch, Mum returned to the paid workforce. Dad was able to give up his secondary jobs, and I joined the others swimming — training morning and night. Dad's work was up at Kaiapoi, so Mum took the early morning run, then he would take us at night.

One Saturday Dad and Mum had gone to Kaiapoi to help my grandparents shift house. Kathy, Dawn (my foster sister) and I were at home. We had a bit of a quarrel and somehow I put my hand through the glass door. My thumb was literally hanging by a thread. Kathy ran down to the doctor who lived nearby and Dawn phoned my parents in Kaiapoi. The doctor wouldn't help. He just said I would have to get to Accident and Emergency at the hospital. Dad got home from Kaiapoi in about ten minutes and took me to the hospital.

I had to stay in bed for over a week, with my hand held up. Dad made a sling, which was suspended from the ceiling, and made a fuss of me. Anyone from a large family will know how nice it is to be the centre of attention, even if I did hate the inactivity of being in bed. During times of sickness, Dad would always bring us our favourite treat — a bottle of Alexander's lemonade.

One August we billeted hockey players for a secondary schools' hockey tournament. The weather couldn't have been worse. It rained the whole week they were there. We didn't have a dryer, as Dad had always dried our washing during wet weather at the freezing works. All through the week he took load after load of washing to the works, to ensure the girls had clean dry uniforms and track suits each day. Even when we were small and generated huge piles of washing, including nappies, Dad had always taken it to the works to be dried. He was never embarrassed. I am sure many of his fellow workers probably cursed him for taking up so much space in the drying room.

Shopping was another thing that never worried Dad. He would do any shopping asked of him. He honestly must be one of the least sexist men in the world . . .

All through his married life my father has cooked wonderful Sunday roasts. When any of us are overseas, we really look forward to coming home to one of these roasts. Even now every Sunday sees at least two or three of the family home with their children to enjoy this special treat. He also prepares the vegetables each night — isn't my mother spoilt?

But our 'bench wiping' obsession, a habit picked up from Dad who can't go past a bench without wiping it, mystified my husband Scott, and in fact the partners of all family members.

And one of my fondest memories of childhood is of those

extra blankets going on when the cold winter nights came. Dad would always come in to check that we were warm enough, and if there weren't enough extra blankets to go around, on would go his old army coat — kept especially for the purpose, I think.

While we were at high school most of us worked at one time or another at the Strollaway Bar, well known in Christchurch for its freezes and thick shakes. The family pattern was to save up and put a deposit on our first motorbike, a Honda Step-Thru (the first 50 cc step-thru, rather than leg-over motorbike, and specially designed for women). Later on we graduated to bigger bikes. How my poor father worried about us on the bikes, and as the others got older and went out on Saturday nights, he would never go to sleep until that last motorbike had zoomed up the hill. Even now he never goes to sleep without praying for our safety. Mind you, he never had much cause to worry about me because my social life was pretty much zilch at the time. From the bigger bikes, we went on to small cars and the dear old VW was our favourite. Dad was quite happy about this because he regarded the VW as a sturdy car.

At the age of fifteen I gave swimming away. I didn't do as well as I hoped I would, and no matter how hard I worked, I only seemed to get second or third at national age-groups, and this never satisfied me. Also, I was a pretty bad sport and was, I think now, jealous of Kathy's swimming successes. I think Dad was especially disappointed when I gave it up. However, my parents suggested I try cross-country running as a way of easing myself into something different. I enjoyed several years of cross-country, track and road running before again giving up because I couldn't quite reach the top. Again Dad was disappointed, but as long as we were well and didn't injure ourselves, he was OK about it.

I completed my seventh-form year at school as Head Girl. I didn't particularly enjoy this position which was probably given to me for my sporting ability and because I helped our Phys Ed teacher, Mrs Barnett, in the organisation of many of our sports days. Being Head Girl rather sets one apart and I found it quite a lonely experience.

I applied and gained entrance to training college, but I didn't get the satisfaction I had hoped for, and left for a three-month stint in the Territorials. Dad enjoyed coming out to see me at Burnham; he had enjoyed army life himself in Japan and Korea. My mother, who was in the peace movement, wasn't at all impressed. I then applied for radiography and completed the two-year course satisfactorily. My sisters Maureen and Philippa also did radiography courses. This was an interesting and satisfying career, and my father felt great pride in us.

But around this time (1981) my father found other things to worry about when Mum, Kathy and I became involved in the Springbok Tour protests. My father was against the tour, but not actively involved in protesting. Mum, however, had a leadership role, and we wanted to support her. Kathy and I went to Nelson to be part of a demonstration there. Dad made us promise to phone him and let him know that we were OK. All had been quiet and in the early evening we made our phone call to report that all was well.

We joined a picket outside the Rutherford Hotel where the Springboks were staying. Some smoke bombs were passed around and, for the relatively small misdemeanour of throwing one of these, I was later charged with using an explosive. I have never understood how on earth my harmless little smoke bomb had suddenly become an explosive in the eyes of the law. I was initially charged with disorderly behaviour and had to spend a night in the cells in Nelson, which I found pretty upsetting, but nothing compared to the trauma caused by a five-day High Court hearing as a result of the explosive charge. Until this time, I had believed that if you were innocent you couldn't be found guilty. I certainly lost my innocence then. My mother came with me to the trial in Nelson while my father stayed home worrying and reading newspaper reports of the trial. However, I have never had any regrets about my involvement in this moral issue. It was inconvenient not to be able to compete in the USA for a long time but even this hurdle was finally overcome.

I subsequently lost my job as a radiographer in Christchurch hospital, and shifted to Darwin, which was for me the loneliest

'...our "bench wiping" obsession, a habit picked up from Dad who can't go past a bench without wiping it, mystifies my husband Scott...'
Her father takes Erin into the church on her wedding day. Sister Philippa is in the background.

place in the world. However, my sister Alison was also living in Australia and we both settled in Sydney where my triathlon career began.

My dad has played a crucial part in my life to this very day. He is the backbone for us, always there, always steady, always loving. Seeing me receive the Sportsman of the Year Award in 1989 gave him special pleasure. I will always have a special spot in my heart for him, and remember him as the most wonderful father anybody could wish to have. Nowadays he delights in his grandchildren and having them to stay. He can still be seen at night, sneaking in with that extra blanket, or coat or dressing gown, whenever he thinks they might be cold.

✦ ✦

ERIN BAKER is one of a family of eight, six girls and two boys. She has devoted most of her life to sport. She was a Canterbury age-group swimming representative, but at fifteen she turned her sights to running. Twice she won the New Zealand secondary schools' road racing title and many Canterbury cross-country and road racing titles.

While working as a radiographer in Australia, in 1983, she decided to compete in a triathlon event, hoping to win the prize of a return air ticket to New Zealand. She found she excelled at this demanding sport, and became a full-time triathlete in 1985.

Her major successes have included the 1987, 1988 and 1989 Standard Distance World titles, the 1985 and 1988 Nice Middle Distance World Championships and, greatest of all, her 1987 and 1990 wins in the demanding Hawaii Ironman Long Distance World Championships. In 1988 and 1989 she was voted Triathlete of the Year in the United States, the first time a non-American has won such an award. In 1990 she was the overall winner of the first World Series Ironman championships, taking three firsts and one second in the four Ironman events in which she competed. Erin Baker won the world Women's Duathlon title for 1991. Her endurance and determination have become hallmarks of an outstanding career and she is unquestionably the world's top female triathlete.

Cattle in Mist

A postcard from my father's childhood —
the one nobody photographed or painted;
the one we never had, my sister and I.
Such feeble daughters — couldn't milk a cow
(watched it now and then, but no one taught us).
How could we hold our heads up, having never
pressed them into the warm flank of a beast
and lured the milk down? Hiss, hiss, in a bucket:
routine, that's all. Not ours. That one missed us.

His later childhood, I should say;
not his second childhood — that he evaded
by dying — and his first was Manchester.
But out there in the bush, from the age of ten,
in charge of milking, rounding up the herd,
combing the misty fringes of the forest
(as he would have had to learn not to call it)
at dawn, and again after school, for stragglers;
cursing them; bailing them up; it was no childhood.

A talent-spotting teacher saved him.
The small neat smiling boy (I'm guessing)
evolved into a small neat professor.
He could have spent his life wreathed in cow-breath,
a slave to endlessly refilling udders,
companion of heifers, midwife at their calvings,
judicious pronouncer on milk-yields and mastitis,
survivor of the bull he bipped on the nose
('Tell us again, Daddy!') as it charged him.

All his cattle: I drive them back
into the mist, into the dawn haze
where they can look romantic; where they must
have wandered now for sixty or seventy years.
Off they go, then, tripping over the tree-roots,
pulling up short to lip at a tasty twig,
bumping into each other, stumbling off again
into the bush. He never much liked them.
He'll never need to rustle them back again.

FLEUR ADCOCK

Sue McCauley

◆ ◆

TO MY FATHER

*I*n fifty years I remember only two personal comments you have made to me. That may be a record. Perhaps there were others and I have forgotten them, though that feels unlikely. In fifty years I doubt that I have made two truly personal comments to you. We are not a family that wears its heart on its sleeve.

The first personal comment was after you had watched me running. *After* or *from* something, for sure —I was not a child who ran for the heck of it. You said that watching me run had been a distressing experience. You couldn't believe that you, who had run in competitions (indeed your running prowess had become a part of family mythology) could have fathered a child so inept at putting one foot behind the other at speed.

The second personal comment came about twenty years later, when I had just become a solo parent.

'But you're tough,' you said. Meaning resilient, I suppose, for we were talking about my situation. I was privately astounded: *that's how my father sees me*. For it was never how I'd seen myself. Dogged, perhaps, but precarious and fractured — an emotional wimp. *Tough*?

Later, when I thought back, it seemed to me that you must always have seen me that way. So perhaps it was true. Or at least no more inaccurate than any other assessment of a person's nature. And I realised that, in the same way, I had always seen you as *kind*. Above all, in my mind you were always *a kind man*. And that I know to be true, but I wonder now if perhaps we didn't, both of us, select those characteristics in each other that it suited us best to believe in. A kind of emotional shortcut through

'... but I wonder now if perhaps we didn't, both of us, select those characteristics in each other that it suited us best to believe in.' Sue and her father, centre.

the thorny undergrowth?

You will argue that my first sentence here is absurd. That there have been assorted personal comments I must remember. And that's true, but I refuse to count wry comments about my clothing or the colour or state of my hair because I've always taken those to be a statement — not about me, but about the speed at which the world changes. Though, in fact, if you and I belonged to the same generation our lives would still have been foreign countries with mystifying rituals and alien customs.

When I was eighteen I went to a fortune-teller in Napier. A workmate had told me how two friends had visited this fortune-teller, and one had been told of romance, children, happiness. But, when the second friend stood before her, the fortune-teller made an excuse to cut the appointment short. The second friend ran angrily out from the fortune-teller's house, feeling cheated. And was hit by a car and killed.

I suppose this was an urban myth, but at the time it made going to the fortune-teller in question feel like a daring act. What if she had nothing to tell *me*?

In fact she said very little. Only that I was no longer living at home (which I knew already) and that I was soon to leave Napier for good (this turned out to be true). Then she looked at me intently and said, 'When you next go home and you step off that train you should try hugging your parents. There is not enough hugging in your home.' I thought, *she even knows I go there by train.*

I have friends that are heavily into hugging (that won't surprise you — that's the kind of people you expect me to hang out with), and I have friends who are heavily into family communication and discussing their emotions. Who can say, '*I love you,*' with the ease of American sitcoms. They think anything less than they exhibit is emotional deprivation. They do not understand the caress of silence, the comfort of the unsaid, and I don't know how to explain it. Not to them.

I can talk about land, plants, animals, birds — the things that nurture us best, and most kindly, demanding nothing in return — and how they have no need for *declarations.* I can say that in the simple existence of nature is the only kind of truth or caring that, finally, matters. That words and gestures are prone to corruption and misinterpretation. In my heart I have an absolute sense that this is true — but in saying it the words become poncy and didactic.

But you will know what I mean. For it is the most precious thing you have given me; that sense of meaning and harmony in nature that is absolute and needs neither explanation nor exposition. In my heart I recognise this, it makes sense of the world and stops me from jumping off bridges. In my heart I know (for you have shown me) that love is hills and riverstones and that words are at best suspect.

Yet I have chosen to build my life around words.

Each day I play fast and loose with them, I take them for granted and I invest them with a sense of importance. But I am your daughter and all the time I know my words are always irrelevant, sometimes untruthful, and occasionally treacherous.

For a writer this is not a comfortable thing to believe.

Fortunately I am tough.

SUE McCAULEY was born Susan MacGibbon in 1941, in Dannevirke. She has one older sister with a wonderful imagination who invented complicated games in which 'we were each a whole extended family of happy primitive bush-dwelling people'. Sue's father was a farmer — mainly sheep, some cattle; her mother, who died when Sue was very young, was a school teacher.

'My father remarried when I was eight and my step-mother talked him into letting us ride our horses to school. Mine was a Welsh pony called Viti because she had South Pacific connections.'

Sue spent four years at Nelson College 'nursing a bad attitude', and a year as a nurse aide. Since then, apart from casual jobs, she has always worked as a writer of some kind — copywriter, journalist, freelance writer, etc.

An 'ill-advised' marriage at twenty-one to a fellow journalist resulted in two children, but ended in divorce. Sixteen years later Sue remarried — not a journalist. She has lived, at various times, in Waitahora, Nelson, Dannevirke, Napier, Wellington, Leeton NSW, Melbourne, New Plymouth, Waiheke Island, Umawera, Okaihau, Auckland, Masterton and (at present) Christchurch. She claims she does not like shifting house.

She still works as a writer.

Penny Brothers

◆◆◆◆◆◆◆◆◆◆◆◆◆◆◆◆◆◆◆◆◆◆◆◆◆◆◆◆◆◆◆◆◆◆◆

SCIENTISTS

Separation of identity from that of parents and family comes differently for everyone. Apart from being plump and brainy, both serious drawbacks among one's peers, I had a relatively easy ride through adolescence. I worked hard at school, my friends generally met with parental approval and socially I was a late bloomer, so I never went through a phase of teenage alienation from my parents. The need to assert my independence crept up on me slowly and in early adulthood rather than adolescence. My mother remains one of my best and closest friends and I have never felt the need to rationalise her influence on my life. It's not so straightforward with my father.

Dad was a self-confident, gregarious and articulate fellow. He always came across as a great debater and raconteur, whether around the family dinner table or in wider circles. As a youngster I looked up to him, thought he was wonderful and assumed that everyone else thought the same. I can remember well a sudden dawning of awareness on my part at the age of about eleven or twelve that perhaps he wasn't always right, that perhaps his firmly held opinions were just that, opinions rather than facts, and that perhaps there were people in the world who didn't agree with him. The acute feeling that I can still recall was like discovering that some great, safe, solid and utterly dependable object had its weak places, after all — and the more I looked the more I seemed to find. I am still aware of worrying about what others think of him; especially as I now work in the same institution where he made his career for over thirty-five years.

Nick Brothers, my father, was born in Taihape in 1924; the

'I always felt that these years away were something really special that our father had been able to give us.' On the boat home from England, December 1960, Penny sits between her father, Nick and her brother, Peter.

second son of a railway employee who was a guard on the main trunk line. My father remembered riding on trains with him, but he cannot have known him well as his parents divorced when he was eight, and his father died when Dad was about fifteen. When his parents split up my father moved with his mother and brother to Auckland, where his mother ran a small farm in Avondale, and took in paying boarders to help make ends meet. Despite his non-academic family background Dad was a keen scholar and resisted pressure to leave school and help out on the family farm. He went on to study science at Auckland University where he met my mother Margaret, also a science student. They married shortly before leaving for England where Dad did his PhD in geology. My older brother Peter was born just after they returned to New Zealand, and I came along five years later, in 1956, followed by two sisters, Trish and Philippa, within the next five years.

Dad seemed determined to give each of his children the advantages that he had been denied. When we complained about homework he would tell us that when he was young he had to take a lantern out to the barn to do his as it was the only place he could find where he could work uninterrupted. As soon as each one of us reached the homework age he installed a sturdy kitset desk and an anglepoise desk lamp in our bedrooms. Everyone in the family is now a great reader — a habit instilled by a weekly Friday night visit, with Dad, to the Grafton library where we would choose our books for the week. They were then confiscated until Saturday morning when we would find them in a pile by each bed when we woke up, topped with a chocolate fish.

The same Friday night outing included visits to the hardware store and plant shop in Mt Eden village, where Dad would stock up on supplies for the weekend's projects around the house and garden. With two parents who were keen gardeners, the whole family (at least while we were young) would spend weekends mostly at home. We were encouraged to be part of the projects Dad undertook although this often meant hauling loads of hedge clippings down to the trailer, or standing for hours holding stakes in place while Dad got the levels right in order to build boxing for a concrete job. He was a thorough and meticulous worker. Everything he did was designed and executed to super-sturdy solid specifications. I remember thinking that other kids seemed to do more exciting stuff with their families on the weekends, while we always just hung around home. Though there were compensations.

About 1958, my parents bought a section in the Bay of Islands and built a bach. We would spend a month up there in summer, as well as shorter periods at Easter, May and August vacations and Labour Weekend. What Dad created there for the family was something really special. I think my own sense of family grew deepest during our holidays up north, and I think that's where I also learnt from Dad how to really love the physical qualities of a place — the surrounding hills and bush, the beaches, each with its own special character, the changing weather and the corresponding changes in the sea and land. He seemed to work as hard 'on holiday' as he did around home, and again we were part of many of his projects: standing by while he smoked fish; helping to build enclosures around the pohutukawas he planted on the foreshore to protect them from browsing animals; sanding and painting the small sailing boats. But in addition to the never-ending projects there were family picnics on secluded beaches, walks in the surrounding hills, and fishing, either with nets for flounder or yellow-eyed mullet, trolling for kahawai or drift-fishing for snapper. I learnt from him the rudiments of small boat sailing in a P-class while he patrolled behind in the dinghy with the outboard. I had to follow his shouted instructions faithfully, even though these might eventually lead to capsizing the boat (all part of the learning process). Later, on every boat trip around the Bay of Islands he would point out the same landmarks and hazards, hidden or obvious, over and over again. Now I cannot help myself doing the same thing when out in the boat with my husband or sisters.

As part of Dad's university job as professor of geology he was able to spend a year, every seventh year, on sabbatical. This meant that the whole family was packed up and transported by sea to some distant location where we would be installed in a new place to live, attend a new school, and be exposed to many new experiences. As a result I spent a year in London (aged three), a year in Berkeley, California (at ten), and, seven years later, a year in Athens, Greece. The time in Greece had special significance as we were ourselves an eighth Greek through our paternal great-grandfather, a Greek who had settled in Dargaville, and run a successful fishing business. One of his thirteen children was Nana, Dad's mother, who had definitely inherited the Mediterranean temperament.

I always felt these years away were something really special that our father had been able to give to us. While living overseas we would attend the local school, which didn't always offer continuity with our studies back home, but Mum and Dad must have felt we could easily overcome this and that the travelling itself was an important part of our education. However, back at home, progress at school was accorded great importance within the family, even though this was not accompanied by overt pressure. Doing well at school was expected of us, and a report card with straight A's was usually received with mild satisfaction that all was going according to plan, rather than with great expressions of delight or congratulation. I remember a schoolmate telling me she had been promised a new bike if she got straight A's — certainly no particular rewards, material or otherwise, were offered by my parents for doing well at school. It may be true that children respond better to high expectations, but looking back it was difficult for me to know if, or when, I had done well enough. Being involved in teaching himself, Dad had some ideas about the process which, to me as a teenager, seemed somewhat out of touch with reality. For instance, exams were to be enjoyed, rather than feared or endured. I remember coming home after what I felt had been a disastrous exam and pouring out a tale of woe to Dad, who offered his standard response: 'Well it sounds like you enjoyed it, that's the main thing.'

Certainly my choice of career in science was a direct result of family influence. Growing up in the sixties and seventies, the golden age of modern science, with a father who was a geologist, a mother who had a masters degree in botany, and an older brother studying maths and physics meant that there was little doubt about the direction I would take. This was not openly stated, but it was an atmosphere that prevailed. Science and continued academic study were the only real options. Certainly this was the route that I took, studying first BSc then MSc in chemistry at Auckland University, followed by PhD at Stanford University in California.

My first year as a student at university marked a huge change for me. I joined the University Tramping Club and this quickly became the new focus for my life. I threw myself whole-heartedly into tramping, rock-climbing and mountaineering, and made a heap of new friends, both men and women, in a way that felt much more natural than the angst-ridden social occasions I had endured during my schoolgirl days. Strangely, though, I never felt sure of Dad's approval of my new interest, yet I'm sure my affinity for physical landforms, river valleys and mountain ranges came from him, and certainly geologists spend much of their time tramping. But geologists might tramp over rugged terrain with a heavy pack to get somewhere specific, to make an observation or collect a sample, whereas trampers, Dad asserted, covered rugged terrain with a heavy pack just to see how fast they could get from A to B, all in a red haze. In a similar vein, he maintained, geologists work with rock to study and understand it, whereas rock-climbers are simply hanging on for dear life without caring whether it's sandstone, granite or greywacke.

In the same way, while I couldn't have followed more closely in his footsteps than pursuing academic study all the way to PhD, followed by accepting a lecturing position at the University of Auckland, exactly as he did forty years ago, it was somehow all marred by the fact that the science I chose to pursue was chemistry. He gave me the impression that he felt, in some subtle way, chemistry was a science inferior to geology — not that I should have studied geology. After all, he would tell me, geology is *the* fundamental science; cavemen were wandering around bashing rocks with other rocks long before anyone worried about atomic or molecular structure. He never quite admitted or acknowledged that I find chemistry as rich and stimulating a subject as he must have found geology. Only once, in a weak moment, did he admit to me (not seriously) that geologists studied geology because they found chemistry too difficult.

Together and individually, my parents visited several times while I was studying at Stanford. One of these occasions, when Dad stayed with me for ten days, came at a time when I was at a low point with a bad case of the PhD blues. I dearly wanted to be able to talk it over with him. I felt that with the benefit of years of experience he would be able to give me advice and encouragement, but somehow I couldn't break the ice, feeling perhaps that his aspirations for me were so confused with my own that neither of us could possibly be objective. We had some good times together, with trips to the wine country and an oyster-eating expedition, and I accompanied him on field work in the hills around the San Francisco Bay Area, yet I spent the whole visit in a state of increasing tension which didn't break until after he left, and which I never really resolved.

Rationally, I'm sure Dad didn't disapprove of my interest in mountain recreation beyond a parent's natural concern for his child's safety in a potentially hazardous pastime. Similarly, I'm sure he was proud of my achievements in my chosen field of study. The indefinable undercurrents that I felt are probably in my own mind, the result of years of well-meaning ribbing, my inability to be able to determine just when I have done well enough, and perhaps Dad's inability to express pride and approval in a way that I understood.

I may never know. Dad died almost four years ago, quite suddenly, after being ill with lung cancer for only two months. It seemed inconceivable that such a larger-than-life figure should have moved on out of our lives so quickly. He still doesn't seem too far away. When I visit Mum, still living in the family home in Epsom, it is just possible that he might be pruning fruit trees down in the garden or working on a manuscript in his study. Up in the Bay of Islands he is even closer; working down in the boatshed, or out fishing in the boat just out of sight around the point. He died within a month or two of my taking up the lecturing position at Auckland University, so he and I never quite got to be colleagues. I know that he was pleased about my job, and that he liked my husband David and was delighted by our marriage. If David and I can do half as good a job of providing a happy, secure and stimulating family and childhood environment for our own child as my parents did for me, then we will be doing well.

✦ ✦

PENNY BROTHERS was born in Auckland in 1956, and grew up in Mt Eden and Epsom. She attended Maungawhau Primary School and St Cuthbert's College and went on to study at Auckland University, completing a BSc and MSc in chemistry by 1978. She spent some periods overseas with her family — a year each in England in 1960, in California in 1967 and in Greece and Europe in 1974. In 1979 she went back to California, this time on her own, to study for a PhD in chemistry at Stanford University.

During her university years in both New Zealand and in California, Penny devoted much of her recreational time to tramping, rock-climbing, mountaineering and cross-country skiiing. Highlights were completing ascents of several 'big walls' (multi-day rock climbs) in Yosemite Valley, California, and in 1980 joining a US and Indian women's climbing expedition to the Himalayas, when she was in the summit team which made the first ascent of Brigupanth (7200m).

In 1986 she returned to New Zealand with David Ware, a fellow chemistry student from Stanford, and they married in 1987. There followed two years as a post-doctoral research fellow at the University of Auckland, before Penny took up a position as lecturer in chemistry at Auckland.

She spends less time in the mountains these days, but still enjoys outdoor activities like swimming, triathlon and orienteering. She lives in Hillsborough, Auckland, and she and David had their first child in late 1991.

To My Father, M.H.K.

My father, who at 82, three years
and twice my age, can still terrify
with an intermittent Napoleonic bark
I went white inside at as a child
a tennis-player with an un-putaway bike
or a huntress become a forlorn rose-bed weeder
ours the normal family sins

now frail and thin, frets against
his uselessness when his eyes cloud up
his breath coming in fits and starts
cleaned through an air-pump three times a day
and then on a good one, perambulates
the lawn with my mother to survey the progress
of a troop of new sweet-peas along the trellis

Captain Kemp who wrote back from the war
thanking my aunt or grannie
for the knitted socks or fruit cake
all the company enjoyed; life's not
much good here — I'm not grousing
it's the same for all the chaps —
and we did see the Pyramids.
On the ship back home he gambled for & won

mother's diamond rings, being quick at cards
& billiards; and now, serving her sherry
on the silver platter, tells again the story

of the belly-dancer who might have been
our mother. I first heard Gershwin & Cole Porter
through the glass door, that let you peep
at sparkling mothers in strapless party dresses

& Morice, hospitality itself at the piano.
Though I always wished him leather-elbowed
tweed-jacketed and wise, with pipe and books
he preferred burning his eartops
in the Coromandel summer sun, up-ended
over the intricacies of the outboard motor's
splutterings & how to get us up on water-skis.

Now, my mother must prepare for him daily, make
soup or the filled bread rolls he likes at lunch
while listening as she reads aloud when the mail
with our letters comes. Daily she consorts
his ups and downs, together they watch t.v.
talk to visitors. Perhaps she wishes he was the kind
who'd read more, so books could give him the things

she knows of, in the blanks.
He says he's not afraid of dying. His dream's
to be put to sea in a boat like ours was
with the bung-hole out and gently to sink down.
This man, my father, is given to our family
to hold close. My mother will read him this
when the next mail comes.

JAN KEMP

JAN KEMP was born in Hamilton, New Zealand in 1949. Since graduating from the University of Auckland MA (Hons) in 1974, she has lived and worked in various Pacific and Asian countries, including Australia, Vanuatu, Papua New Guinea, Malaysia and Hong Kong. At present she teaches English at the National University of Singapore.

Her latest collection of poems, *The Other Hemisphere*, follows two earlier books *Diamond and Gravel* and *Against the Softness of Woman*, both now out of print. Her first collection of short stories *The Cook, the Consul and the Crazyman* is to be published in 1992 by Hazard Press in Christchurch. She is currently completing her first novel, *The Last Married Man*.

Jan Kemp held a PEN-Stout Fellowship at Victoria University of Wellington in 1991.

Jan Kemp and her father.

Waimarama Taumaunu

•••

Dear Dad

Last week George and I went to Mak's funeral. We couldn't quite believe that he was dead. George talked about his own father's death, and it frightened me. I couldn't bear you to leave me Dad, not yet. With you around, I have always felt safe.

Safe enough to put a scrum down with your Te Aute team — with no pants on, as you have laughingly reminded me. Safe enough to climb out of our school house and into the principal's house. Safe enough to destroy both the principal's wife's expensive cosmetic collection and her eiderdown in one afternoon's play. And safe enough to fall asleep amidst the debris.

You were always there when I needed you. Like the time I came home from netball, terribly upset. I had just started my period and that day I had forgotten about it. My new purple jeans were a mess. I don't know now what upset me the most — ruining the jeans, my embarrassment, or whether I was just tired. You didn't know either, but you patiently pacified me — without embarrassment or irritation. In so many ways you are a man ahead of your time.

In other ways, however, you are right back there with your cousin, Neanderthal. Remember my first 'date' with a boy? Never mind that there was another girl with us, and that his mother picked us up and dropped us off, and that we were going to the two o'clock pictures! You made me take off 'those nylons', you made me change my dress and my shoes, and you made me wear one of Mum's ugly cardigans. I was eleven years old and boy, did I hate you. My hatred however, would only have lasted

until the next time you practised netball passes with me, or we discussed the state of netball in New Zealand, or you gave me golf lessons.

And there have been times when you have embarrassed me more thoroughly than I could ever have dreamed possible. Like the time you dropped me at the airport to travel to nationals, and then cornered the coach to tell her who her top line-up should be. Contrary to her opinion, you included me in the team. Much later you did the same thing to Lois Muir. Luckily Lois always enjoyed your opinions, however wild and wondrous they were.

There have also been times when I have seen you hurt and I have felt like crying. The night we drove home after the birth of our youngest, I remember feeling so helpless. Mum and Ana were both in intensive care and I was the only person who you could talk to. But I was too young to really help you.

And on New Year's Day in Whangara. It was very early in the morning and I woke up to find you setting up our table for a party. When I asked why, you smiled and sat down and explained 'tin-canning'* to me. We looked out the window together and saw a group of about fifteen of our relations singing and drinking

* celebrating the New Year by visiting and partying at different homes

next door. I knew you were excited and so I was too; and we waited together in sweet anticipation on our old couch.

Only two people came. I watched them debate the issue at our front gate and I watched most of them shake their heads and leave. I wanted to run out and make them come in, but I couldn't.

You, of course, never really showed how you felt — but I knew. Just like I knew at Pa's tangi when we stood holding hands as they covered him for the last time. I knew too when you held my hand on the way to my wedding — tightly, silently, staring at nothing out the car window.

I remember when one of the boys said something derogatory about you, Mum said, 'Don't ever talk about your father like that, he is the finest man I know.' I agreed with her then, and I still do. You are the person who I most admire in the world. I have had a lot of luck in my life, but I feel most lucky to have been born your daughter.

Do you remember when I made my speech at your not-so-secret sixtieth celebration? 'Ka nui taku aroha ki a koe, engari kei te mohio kē taua.'* I knew you were touched. I could tell because you got grumpier and more miserable as the night wore on. Even though you had hinted for ten years, since Uncle Brown's birthday, that you, too, wanted a big sixtieth!

I watch you now with your mokopuna and I can't wait for the day that my children join them. And that's why death makes me anxious, Dad. I want you to be there for my children. To play with them, to teach them, to growl at them; to love them; and to make them safe. Just like you did for me.

I love you very much Dad, and you are not allowed to leave me yet. I need you to be here for me for a little while longer.

Arohanui

Wai

* 'I love you very much, but we already know that.'

WAIMARAMA TAUMAUNU was born in 1962. Her parents are Hone Meihana Taumaunu of Ngati Porou iwi, Ngati Konohi hapu, Whangara-mai-tawhiti marae, and Maire Joyce Taumaunu (née Hopkinson) of Ngai Tahu iwi, Arowhenua hapu.

She was educated at Riccarton High School and Canterbury University where she gained a BA (History) in 1983. She then attended Christchurch Teachers College where she trained as a teacher and subsequently taught at Upper Hutt College and Wellington High School. In 1990 she joined the Hillary Commission as a programme manager for Maori Sport.

In 1978 she first played representative netball for the Canterbury Netball Team and played for them until 1984. In 1981 she was chosen as a New Zealand netball representative and in 1989 she became captain of the New Zealand netball team, a position which she held for three years.

In 1985 with her move to Wellington, she joined the Wellington Netball Team and continued to play for Wellington and New Zealand until 1991 when she retired from representative netball.

Waimarama Taumaunu won the Maori Sports Personality of the Year, 1991, and was awarded an MBE in the 1992 New Year Honours list.

'Ka nui taku aroha ki a koe, engari kei te mohio kē taua.'
Waimarama Taumaunu with her father, Hone.

Tessa Duder

✦✦

FATHERS I HAVE KNOWN

A satisfying aspect of Duder's books is her depiction of mothers and family life . . . the creation of mother characters who cope with the many demands of children and husbands with energy, the occasional outburst of frustration and above all, highly developed organisational skills . . . fathers are more shadowy . . . '
Helen Watson, *Broadsheet*

Shadowy, therefore without substance or influence? Or does closer examination show that these fathers cast very long shadows?

It's quite alarming, the thought that sooner or later — and in the 1990s, with New Zealand fiction growing in stature and recognition, probably sooner — the academics and literary commentators will begin to scrutinise and critically analyse my books and therefore me. Reviews, good, bad and odd, I have grown used to, but the academic poking around in the corporate body of my work is another matter.

Allow me to forestall the academics and try a spot of stand-back analysis myself. How does this woman writer, much read by children, depict men in general, fathers in particular? From a feminist perspective? Stuck in the fifties with nuclear families, the sixties with the new permissiveness, the seventies with feminists and alternative lifestylers, or the eighties with yuppies and New Age men? Where, as they ask these days, is she coming from?

Actually, they make an interesting group, the fathers of my six novels. *Night Race to Kawau* has Nick Starr, the decent well-meaning family man contrasted with men who regard it as their God-given right to leave their families weekend after weekend for the bonhomie of round-the-buoys yacht racing . . . or by implication, golf, drinking, handy-manning, watching footie, the office, or the hundred other ways men avoid involvement in family life.

Jellybean has two adult male characters, neither wholly admirable. Ten years before the period of the book, Jellybean's

206

philandering father abandoned his young pregnant wife; her mother's first love Gerald was not prepared even temporarily, to leave his own musical ambitions and life in London for a life together in New Zealand, though he redeems himself in the course of the book by his sensitivity to Jellybean's reaction to his reappearance in her mother's life.

And what about the four books of the *Alex* quartet? There's Maggie's smoothly dressed father, always 'away on business', remote to his wife and two daughters, and probably, though I don't even hint so in the books, maintaining expensive affairs in Singapore or Sydney or his other ports of call, even Auckland, if the truth be known.

There's Andy's old man, a pompous, pipe-smoking bully, with a silent, repressed wife, and a son whose every achievement is not quite good enough, but for whom a medical career is mapped out. There's Julia's father, another bully, but tougher, favouring his son's education and only agreeing to Julia's ambitions to study medicine because of a grubby deal that she remain quiet about an Italian cousin's sexual advances. Mario, the cousin, the family man who cannot keep his hands to himself, even with fifteen-year-old asthmatic 'rellies'. Keith's Scottish father, who walked out on his wife and three children, one a Down's Syndrome child, for a secretary seventeen years younger. And there's the Hamilton family: Alex's eighteen-year-old cousin Ginnie forced by her father into a shot-gun wedding, power over the unhappy young couple maintained on both sides by threats of disowning, and trusts for the baby; Ginnie's pregnancy going wrong and the imminent young father (another one) ostentatiously having it away with his secretary.

And Tom, the major new character of the third and fourth books; born illegitimate in England in 1938 (when the words bastard and illegitimate still carried a weighty stigma), his father high-born English, his mother not surviving the birth, the natural father only too pleased to sign the child away to its New Zealand uncle. The uncle turning out to be another overbearing bully, a wealthy Taihape sheep farmer who fathered only daughters, and sees Tom taking over the running of the farm; who refuses to

'I was born in November 1940 and was about two and a half when he was invalided home from the Middle East.'
Tessa with her father, then Captain Jock Staveley, MC.

acknowledge that Tom might have other ambitions, objects fiercely to that ambition being music and denies him help through university, eventually driving him away from the family, and from New Zealand.

Well! Now that I lump them together for the first time, I don't much like what I see. I could, if nailed down to the floor, name a real-life, near-equivalent model for each one of them, though of course I won't; writers don't, ever. In defence, like Fay Weldon, I proclaim I'm not anti-men. I simply write what I see happening and what I hear being said around me. But it would be easy and understandable for a critic to conclude that, like Fay Weldon, though less acerbically, this writer has a rather jaundiced view of men in relation to their womenfolk and children. Do not her fathers tend to be dominating and demanding patriarchal figures, not open to compromise or negotiation, supremely selfish, narrow-minded, disloyal and weak? Though secondary characters without much dialogue, with their actions, demands, and pronouncements in the background, they cast long shadows over their children's ambitions and lives; their wives cope, heroically as they always do (oops, is my bias showing?) as best they can. The children, for the most part, rebel.

And in all fairness to myself, the women are not without their faults: Mrs Starr, though lacking confidence, can be cuttingly sharp-tongued, Jellybean's mother can be accused of being insensitive and selfish, Maggie's lonely betrayed mother is the archetypal swimming (or ballet or whatever) pushy mum, her hopes and talents early stifled by her own father, charming, snobbish, ambitious, cunning and ruthless. Alex herself pushes her luck for readers' sympathy. She can be egocentric, pig-headed, hard and calculating.

One father, though, I've so far purposely excluded. For he, despite what you might conclude with all the foregoing evidence, is the nearest to my own experience. Some reviewers have objected to Alex's family as being almost super-humanly supportive, unrealistic and implausible, even for the fifties. Was it, or is it now, possible for two parents to be so long-suffering, unselfish and wise?

Meet Jim and Helena Archer, supportive parents of the tall and stroppy Alex through the trials of the first book, through the difficult winter of the second book leading up to the Rome Olympics, and her crossroads summer of the fourth, the aftermath of Rome. They hardly appear in the third book, with Alex in Rome, and play only supporting roles in the fourth as she struggles with her decisions regarding school, exams, swimming, Saint Joan, and whether she can or cannot trust Tom Alexander. As Paul Zindel has written, books for teenagers should have the parents and families in secondary roles; their major problems with their sexuality, their relationships, limits, rebellions, are being worked out elsewhere, outside the home. During the eighteen months of continual stress depicted in the four books, taking Alex from just fifteen to a mature sixteen and a half, Jim and Helena Archer wisely and quietly wait.

But this is not to minimise parental influence, especially of fathers, since one thing is clear from my earlier roll-call of fathers: that their potential for negatively, even destructively, influencing their children is far greater than mothers who, in my experience anyway, use all their energies simply keeping the show on the road.

The imperatives to boys: study harder, do better (than me, though earning my jealousy), be stronger (ditto), earn more money (ditto), grow taller, play footie harder, don't play soccer, do play the field, don't play the violin, do mow the lawn, get a proper haircut, don't drink and drive (though I do), stand up for yourself, son! And to daughters: don't be rude to your mother (though I am), don't ring up boys (we want to do the chasing, keep the initiatives), unemployed girls can help at home, okay fine, go to art school (you're only filling in time, or, it's a waste educating girls), choose, lass (career or marriage?).

But Alex's battles are not with her parents, except on those few occasions, mostly in the second book, when she temporarily exhausts their patience. Their expectations of her are high but not burdensome, their love unquestioned, their practical help regular and freely, generously given. It's an interesting thought, how the tall craggy Jim, a former naval radio operator who works in the

Post Office, would have coped with his first-born being male, rather than the strong-minded Alex. I believe it would have made no difference; it's very logical to me that many outstanding women have apparently been first-born children, given the same support and high expectations as sons.

So, Jim Archer's my tribute, I suppose, to those family men I know who *do* — to the best of their abilities — spend time with their families, support their wives, support their children both male and female to do what they, the children, want to do with their lives, don't go off with the lads and don't play around; who somehow juggle their working lives and their family lives, compromising nothing except their image as macho men. Not often heard about these days, as the media tells us frequently about the victims of abusive fathers, or of partners and children stranded and living on a pittance, about fathers working six days a week to keep their jobs, or corporate bosses always 'in a meeting' who have been quoted as thinking that time spent with families is time wasted to the company.

But I insist they exist, these conscientious gentle if rather tired family guys. I resist the notion that Jim Archer is unreal, an impossible even righteous, even priggish role model of fatherhood, even for the fifties. I know some Jim Archers, even now, can count them on the fingers of more than two hands. I have one for a husband. And I had as a child, and still have, one for a father.

My father and I had an unpromising start. He never saw me as a baby, so that he could slowly learn fathering skills. Newly qualified as a doctor and newly married, he went off to the war in the early forties, aged twenty-six. I was born in November 1940 and was about two and a half when he was invalided home from the Middle East. Family tales say that he finally arrived at the house in Albert Street in Palmerston North late one night. The next morning my Italian grandmother dressed me in my best dress, put a Union Jack in my hand, and well-meaning but unwise, sent me in to see my father. I promptly came out howling, 'There's a man in Mummy's bed.'

Another family legend has it that from birth I was extraordinarily like my father, with the same facial structure, long and assertive nose, broad forehead, blue eyes which I'm told look straight and hard, fine mousy English hair. So alike that my mother has always said she could have sent me as a baby unlabelled to Egypt, and I'd have found my way to Captain Jock Staveley, MC.

As adults we share the same facial likeness, an argumentative and opinionated nature, and a sense of outrage, well exercised during the eighties. Rogernomics under a Prime Minister he never admired, user pays, tomorrow's schools, the dilution, even disintegration, of the welfare state and general standards of behaviour. This, he says, is not the New Zealand he helped fight a war for, the New Zealand he loves. This is not the public hospital system where he spent his whole working life, developing for Auckland a freely available and internationally renowned blood transfusion service. The service is still free (heaven help us when we introduce money to the transaction of blood and organs as they have elsewhere), but these days, with AIDS and less community goodwill around, it's more difficult to ensure a year-round supply of blood. I cannot disagree with much of his disillusionment.

We also share a single-mindedness which, in the family, is known as the Malfroy factor. His mother, who grew up the daughter of a French saw-mill owner in Hokitika, was strong-minded, single-minded, robust, self-disciplined, ambitious for herself and her family, quick of movement and mind, talented artistically, especially in music, a striver for excellence verging, some say, on the obsessive, with the stamina and stoicism to match, and given to migraines. In middle life she wrote a novel about her West Coast days. Sadly, it was destroyed.

As adults, there are some things we don't share. Like many women of my age, getting less exercise that I should, I'm on the round side of ideal weight and have been since I gave up competitive swimming at the age of eighteen. He has always been tall, very angular and bonily thin, and after a lifetime of long daily walks, extremely fit, and not particularly interested in food except for a passion for fruitcake. He became a familiar figure striding daily, at a pace most people run, through Newmarket, Auckland, walking home for lunch, then back again, maybe three kilometres each way, 12 kilometres daily, for the best part of thirty years. I hate walking, except along beaches, and never wanted to climb mountains.

Before the war, and before marriage, he did a considerable amount of tramping in the Southern Alps and a modest amount of climbing in the years when my brother and I had left home and there was at last some discretionary spending money. During my early teens in the early fifties, we spent our summer holidays in rented cottages at Taupo. The altitude was 'good for us', Auckland sea-dwellers. And here my father was able to 'share' his passion for climbing with our annual trip up Mount Tauhara near Taupo. Every year on arriving in Taupo, I'd say to my mother — never a climber since her honeymoon spent scrambling up the Franz Joseph glacier behind my father — 'Let's get it over with.' I look back now and wish Dad had been happy, or even able to take a whole half day to do the climb, and, once on the summit, to relax and enjoy the view. All I remember is heaving my way painfully in his relentless wake to the top, hating every moment of it, in spite of my swimmer's fitness. I last did it as a forty-year-old; at sixty-six he put me to shame, and I don't doubt he'd outpace me even now, though his knee joints might let him down.

Another thing we do not share is his passionate faith and belief in the certainties of science, and by inference scientists being 'right' and their world-view therefore carrying more weight. In a life of service to Auckland Hospital Board which won him first a new Blood Transfusion headquarters, then an OBE, and in 1980 a knighthood, as well as unswerving loyalty from his staff, he waged a constant battle against what he called 'shiny-arsed clerks' of all persuasions. His always was a cut-and-dried view of the world, which allowed little leeway for the unexplainable, for the mysterious interior world of the imagination which is now the world I move in, or for the curiosities of human behaviour which led to, for example, the National Women's Hospital scandal or, as I write, a widespread cynicism about politicians in general and the National Government's election promises in particular. We argued fiercely for years about Muldoon, whom he championed right to the end, and probably still does. He was appalled I supported David Lange, at least in the early years, and twice voted Labour; though we came to agree about his 'arch-villain', Roger Douglas. Now he supports, somewhat less convincingly, Ruth Richardson. Women politicians seem to disturb him, but he voted National on the grounds that Labour had ruined the country, and Helen Clark the health service — so he's stuck with Richardson and Shipley.

It's ironic. In recent years, the growing power of women to challenge publicly the assumed white male hegemony which his generation unconsciously took for granted, and the combined assaults of four stroppy granddaughters have left him constantly on the back foot at family gatherings. I don't believe he is so very dyed-in-the-wool and chauvinist, not really, given what he's actually done for me over a long period of time, but that's how he often comes across. These days, more often than not, I sit back on the sofa in the family home in Northcote and listen to them slug it out.

It's largely to his credit, though, that we have remained close even though our strengths and arguments have, for decades now, mirrored the classic confrontations of science against art, and since 1974 when I discovered Betty Friedan, entrenched male against challenging female viewpoints. He must once have hoped that I'd show some aptitude for science, or languages, which he encouraged. Instead through a school where the science teaching was lousy and languages ho-hum, my strengths even as a child were always in the school's one strong area, the humanities: English, history, the performance arts. He says it was my decision to go at the age of eighteen straight into a newspaper office; I wish now he'd been rather more heavy-handed in insisting on university.

In fact, as I depict in Alex's story, the crucial decisions of my teens and early adulthood were always mine. At least that is how I remember it: no pressure, threats, hints that it was time I went flatting, or time to stop agonising about an unsatisfactory boyfriend. As parents of promising athletes still must, they provided the back-up which enabled me to develop my talents as a swimmer. Mother provided stability and wonderful meals, home-cooking of a style which is now rare, Dad, the transport and moral support at the pool as I worked towards international standard. I have clear memories of Dad dropping me off, picking me up, standing alongside my coach Jack Lyons in the rain at the Olympic Pool both with stop-watches in their hands, a bitter spring wind howling up the pool; of my father sitting frozen until 11 pm at outdoor carnivals at the Olympic Pool or over-cooked in the noisy muggy Tepid Baths, waiting for my last race to be over. Later, when I was seventeen and training for the Cardiff Empire Games, his shaking me awake before 6 am with a cup of tea, just as Jim does for Alex. The difference is that I think whatever success I achieved in swimming was due rather more to Jock's daily encouragement and practical support: unlike Alex, I was never, and still am not, an early riser by inclination. It takes a special sort of person to get you to haul yourself out of a warm bed and go training at 5 o'clock on a winter's morning. For sure, I did the training, but I think now Jock was that special person.

For all adult children, there are events and decisions they wish had been different, and which as adults and parents themselves, they criticise. I received only one real hiding, at the age of about seven, when I wandered off down the road and ended up half a mile away near a house of ill-repute in one of the less respectable roads in Remuera. (There are some, down in the gullies; remember the Bassett Road murder?) From sheer relief, no doubt, the heavy hand came down; I still remember the pink imprint of his hand on my backside, the darkened room with no tea. I now find hard to accept the reasoning behind my being sent away, aged six, to boarding school: they had to weigh up a council school in London, from a grotty basement flat, against a 'decent' boarding school on the south coast. The fees meant a personal sacrifice to a young couple with no savings in London directly after the war, but the experience left its scars on me.

I also look back on my 'sex education' with some amazement. Without the questionable benefit of today's films, television and magazines, which between them educate the young in a way undreamt of in the fifties, my sex education consisted of one fatherly lecture when I was about eleven, to prepare me for the onset of puberty and periods, complete with medical textbook. I then spent the whole of my teens, the fifties era of heavy petting, slowly finding out what today's young would know at half the age. It was not an area of upbringing either of my parents felt comfortable dealing with — Dad despite, or even because of, his medical training. It was probably a fairly common experience for girls then.

Yet I remember one curious and significant incident. During 1958, which I spent training for the Empire Games in July, I also did Stage One English and got to know a worldly Stage Two student with a passion for early opera, Gluck and Handel, and an ability to remove banned books from the locked case in the university library. Henry Miller's *Tropic of Capricorn*, or was it *Cancer*, ended up naively as my bedside reading. My parents read it aghast. Yet what I remember from this episode is not a demand that I never see the student again. The affair ran its course. What I remember, is Dad saying, 'Read the book if you must. Mum and I find it highly offensive, and your boyfriend's action in giving it to you suspect, but this is my opinion: nothing can be considered dirty or distasteful inside marriage as long as both parties fully and honestly want it and agree.' Today's permissiveness — and even my daughters — would question the qualifying need for marriage, but even today, it is a wise rule of thumb for human relationships. Behind mutual agreement is honesty, and who can argue with that as a sound basis for life? In 1958, he was anticipating by thirty years the relaxation of the laws against homosexuals, and the current on-going debate, particularly in America, on what constitutes rape.

Though I have said that our closeness has persisted despite, or perhaps because of, our differing interests and outlook on life, one passion we do share — one which I've no doubt he was responsible for planting and nurturing in me. I grew up in a house where music was always important: my Italian grandmother hummed Verdi, my mother was a fine cellist and, given other circumstances, would have had a musical career; both my parents were always concert-goers, but it was Jock who acquired and played the records of Stravinsky's *Rite of Spring* and *Firebird*, William Walton's *Symphony No. 1* and Henry V film music, Ravel's *Daphnis and Chloë*, Gershwin's *Piano Concerto in F*, Khatchaturian, César Franck, Debussy, Richard Strauss, (though strangely, not Mahler, Dvořák or Shostakovich, much), Tchaikovsky, Elgar, Delius, Vaughan Williams, Resphigi, Prokofiev, the whole of *La Bohème*, *Madam Butterfly*, *Tosca*, in other words the late romantics/early twentieth-century symphonic school, with its daring harmonies, jazz-inspired syncopations, and lush highly coloured orchestrations, which I also grew early to love. He was a fine classical pianist, playing Chopin, Ravel and Debussy, and for regrettably short periods accompanying my mother in Brahms and Rachmaninov sonatas. As a young man he also played a trombone, organised a dance band, composed songs of the Cole Porter type, incidental pieces of the Eric Coates type, and, though not an instinctively sensitive accompanist, could improvise the jazz classics like *Night and Day* as brilliantly decorated solo pieces. He gave me my first piano lessons when I was aged four or five, and taught me, as his mother had taught him, for some five years to about grade four standard. Perhaps it was through those lessons that he learnt, in his early thirties, the early lessons of fathering.

As I think past my teens, and therefore past any similarity between Jim Archer and my own father, I find myself concentrating more and more on the positives of our relationship. I remember constant reminders that I must be punctual, reliable and honest, from someone who himself was punctilious in these things, almost to the extreme. If he and my mother were asked for dinner at 7 pm, they arrived at 7 pm, and nothing would persuade my father that his hostess might be a little grateful if they came at 7.10 pm.

'To thine own self be true,' was a frequent quote. So was the word 'stickability', which is something no swimmer on her lonely laps up and down a pool, or novelist staring daily at a computer screen, can be without. It takes as much stamina to write a novel as it does to train for a sport. It takes stamina for a doctor to earn a knighthood (some of them are earned by hard work and results, not political favours) and stamina to make a marriage work, as my parents have done for fifty-one years. There was always an underlying assumption that the greatest rewards in life are in service to others and come slowly, and only after struggle and hard work.

Through my own twenty-seven years of marriage and through the eighties, as our family grew and my career as a writer developed, I have good reason to believe that my father has been of greater influence and practical support than I realised before I began writing this. Whenever we've had a medical crisis he's been in the background, helping us cope — my first child a breech-delivery, my husband's severe bout of hepatitis in Pakistan, children with broken limbs, one with asthma, two for an appendectomy, one with glue ears, one with eczema, husband with a bad back in spasm, myself with a broken foot, myself again in 1990 undergoing a breast biopsy, which, until pronounced clear, produced the unique sight of him breaking down in tears, this always rational sensible man, who has dealt with tragic leukaemia cases, often children, and no doubt some dreadful war injuries in his working life. Always for my family, and the wider family as well, there has been advice, support, time to listen, consultation with colleagues and reading up medical literature.

In recent years as my writing/speaking workload has got bigger and my husband's engineering firm has, like everyone in the construction industry since the stockmarket crash, been fighting for its survival, meaning nights and weekends spent working, it's my folks who've regularly pulled out the weeds and trimmed the edges around our house as well as theirs. When a commitment to talk to a school or visit an editor has clashed with picking up a child after some activity, it's Jock to whom I've frequently turned for help. He's been retired for more than fifteen years now, not as rich and fulfilling a time for him as he and the family always hoped for; the change from a completely

'Another family legend has it that from birth I was extraordinarily like my father...'
Tessa and her father, now Sir John Staveley.
Photo: Gil Hanly

structured working routine to retirement was not one he or my mother made easily, yet I try not to presume on his easy availability and willingness to help.

And it hasn't always been a one-way traffic. Twice in the past ten years my parents have gone through the exercise of 'it's time we went into an old folks' home'. Both times, my husband and I argued strenuously against it, and to their credit, the old folks listened, and didn't sell their house, and time has proved that a reassessment of their situation is not yet necessary, and won't be, while they can still look after each other.

In the meantime, Jock still pounds around the lawns, taking an hour where every other man of seventy-seven would take three, bashing his bald head on the corner of any open window he is going too fast to see. Mother tries to go round shutting the windows first, and interrupts his circuits by calling him in halfway for tea, but not always with success. She just doesn't get there fast enough.

When his time comes, I passionately hope it comes quickly to this man who has lived life with quickness of mind and movement. I shall remember him as a man of action, a man who acted not for his own benefit, but for mine, and for my mother's and brother's, and his grandchildren's, and for the benefit of many other people he met in the course of his working life as a doctor. A man never easily persuaded to talk about himself or his concerns, but with music in his soul. In his heaven he'll be on a mountain top with a full orchestra, soloist in *Rhapsody in Blue*.

◆ ◆

TESSA DUDER was born in Auckland, where she still lives. She has four daughters and is a keen sailor, musician, theatre-goer and a compulsive reader. As a swimmer in her teens she won a silver medal for New Zealand at the Cardiff Empire Games in the 100 yards butterfly event.

Since then she has worked as a journalist in Auckland and London and has become best known as a novelist. The idea for her first novel, *Night Race to Kawau*, came to her one summer's night in 1978. She has been writing full-time ever since. Her second novel, *Jellybean*, was an American Libraries 'Notable Book' and a finalist for the Goodman Fielder Wattie Award. *Alex* and *Alex in Winter*, the first two books in her Alex quartet, were both voted New Zealand Children's Book of the Year and won the New Zealand Library Association's Esther Glen Medal. The third title in the quartet, *Alessandra: Alex in Rome*, was published in 1991 to much acclaim, and the fourth, *Songs for Alex*, in 1992.

Tessa has also won the Choysa Bursary, and was the first (1991) Writer in Residence at the University of Waikato.

Pulling Faces

MARYILYN DUCKWORTH

This fiction extract is from *Pulling Faces*, first published by Hodder and Stoughton in 1987.

Stuart's children come to visit him. It isn't a regular thing. Their mother believes they should be free to come and go as they choose — unless, of course, she has something special planned which can't include them. This is one of those occasions. Stuart has just embarked on a long prose poem and would prefer to see them at any other time. But here they are on the doorstep, with zip bags and bedding under their arms. He has to make room on the floor for the camp mattresses he keeps rolled up behind the sofa.

Lilian had arranged to have her and the children's bedrooms removed within ten days of her leaving. They were modular additions and were quickly reassembled on his brother's property. His feelings — and no doubt the children's feelings — had taken a little longer to reassemble.

'I hope you've got something to eat this time.' Alex tears open the fridge and pulls a face. 'I thought so. What do you live on? Can we go to the dairy?'

'That dairy's hopeless,' Janice chimes. 'Let's all drive to the supermarket.'

'No, you can walk to the dairy,' Stuart decides. 'I don't want to take the car out just for that.'

'Jesus, thanks a lot!' Alex sneers.

'Make out a list and I'll see how much money I've got. How about crumpets?'

'Muffins,' Janice suggests. 'Fruity ones. Better for you.'

'Chocolate biscuits,' Alex says aggressively. 'If you can *afford* them.'

When the list is drawn up there is an argument about who will walk to the dairy. Neither will give in. Stuart turns the television set on to drown out the noise. He also hopes, not very positively, that the programme will suck them away from their arguing. Janice strides across the room to turn it off — snap. She is a small girl, very crisp and deliberate in her movements. Now she turns quickly and puts out a hand for the papers her father has been working on. She knows this isn't allowed, but scans the lines rapidly before he can leap across to take them from her.

'Sorry, Dad.' She giggles.

'You're not sorry.'

'Well —' She looks to her brother for support and giggles again.

'Have you got a girlfriend, Dad? Have you?'

'Why do you want to know?'

'Nothing. Just that poem —' She winks at Alex. 'I'll tell you later.'

'Don't bother,' her brother shrugs. 'Of course he's got a woman. There must be someone.'

Stuart decides to take this as a compliment. He wipes his hair off his forehead, a gesture of relief that the conversation has become less noisy and abrasive. Even if this is at his expense. He begins to plan the evening meal in his head — there is ox liver in the fridge and plenty of onions.

Janice comes across and perches on the arm of his chair, swinging her sandalled fool. 'Let me see your head, Daddy.'

'What?'

'Your head. I think you're going bald.' She attempts to sweep his forelock back with her little brown hand. He resists, clamping both hands protectively over his head as if she were attempting to remove a wig. 'Show me! I want to see! Alex — come and help me.'

For once Alex decides to help his sister. Between them they trap Stuart in the chair and remove his hands, pulling at the fingers as if they are rip tabs — and expose the receding hairline.

'Look — look!' Janice shrieks gleefully. 'He *is* — he's going bald!'

The boy pretends to fall down on the floor, clutching his stomach and laughing exaggeratedly.

'Cut it out, you monsters.' Stuart smooths his hair into position tenderly.

'Balding at thirty-seven! It must be sex that does it,' Alex says. 'Oh well — it's a small enough price to pay.'

'Who is she?' Janice persists.

Stuart plucks his plastic raincoat from behind the door.

'Where are you going?' Now his son sounds affronted, accusing. Not another desertion, he seems to say.

'I'm going to the dairy. We need milk.' He sees Janice's look of triumph and adds — 'If you want biscuits and stuff you can come with me.'

'Oh, Dad!'

'Do you need us to hold your hand?'

'Please yourself.' He shrugs. And wonders if he can secrete one packet of chocolate biscuits in his raincoat pocket without the outline showing through the plastic. He will produce them later as a peace offering.

'I'll come.' Janice capitulates. 'And you can tell me about your love life. I think Mum would like to know.'

Walking along the windy street which rattles with lorries going to the rubbish tip, he feels Janice's arm tucking into his own. The warmth of her narrow wrist folded over his own larger one, gives him a pang. It doesn't matter if her gesture is meaningless, he responds to it exactly as if it were real filial affection. And noticing his response makes him sad. He begins to tell her about Gwyn, but without, of course, giving anything real away.

Ginette McDonald

◆ ◆

MY FATHER MYSELF

Scott Fitzgerald, I think, defined intelligence as the ability to hold two opposing arguments, one in each hand, and to see merit in both.

My father, James Joseph McDonald, *was* two opposing arguments, broiling away in an uncomfortable eggshell coat of professional respectability.

From him, I learnt what it is to be truly human — to say one thing to placate or disturb, whilst passionately feeling the other.

I'm going away, but before I go away, I've got something to tell
you, I've got something to say
I'm going away . . .

Dad sang this monotonous ditty cheerfully off key on all of our half-year drives to 'the Hutt' — in the sixties the equivalent, in distance and expectation, for our large family to a drive from Wellington to Taihape in the nineties.

When Dad finally went away, very tired and dead on the bathroom floor one raining morning in September 1988, I felt a shard of grief so intense, so pure that I felt as though he'd cut me, cut us all, loose.

'And upon this rock . . .'

For my father; JJ, Jimmy, Mac, Dr Mac, James, was the rock upon which our fragile family had rested. In life, sometimes an obstructive figure, sometimes, often, dictatorial, occasionally seriously silly, we all took our old man for granted. It's a pity that he had to die for us to realise what an example his own humanity

223

'Dad was fond of saying that the marriage proposal, written from a ravaged Trieste two weeks after their first and only date, was the bravest thing he'd ever done in his life.' Ginette in 1952 with her parents, Jim and Joan McDonald.

had been to us. What significant part of our own characters we could point to and say with embarrassed pride, that we were like Dad . . .

It wasn't easy for the old man. He came from an Irish Catholic family who were not in any way lovably eccentric, but for the most part, rather charmlessly mad. It fell to Jimmy, as the oldest and most horrified by the past, to pull himself together, to study medicine, not acting (which was his first love, and at which he excelled as a terrible ham) and to marry — right out of his class and out of his planet — an exotic English-French girl of astounding beauty, upon whom, according to the late Bruce Mason, all the other ANZACS at the Dominion Officers' Club in wartime London had their eye. They were amazed when the shy, awkward young doctor from Wellington succeeded. Dad was fond of saying that the marriage proposal, written from a ravaged Trieste two weeks after their first and only date, was the bravest thing he'd ever done in his life.

But he had to hold on to it — my mother certainly never expected to have seven roiling children in rapid succession, and to remain immured for thirty years in a Wellington that seemed to her febrile perceptions socially and physically straitened. They both held on — and dished out love and discipline in the absent-minded way that comes from being weary most of the time.

I always felt that my father, despite holding fairly objectionable ideas on male supremacy, sort of liked me. Of course he loved me — that was what one did, the Catholic way, but he liked seeing himself in me: the stubbornness, the love of reading.

'Destroy a book and you destroy life itself, lass,' he thundered after Mother Murphy had torn up my Enid Blyton in Standard Two study, pronouncing it worthless. Dad reckoned no book was worthless, and would sit up long into the night reading *Mein Kampf* or *The History of the Mormon Faith*, or *Erotica Through the Ages*, absorbing it all, incorporating even longer words into his considerable vocabulary.

But he *liked* me. I know it. Now this was important in a tribe of seven, all vying for attention — none ever getting enough.

There was a time, very precious to me now, when I crept into his bed every night. I was six or seven and he was forty years older and handsome. I would sneak in, protesting that I couldn't sleep, and he would resignedly let me in beside him. Nearly every night he would be summoned for the inexorable deliveries at St Helen's Maternity Hospital on the hill. He would put on trousers and a bright blue polo neck over his pyjamas and go away, for what seemed like just a few minutes. Then he'd be back, whispering so as not to wake my mother, 'It's a boy,' or even better, 'It's twins.'

He asked me not to keep coming into his bed. He said I couldn't keep doing it. I accepted that. I always knew a little about a lot.

From our fathers we learn about men — how to expect to be treated. So while Dad was outwardly uncompromising with my mother, with his two daughters, we knew that the old opposing argument was clenched in the palm of the other hand.

He was frightened of emotion, of his large capacity for tenderness. 'Instability', any form of self doubt, was ignored. It was all right for him to bellow with rage like a bull — that was a catharsis, but any wallowing in melancholy or introspection reminded him too forcibly of his own dreary family circumstances.

He cried once that I know of. At his father's funeral. His father was a tough old bird. Dad cried and cried. I sat next to him. I couldn't help. I was thirteen and we weren't speaking at the time . . .

I had a turbulent adolescence from which it seemed that Dad and I would never recover. At age thirteen, bored and desperate for drama, I hung around with some bold fifteen-year-old girls who 'did it' and had teased hair and pink nylon hipsters, and white boots. The white boots made my father almost apoplectic with rage — a symbol of licentiousness. He thought I was 'doing it' too, and I, aware for the first time of a little bit of power, didn't disabuse him. The words, 'strumpet', 'doxie', 'vixen', and 'termagant' were hurled at me. He forbade me to go out. I climbed out the window. No lipstick or mascara, but I haunted the Cutex stand in Wellington's James Smith department store.

He was furious that I was growing up. And actually jealous. Jealous. What glee.

I was thirty-three years old and one minute out of a terrifying 36-hour labour before I'd realised I'd finally escaped his expectations for me. I'd had a girl child. He wanted my first-born to be a boy. Ergo, it would be a boy. Isn't that how the world goes? But a girl. Stuff that in your pipe and smoke it, Dad. But he worried like an old bantam when that labour started to go wrong. Typical, standing in the delivery room supping whiskey with my husband, droning away about David Lange ruining the country...

Through the tears and pain, I knew he was deeply concerned, and hiding it in an inadequate, old codgerish sort of way. For a while afterwards, he opined that my labour had been fairly run of the mill, until silenced by glares from my mother. Pretend. Pretend. If you say so, Dad, it'll be all right. Don't let anybody see that old opposing argument.

He didn't encourage me to be an actress, although he smirked proudly on the occasions that he thought I'd got it right.

'Well done, lass,' was what I got, and it's enough.

He talked a great deal about the war. Though he'd been in the Medical Corps and not really seen any action (apart from the time in the Solomons when he and five Kiwis had arrived in a clearing to find six Japs and everybody concerned had looked startled and both sides scattered in opposite directions), the war had provided his release from New Zealand's stiflingly provincial expectations for him. Thus I absorbed osmotically a great deal of twentieth-century military history.

Significantly, since I became a television producer, two of my most successful productions have been set in wartime. He gave me a feel for it, and not just the Second World War, any war, but a sense of history, of the continuum of things, of an understanding that goes deeper than the conscious knowing.

Two opposing arguments in the palm of each hand . . .

I find myself looking for that in people now.

I'm often disappointed.

✦ ✦

GINETTE McDONALD, actor, comedienne, television drama producer and director, was born in Wellington in 1952. Sixteen years later she was introducing her character Lynn of Tawa to the world in a collaboration with Bruce Mason and Roger Hall at Downstage Theatre, Wellington in a late-night review called *Knickers*. She went on to become one of New Zealand's first full-time actors, appearing in numerous Downstage plays, and working in drama on both television and radio.

Between 1971 and 1976 she worked as a professional actor in the UK, with numerous television credits, and in a remake of the movie *Brief Encounter* with Sophia Loren and Richard Burton. Since returning to New Zealand she has produced and/or directed numerous television dramas, including episodes from *Close to Home*, *Gliding On* and *Shark in the Park*. She has won the Feltex Best Actress award twice, in 1979 and 1983, and Best Drama Series, Best Children's Drama awards for *The Fireraiser* in 1987.

In her spare time she debates, cooks, decorates interiors, reads, listens to music and reads as much about military history as she can.

Judy McGregor

‹ ◆ ›

*T*here is nothing as acute or painful as teenage embarrassment. Thirty years on, I still flush at the memory of 'The Sporting McGregors'. 'The Sporting McGregors' was the headline over a newspaper article published by the *Rotorua Daily Post*. There was nothing memorable about the article itself. It was the usual cliché of a family with disparate and/or connected sporting interests. Rob, my father, played golf, his game marred by lack of patience on the greens after massive tee shots. My brother was captain of the 1st XV at Rotorua Boys' High School and surfed, and I had represented the girls' school in cricket and hockey, and was obsessed with surfing. The connecting thread for the newspaper article was that the three of us were all keen on 'wet bum' yachting on Lake Rotorua. Rob sailed a Finn, David crewed with a friend in a Cherub class, and I sailed a P class.

It was the photo that was devastating. Rob wore a McGregor tartan shirt for the shot. That was bad enough. But, horrors, he topped it off with a black beret, French Resistance style. David and I remonstrated about the beret but he insisted on its sartorial elegance and photogenic qualities. I was mortified when I saw the photograph. It was of the 'cheque presentation' type, with the three of us lined up side by side, staring gormlessly at the camera exhibiting varying degrees of self-consciousness. The dominant feature in the photograph was Rob's ridiculous black beret. I refused to go to school for a week, feigning illness.

My other acute memory of discomfiture over Rob's eccentric clothes habits concerned his collection of bow ties. No other fathers in Rotorua in the sixties wore paisley or spotted silk bow ties. Why did my father have to exhibit originality? Rob was a big man, six foot plus, an amateur wrestler in his youth and a powerful swimmer. There is an intrinsic foppishness required of men to carry off bow ties outside formal dress. As a teenager I prayed Rob would not wear bow ties socially and dreaded the comments of my friends.

My brother David was always incurring parental wrath for being too physical with the 'girls' — my sister Robin and I. We developed the defence of crying or whining when the going got tough. 'David, stop hitting the girls,' was a persistent parental refrain.

Christmas holidays saw us drive from Rotorua to the Coromandel Peninsula, boat laden with the tent, to camp at Amodeo Bay. After throwing stones into the water to ward off stingrays, we spent much of each day swimming at high tide at the confluence of river and sea at Amodeo Bay, or in the sea at adjacent beaches.

We were all precocious swimmers taught by Mum when we were three to four years old. David excelled at ducking us as part of water horseplay. On one particular swimming expedition at Amodeo Bay, David persisted in ducking us while my father was trying to read on the beach. Either Robin or I (to my shame I feel it was me) began to whine. David was told to stop. He ignored the warning. He then realised Rob had approached the water's edge and was beginning to swim out to sea. Rob was a big, strong swimmer and easily overtook David. They scuffled in the water and then Rob swam into shore. As he walked up the beach he flourished aloft, for the witness of other picnicking families, David's swimming trunks. Naked and embarrassed David spent 45 minutes treading water. Out the back window of the car, as the rest of the family left for home, I caught a brief glimpse of a naked David running for his togs which Rob had left behind just beyond the high-water mark. I felt guilty, a sister's treachery, when a disgusted David arrived back at the tent on foot. I bribed my way back to brotherly acceptance by giving him my white chocolate Milky Bar.

My father was much kinder to me and my sister than he was

'No other fathers in Rotorua in the sixties wore paisley, or spotted silk bow ties. Why did my father have to exhibit originality?'
Rob McGregor wearing a bow tie.

229

to David. David pioneered the limits and boundaries of acceptable childhood and teenage behaviour. He was the eldest child and the boy. He had a physical relationship with my father. My father hit him as physical discipline on occasions. Those were the days when parenting included the wisdom that a good whack was necessary when a youngster was out of line. Rob also taught David amateur wrestling holds and the two of them would clinch and tumble on the back lawn or in the lounge. I remember Rob retired from these contests the first time David became big and cunning enough to pin him on the floor and win a concession of defeat.

I had quite a different relationship with my father. I do not remember a physical relationship beyond the perfunctory good-night hugs between children and parents as we were packed off to bed. Nor can I recall Rob expressing emotion, other than his flashes of anger. And he disliked displays of emotion. He could not abide tears. When my sister Robin had her first teenage 'ding' in the car, she and I conspired that as soon as she was sent in to tell my father on his arrival home in the evening, she would burst into tears. He would be so irritated by the tears she would escape harsh punishment. It was a flawless strategy. Immediately she began to cry Rob said, 'I can't stand the sight of females crying.' Robin claimed that she had hit the squash centre building in Rotorua by careless use of her foot on the accelerator. Both David and I were suspicious of this ridiculous story but the damage to the car was consistent with the fabrication. Many years later Robin disclosed she had been 'stacking' the car on the dirt track road at the back of Government Gardens and the car had spun into Lake Rotorua by Sulphur Point. The dent in the front of the car was caused by the tow truck winching the car from the lake.

The absence of a physical or emotional dimension in my father's family relationships meant we seldom saw him and my mother touching, kissing or hugging. While there was affection for us there were seldom open expressions of emotion.

My father did possess a notoriously explosive temper. He was car-mad, and much of his frustration at the idiocy of other motorists was expressed through a tirade of invective hurled out of the car window as he overtook. Car travel with the family was always fraught. No one was immune from Rob's motoring mania; little old ladies, potterers, men with hats, traffic officers. But he possessed a special hatred for road-hogging caravans. They would receive particularly manic treatment. And because of Rob's taste for exotic cars, we were conspicuous. I remember my surprise going on a car journey with a girl friend and her family and finding that they played 'I spy' to ward off bitumen boredom. The only game my brother, sister and I played on our family outings was trying to slide down the back seat during Rob's rages so we could avoid identification. I am convinced that nervousness about my father's demonic driving behaviour induced regular car sickness. At much the same spot in the Mamaku Forest, between Rotorua and Tirau, the car would have to stop while I was ill on the side of the road. At times I left it too late and once I vomited down the back of Rob's neck as he was manoeuvring to a halt. He was remarkably civil about it considering he was possessed by demons every time he slid behind the wheel.

Rob was the antithesis of the Kiwi do-it-yourself ethic. He was incompetent at any small, domestic or leisure chores. Give him a spanner and the nut would fall off. Give him a screwdriver and the screw would cross-tie itself.

Yachting expeditions were nightmares. My excitement at the thrill of wind, water, sail and competition would be tempered by the knowledge that the whole yacht club would be treated to the spectacle of bad temper that accompanied Rob's attempts to set the mast of my P Class yacht. In those days masts were attached to the deck of the yacht partly by three wire stays. The trick was to ensure the tension of the stays prevented the mast from jumping out under the pressure of wind and causing the yacht to capsize. Rob seldom perfected the technique. Inevitably in a big blow my mast would jump out and the entire rigging collapse on to the deck of the yacht. Once I drifted around to Sulphur Point, which is an eddy in Lake Rotorua, clinging grimly to the collapsed rigging and the boat. I was not spotted by the rescue craft for half an hour. I was saved from hypothermia by digging my toes into the sand and locating the pockets of thermal activity on the lake bed. When the Laser yacht was designed, an innovative feature was the placement of the stay-less aluminium mast down through a hole in the deck of the fibreglass moulded yacht. It is impossible for the mast to jump. My brother and I bought one immediately.

Rob's parenting style meant he was not a great disciplinarian. He was sometimes used by my mother as the last-resort tactic. 'Wait until your father comes home' contains all the frustration of a parent who had to suffer and survive the first wave of unreasonable, worrying and mystifying behaviour.

I always suspected Rob felt uncomfortable about the hypocrisy of lecturing me about being late in, when he had arrived home only minutes earlier himself. One night during a holiday stint as a waitress in slave-labour conditions at Tudor Towers, then Rotorua's prestigious restaurant, where the apotheosis of dining was T-bone steak, eggs and chips washed down with a bottle of Waihirere sauterne, I joined the staff for an after-work party. I left to drive home at 2 am, two hours after family 'curfew'. In those days Lynmore was a rural suburb on the outskirts of Rotorua. Rob's car business meant we drove separate cars. My brothers and I perfected the skill of freewheeling with the lights off down Lewis Road into our property, through the gates, down the enormous drive and coming noiselessly to rest between the giant silver birch trees. We could then creep around the side of the main house to our sleep-out, nicknamed 'The Shed', and avoid recriminations about lateness.

'The Shed', a sleep-out with two bedrooms, provided relief for my mother from David's hopeless sloth and my own sulky, rebellious teenage temperament. I can't remember David making his bed in the three years we lived adjacently in the sleep-out. Mum would hand him clean linen every week but to disturb the bed meant cleaning off a vast amount of sporting gear, David's cat Misty, my dog Lee (how could any *real* dog start life with the pedigree name of Annabel Lee of Enchanted Hills) and assorted detritus — animal, vegetable and mineral. 'The Shed' had a connected passage between the two bedrooms and both of us pilfered Rob's liquor supplies and kept a secret cache of beer and gin behind the wooden beams in the passage.

This particular night when I crept into my bedroom I found Rob waiting for me. He had arrived home only minutes earlier and had been dispatched by mum to remonstrate with me. He was clearly too embarrassed to enter enthusiastically into the role of the aggrieved and frantic parent. He knew I knew he was only just home himself. We sat at 2 am chatting about trivia until he said goodnight and went to bed. I have no doubt he told my mother he had torn strips off me and I had been penitent. The next day there was a conspiratorial silence between Rob and me about the incident and it was never mentioned again.

Not long after, my father's businesses failed and my parents separated. I had been only marginally aware of my mother's loneliness and aloneness and the brave concealments she made. My most vivid childhood memories of my father were related to holiday periods because that is when we saw most of him.

My parents' separation and financial crisis coincided with my first year at university in Hamilton after two years at training college. I was physically separated from the drama and anguish, and self-absorbed enough to single-mindedly block out much of the pain. I feel enduring shame that I did not offer Mum more emotional and physical support at this time.

Later when my parents remarried we saw that both Mum and Rob had the opportunity for second-chance happiness. And we had a bonus parent in stepfather Ross. Ross was kind, gentle and interested in New Zealand, in life, literature and music.

My relationship with my father changed during my adulthood. For many years he exiled himself overseas. Of the children, I was the one who kept up most contact with him. I spent holidays with him in Australia when he was in the transport industry and in Papua New Guinea where he owned pubs. During this period our relationship was cautious as we avoided examination of the bitterness and guilt concomitant with his separation from Mum, and it was an artificial relationship marked as it was by the limitations of holiday visiting. To Rob during this time I credit some of my fervour about journalism. Both he and Mum had been prodigious readers. Our house had been filled with periodicals, books, and alternative publications. Rob's stint in Australia coincided with the establishment of the weekly publication there, *Nation Review*. We would spend time together analysing the political commentary of Mungo MacCullum, and pondering the incredible cartoons of Leunig. We bought each other collections of Leunig cartoons for Christmas. Rob had better luck converting me to his journalistic tastes than he did encouraging any interest in his other passion, the music of Liszt.

Another persistent association I have of my father relates to food and drink. Rob drank too much for most of his life. He also enjoyed a large appetite cultivated by Grandmother Rose, who is now ninety-four years old. Gran was a Cornish publican's daughter and a wonderful cook. She ran a bakery in Tauranga, a guest house in Rotorua and housekept at the old Brents Hotel in Rotorua for many years. Gran would do the weekly baking for our family and either David, Robin or I would be entrusted with walking back with the tins from Lynmore Avenue to Lewis Road. David claimed the record for eating five Neenish tarts and re-arranging the rest to look as though they had not been disturbed. I remember suffering acute indigestion when the baking included chocolate caramel squares and I ate three too quickly on the baking delivery run. The Heart Foundation would have had a fit at one of Gran's most popular sayings: 'It must be good for you, dear, it's got all that good New Zealand butter and sugar in it.'

Rob returned to New Zealand when he retired. The cancers he was to die of were beginning to consume his body. Living in the tropics for many years and being blond, meant he suffered badly from skin cancers. He also had cancer in his back. During his last years he lived at Waihi Beach and I would drive to see him whenever I could. A terrible poignancy marked these visits. I am sure he regretted his missed opportunities in terms of relationships with his children, but he was too sick to reinvigorate them or redeem himself. When he was dying in Waikato Hospital, his second wife Dawn and I were at his bedside. The morphine cocktails meant he had only moments of clarity. In one of these he sat bolt upright in bed and said distinctly: 'I do not want to die and leave the two girls I love most.' The sadness was unbearable.

✦ ✦

JUDY McGREGOR was born in Rotorua Hospital in 1948. She has an elder brother, David, and a sister, Robin.

Her father Rob Roy McGregor was a small businessman in Rotorua. Judy was a foundation pupil at Lynmore Primary School and attended Rotorua Intermediate and Rotorua Girls' High School. She was suspended from high school for writing a letter to the local newspaper and signing her name. At the age of sixteen, Judy left Rotorua for Hamilton Teachers' College and then Waikato University. At Waikato, she founded and edited the student newspaper *Nexus*.

She worked as a reporter on the *Waikato Times* and was the *Dominion's* correspondent in Auckland. She also wrote columns for the *Dominion* and *Sunday News* and was both news editor and editor of the *Sunday News*, and removed 'page three girls' from the newspaper, which recorded its highest ever circulation at the time. In 1982 Judy won the inaugural Nuffield Press Fellowship at Wolfson College, Cambridge. More recently Judy was editor of the ill-fated *Auckland Star*, and she now teaches communications within the Faculty of Business Studies at Massey University. She holds a BA from Waikato, an LL B from Victoria and is currently completing a post-graduate law diploma from Auckland. She is married to John Harvey, editor of the *Evening Standard* newspaper in Palmerston North.

'My relationship with my father changed during my adulthood . . . To Rob during this time I credit some of my fervour about journalism.'
Judy McGregor.

Before the Fall

After the bath with ragged towels
my Dad
would dry us very carefully:
six little wriggly girls,
each with foamy pigtails,
two rainy legs,
the invisible back we couldn't reach,
a small wet heart
and toes, ten each.

He dried us all
the way he gave the parish
Morning Prayer:
as if it was important,
as if God was fair,
as if it was really simple
if you would just be still
and bare.

RACHEL McALPINE

Rachel Garden

◆ ◆

REFLECTIONS

One of my early memories, when I was perhaps around five years old, is of sitting in the back of our van with other children, conjuring up my father's image and thinking quite fiercely: 'He is so handsome. Not one feature, nothing about him, could be changed to make him more handsome.'

I remember this clearly, perhaps because of the intensity of my feeling. Looking back it seems an oddly visual occasion — I sat there, in the back of our Landrover, and imagined my father's face and form, studying it for any imperfection, and room for improvement.

I don't recall ever judging other aspects of my father, let alone with such intensity. He was simply accepted as a distant, quiet but powerful presence in a boisterous household.

I have four siblings, and with two sets of twins the five children were very close in age — less than five years between the youngest and oldest. In fact twins were the oldest, my brother and sister, and twins were the youngest, my sister and myself. In between was another brother, the special 'single' of the family. My mother was proud of the fact that there was no 'oldest' or 'youngest' individual in our family.

We were all particularly close to our mother. This relationship was full of words; we talked, read, argued, discussed. Our mother, although frequently ill, was with us all day long. Warm, intimate, articulate, she was central to our lives.

My father was quite a different presence. Looking back I can see that he was under great stress in our early years, as he was working in Hamilton while we lived on a farm outside

'One of my early memories . . . is of sitting in the back of our van with other children, conjuring up my father's image and thinking quite fiercely: "He is so handsome. Not one feature, nothing about him could be changed to make him more handsome."'
Rachel is leaning on the front of the school bus.

Morrinsville, half an hour away. My mother's illness, and the fact he was running a farm as well as working by day, meant he spent much less time with us. But when he was with us he seemed to me remote, less well known, sometimes even slightly to be feared. Above all, he was silent.

As a very small child I had less to do with him than the others. I avoided him, just as I avoided other people. My twin sister was vibrant, engaging and outgoing, and was firmly his favourite. She could enliven him, joke and laugh and answer him back. I was shy and awkward and viewed their relationship with amazement. I don't believe I felt jealousy; it was a relief not to be expected to take part.

When I was around three years old my mother taught me to read, to help conquer my shyness. I remember to this day the revelation and joy of these lessons, and the tremendous sense of discovery and empowerment that came with being able to read. The time spent with her every day, in our sitting room or on our verandah, learning to decode the written word — these were special times! Reading lessons soon became the centre of my days and the source of reward and punishment: 'No new words today', was the threat when behaviour was bad, and I can still remember its effectiveness.

Looking back I rather regret that my mother didn't teach me some arithmetic. I would have loved to discover numbers back then and the revelation of learning would have been even stronger. In learning to read I was discovering a system of rules devised and used by people to communicate with each other. Mathematics reveals a world of concepts and language which is more beautiful and has less dependence on people, and which is easily enjoyed and appreciated by children.

Learning to read occupied my preschool years and brought me closer to my mother. There was, however, no such time spent with my father. As far as I recall he played no role in my reading. In fact I think it likely that he spent very little time with me at all.

As I grew up I slowly became more confident of his affection. My sister was still the apple of his eye. She was often ill with asthma throughout our childhood, occasionally very ill indeed when she would seem to fight for her life. It was not unusual for her to have to spend weeks at a time in bed. She put up with this situation with remarkable cheeriness and good nature.

After a particular long illness I remember my father drawing me to one side and telling me how lucky I was not to be ill, and how much I should try to help care for my sister. I remember watching him deliver this message, half-wishing that I could be ill and enjoy this same kind of attention. But mainly I remember the unusual situation of my father having a private and serious conversation with me. I watched him search for the words to express his love for my sister, and my obligations to her.

Over the following years a real, though always distant, friendship grew between us. I also began to recognise similarities between us — to see myself in his character. My father was not very happy in these years, and was often moody and depressed. He was also becoming increasingly deaf, and this emphasised his remoteness from the family. Even when the noise and clamour of five teenage children surrounded him at meal times, he would be aloof, often gloomily preoccupied in a world of his own.

I was growing increasingly moody and depressed myself at

this time. I remember once, as a teenager, getting up around 2 am during a sleepless night and having a hot drink in the kitchen. My father appeared at the door and joined me. We sat together into the night, sipping our drinks. We were both silent, but by now there was an unspoken language between us and I remember feelings of warmth and support coming from him. We were fellow beings.

I enjoyed the quiet of night-times. Quite often as a teenager I would sit talking for hours into the night with a friend, a local boy I had known for several years. On one occasion my father drove past us. It was very late and he walked back up to us. He did not argue, object, or indeed say any words to either of us at all. I simply joined him in walking back to our house. His silence seemed then, and still does seem, enigmatic to me. He did not appear angry, did not discuss or explain or argue. We simply returned to the house in silence and never discussed the matter.

My father was not alone in the family in relying on unspoken communication. The rest of us talked far more and considered ourselves emancipated and unrestrained. But there were, in fact, complex unspoken rules that governed our family conversations and barred certain topics. How to handle one's feelings and how to behave with the opposite sex were among these rules.

I began to feel restless and frustrated as I moved from intermediate to high school. My family had by now lived in Hamilton for a few years, in fact since the older twins started at secondary school. We all eventually went to high school at Fairfield College, as my mother favoured co-educational schooling. My parents had carefully investigated the school when the elder twins went there but, by the time our turn came, the enlightened headmaster had left, and with him most of the good teachers and the standard was very poor, though I remember art classes with real affection.

I believe that maths and science teaching at school favours boys over girls. It tends to be taught as a series of problem-solving techniques without presenting a unified or conceptual view. I believe girls prefer a more conceptual, logical and 'overview' approach, and are less likely to want to work through details of a specific problem without understanding the principles involved. Girls therefore tend to do less well in tests and find less interest in the subject if it is taught by limited teachers. Later, when I taught logic at university, I almost always found women clustered at the top of the class. Once the fundamentals were clear to them they did very well, but they were much less willing to learn strategies of problem solving without the basic understanding.

Certainly I found neither maths nor science classes at all enjoyable at school. I still remember with great dislike our science teacher who kept the same notes on the board for all classes, so that those of us in higher streams were regularly given free periods in which to run riot until the slower classes had caught up — and this teacher was head of science in a school of over 1200 pupils! I recall after some physics test, probably in the fifth form, being called back after class by this teacher who told me I showed a true aptitude and should continue with physics at university. This single act of encouragement came from a teacher who was actually too lazy to teach. The fact he thought me good at physics simply made his own attitude to teaching seem worse, and I remember the complete derision I felt for him.

Maths teaching was similarly dreadful, with the exception of one part of my third form year when I was lucky enough to be in a class trying out a pilot set theory course. The teacher involved left soon after, and those who followed were uniformly poor. I remember particularly the head of department attempting to teach calculus in the sixth form, a subject vibrant with interest to me. He taught mechanical methods of problem solving but could cast no further light on the subject. When pressed to discuss the nature of infinitesimals, for example, I remember he would tell us that infinitesimals had no size at all. When asked to explain how they could make up a length he would only smile enigmatically and say, 'Isn't it amazing?' I realised with a shock that he did not understand his subject.

My father, like my mother, was a scientist, yet I cannot remember talking with him about the details of what we did at school. I remember his general interest in my progress and his

'With a first class honours degree I left for Canada in 1975 to join a large philosophy graduate programme which specialised in pure mathematics and physics.' Rachel with her father in Philadelphia in 1975.

pride in my achievements, but there was no real sharing of knowledge or experience.

I gradually became more and more frustrated at school and eager to leave. By this time I was studying Russian on my own at home, hoping to appreciate Dostoevsky and Tolstoy without translation. I was probably motivated by the thought that I could get on just as well without teachers at School Certificate and University Entrance level. I also read voraciously, especially through boring classes. I had no clear idea of what to do after school but I had a ferocious impatience to leave. I left as soon as University Entrance was accredited to me.

My mother arranged for me to spend a year in the United Kingdom, something my elder brothers and sisters had done with apparent success. I suppose my father agreed with this arrangement. However, for me the year overseas was a time of enormous stress and change and of near catastrophe. There were good times, especially travelling in Africa, in Europe and working in London at the end of the swinging sixties. But the upheavals took their toll. Looking back, I was completely unprepared for the sudden onslaught of adult life as I was cast, at age seventeen, into a world unlike any I had known. How could one guess what to do, how to act?

In 1970, returning to New Zealand after more than a year overseas, I felt adrift from my family, adrift from life generally. I enrolled at the University of Auckland in mathematics among other subjects simply on my mother's advice, since she herself regretted not having studied it further. All during this difficult time, my relationship with my father continued to unravel.

But first year mathematics was a revelation. I was particularly lucky in the courses and teachers I encountered. A detailed course on the theory of calculus was a total delight. I did extremely well, with an A+ in maths. My second year should have been great.

However, by now I was at odds with the world in general; my father included. I was flatting and did not often visit home. Occasionally I would arrive with the man in my life, and could feel my father's hostility. After some wild moments on the first few occasions, he decided to adopt the simple strategy of behaving as if these young men were not there. Quite a good test of character for the young men concerned.

Somewhere around the end of my third year I started to take control of my life. I began to study more attentively, to enjoy the subjects which truly interested me and in 1973 I went to Wellington where I spent two years at Victoria University completing an honours degree in mathematical logic. The courses offered were outstanding, as was the standard of teaching — in fact they designed a course in logic and mathematics especially for me. With a first-class honours degree I left for Canada in 1975 to join a large philosophy graduate programme which specialised in pure mathematics and physics.

I soon discovered in Canada that I was an experiment — the first woman admitted to the prestigious philosophy of the science programme which had over fifty men enrolled. Women, according to several lecturers, were incapable of philosophy. And philosophy of mathematics and science must be out of the question! How I enjoyed avenging myself over the next few years. I immersed myself in philosophy, completing an MA, fitted in a first-year course at the local art school, and I moved on to a PhD in the foundations of quantum mechanics. The freedom, combined with the quality of the resources, suited me well, and I even won a prize as top graduate student at the university.

But ten years in an academic environment was enough. I retired, after some lively conferences, to the mountains of Wales. There I lived in an ancient house of my mother's, to be near my grandmother, and to get back in touch with something beyond the academic world. In fact I soon gained a husband, a New Zealand friend fresh from a spell in Antarctica. Quickly, we had one, then two, then four young children. At this time, we began a computer software company, and I became immersed as well in writing a book commissioned by the British Institute of Physics.

In 1986 our hill farm was doused with radioactive fallout from the Chernobyl accident. Initially we lived on bottled water and imported vegetables. After a year, however, the contamination was still serious, and we left for New Zealand. In fact, the radioactivity reappears every spring in the new growth of grass on this mountain farm and it is still designated a restricted area, still grossly contaminated, five years later.

Coming home to New Zealand meant coming home to my family. I had already found that having children fundamentally altered and enriched me and as my children engulfed my life, I also came to a new understanding of my own parents. By the time we settled in New Zealand, my eldest child Emily was seven, the twins, Sally and Dan, just turned six, and our youngest daughter Kitty was two years old. A couple of years later in New Zealand our youngest son, Tom, was born.

Now that we live in the same country, my father and I have grown to be friends again. On their first meeting my father treated my husband like all the men in my life, ignoring him for several days, until he needed an expert opinion on the physics of car batteries which my husband was able to provide. Subsequently they have developed a warm friendship. It seems to me that those two have probably had longer and more lively conversations than my father and I managed throughout my entire childhood.

Our children provide me with a new link with my father. I watch his relaxed and warm interaction with them with great enjoyment. Perhaps if we had our time over again, he and I, this is how it would be with us.

◆ ◆

RACHEL GARDEN is a mathematician and philosopher who works in the foundations of quantum mechanics. She was brought up on a farm outside Morrinsville, near Hamilton and she attended Fairfield College in Hamilton, and Auckland and Victoria Universities, before moving to graduate study in Canada.

She writes academic articles, regularly reviews mathematical papers and is the author of *Modern Logic and Quantum Mechanics* for the British Institute of Physics which gives the mathematical arguments for her interpretation of quantum theory. The book was well received internationally and she is currently writing a less mathematical account of her views. Her particular interest is the probability theory used in quantum mechanics, and she argues that many of the peculiar features of quantum theory can be traced to limitations of the theory and do not reflect 'real' peculiarities at all.

Rachel and her husband Peter are co-founders and directors of a computer software company, Cashlink, which has offices in Britain and in Auckland. Software development for the company, which produces and markets accounting software, is now based in the Coromandel Peninsula where they live with their five children.

Since returning to New Zealand from the United Kingdom, Rachel has been an active environmentalist in the anti-mining movement on the Coromandel, and also in other campaigns including the protection of Antarctica, energy issues, and resource management. She received a 1990 medal 'for services to New Zealand and to the energy sector', and is currently chair of the Pacific Development and Conservation Trust, set up to distribute funds received by New Zealand from France 'in settlement of the Rainbow Warrior affair'.

Pauline O'Regan

◆◆◆

MY FATHER AND I

*L*et's begin with my father. I'm writing this on his birthday. He's 121 today! Every year, without fail, I remember his birthday and yet I'm not all that good about birthdays even when people are alive. His is certainly the only one I celebrate after death. Each year I know exactly how old he is. I wonder why this is so? Perhaps it's because he made sure we all knew that he was born in the year of the Franco-Prussian War, 1870. I taught the Franco-Prussian War to sixth formers for thirty years. Perhaps that's why I always remember. It's hard to know with my father.

He was born on the Charleston goldfields near Westport and he never moved far from his birthplace. When the gold petered out, his parents took up farming in the Inangahua Valley and he grew up there. The farm had to be carved out of the bush and even when they were small, he and his brothers had to work hard, picking the last straggling roots out of the cleared ground and piling them up for burning. Bitter frost or drenching rain made no difference. The person who saw that they never slacked was their mother, my Grandma O'Regan. I never knew her, but I know she was a strong woman — many would have it that she was a hard woman. But I never heard my father say that. I think he knew that it was because of her iron will that, at the age of eight, he was sent away to school. She had not come halfway across the world to a new country for nothing. Her children were going to get the opportunity for the education that she, no doubt, had been denied. Her son, John, never forgot to whom he owed his schooling (all four years of it) and he carried his gratitude to the grave.

It was no ordinary thing to go to school if you were a small boy in the Inangahua Valley in 1878. But Grandma O'Regan had a sister who lived at Totara Flat in the Grey Valley, some 40 miles away, and at Totara Flat there was a school. So Aunt McKee took in her sister's children to live with her so that they could be enrolled with Dr Campbell. Dr Campbell was a Scot with the Scots' passion for learning. Between riding for miles on horseback through rough bush, fording flooded rivers to deliver babies and set broken legs and heal every possible ailment (he was a very good doctor), he taught school. He was also a very good teacher.

My father loved Dr Campbell. His presence was so real in our lives that I always thought I had known him too, though of course I had not. It seemed to us, to hear our father talk, that each school day must have been filled with the works of Shakespeare and Robert Burns to the exclusion of all else. But, of course, that was not so. Mathematics and English grammar and spelling and the rudiments of Latin were also part of it. Where else could my father have acquired his fine writing hand which was the irrefutable mark of having had 'the schooling' in a pioneer country? And where else could he have learned Aesop's Fables off by heart? By the time I knew him, what with the plays, the poems and the fables, he had enough quotes to cover every possible exigency in our lives.

The other gifts my father had sprang rather from his genes than from his schooling. He had a sense of humour that was so integrated into his personality that it would be impossible to imagine him without it. In those days people had so little to amuse them that they honed their humour to various degrees of fineness for sheer enjoyment. They were always on the alert for the paradox in life, the irony, the pathos and the bathos. But my father's humour had another dimension. He could perceive all the strange quirks in human nature, his own and others, catch the subtleties, the evasions, the ambiguities, the metaphor, capture the exact inflection of the voice, imitate the body language, reproduce an accent, recall a unique turn of phrase, and then tell the story. He was a born storyteller — that most ancient of all the

'He stood me on the kitchen table to recite twenty-four verses of *Lucy Gray* for their edification and exclamation.'
Pauline O'Regan at three, half way to the table.

arts and one sadly neglected nowadays. In the land of his forebears he would have been given the honour due to the seannachie, the one who knows how to blend voice with meaning, who, in telling a story, can give a mysterious signal long before the time, that there is laughter to come, or tears, the one who, more than anyone else, can hold a mirror up to human nature so that we can look on our foolishness and our greatness with equal acceptance. My father had all that. He had a lot more too.

I was born, the youngest of a family of four, when my father was fifty-two years old. He was a farmer by this time, still in the Inangahua Valley. I don't think I was altogether expected, as mother was already forty-five. If at first they had reservations about my pending arrival, I think they must have soon come to make the best of it because I have never felt the slightest twinge of rejection.

My early relationship with my father was very close. I was the darling of the family, the baby, and I was the apple of his eye. At this distance I can see why he never tired of me. He left all the rearing, the necessary checking, the pruning of the wild growth, to my mother, a matter to which she often took public and emphatic exception. He did little more than delight in my early signs of intelligence, my prodigious memory for the stories and the poetry that he taught me and my capacity to win the admiration and interest of everyone who came to the house. Mind you, some of their interest may have worn thin when he stood me on the kitchen table to recite twenty-four verses of *Lucy Gray* for their edification and exclamation. He loved Wordsworth and was as unable to discriminate between his great and his lesser verse, as was Wordsworth himself.

It was in the course of telling me a story that I came to have the first shadow of doubt about my father, or at least the first small suspicion that he was not perfect. We had a particular ritual every night. When I was tucked up in bed by my mother, I would refuse to go to sleep until he came and told me a story. He always told me one of Aesop's fables. I fought sleep as I begged for another and another and another. He would tell each tale in his

248

own lively way and at the end of each one he would drop his voice and take on a solemn stance to intone the moral. He always began the moral with: 'Ah!'

Ah, envy not your neighbour's lot. Be content with what you've got!

That was one of my favourites, the one about the dog which was walking across a bridge with a piece of meat in its mouth. It looked down and saw its own reflection in the stream below and thought it was another dog with another piece of meat. It opened its mouth to grab the second piece, and lost its own meat into the water. 'Ah!'

Then there was the crow that had a piece of cheese in its mouth. And the fox who wanted it. The fox told the crow how beautiful it was. If only its voice were as beautiful as its looks, it would be queen of all the birds. The crow promptly opened its mouth and gave a loud caw and down came the cheese to the waiting fox.

Ah, we must always beware of flatterers!

Ah, slow and steady wins the race!
Ah, they who laugh last laugh best!
Ah, one good trick is better than a thousand bad ones!

Of course he tired of the storytelling and of course I had to go to sleep. That was the purpose of the exercise entrusted to him. So he would say, 'Now this is the very last story!' But I would have none of it and, unlike my mother, he had no practice in being firm with me. So he used to tell me that he had to stop because he wanted to say his prayers. There was no answer to that. He would sit very still, 'saying his prayers' and I would eventually go to sleep. But never before making a mighty effort to stay awake. 'Are you finished your prayers yet?' No, he was never finished! And that's how it happened that one night my mother came to the door to see if I was asleep and I had to explain that we were not finished yet, we were just waiting until Dad had finished saying his prayers. It was at that moment that I saw something in her eyes as she looked at him, barely perceptible, but enough to arouse my curiosity and to make me store that look away for examination later. It was then that the thought that could not be believed, could not possibly be true, entered my mind. He was tricking me! It was just as in one of his fables, the one about the donkey that had to carry heavy bags of salt. The donkey discovered that if he fell into the river as he waded through, the salt melted and his burden became light. He did this many times until one day his master saw through his trick and loaded him up with sponges. The donkey 'fell' again into the water and could hardly stagger home under the heavy weight.

Ah, you may use a good trick once too often!

My father had used a good trick just once too often. And he'd used it on me. He was not perfect after all. And if he were not perfect then neither were all the other adults in my life. I think I was three years of age at the time. It was hardly the end of innocence, but it was a first step.

As I got older I grew past the age for storytelling, made friends of my own at school and became more independent, if not more wilful. I gradually began to distance myself from my father. I became more critical of him, more ready to assert my will against his, less sensitive to his love for me and his need of my love in return. His stories became 'old yarns' that I'd heard too often before. His sense of humour, his cheerfulness, his certainty that 'everything happens for the best' irked me when we didn't have the money for all the things I wanted. Perhaps if he were more serious, more businesslike, we would be better off. He still initiated virtually all the humour in our lives. Even as a stroppy teenager I was still captivated by his warmth and wit. I would join in the family laughter in spite of myself. But at other times I would see only what was wrong with him. I made him the scapegoat of my adolescent immaturity in a way that I never dreamed of doing with my mother. I knew my mother would never have tolerated it.

I grew up the day my mother died. I was eighteen. My father was wordless in his grief and for a long time his light seemed to have been extinguished. I could only strive to understand, and to bring a new sensitivity to my love for him. They had seemed so

matter-of-fact, my father and mother. I slowly absorbed the truth that there is something between a husband and wife that has nothing to do with their being a father and mother, nothing to do with their children. That was a profound shock. I had believed until then that I was entirely necessary for their happiness, if not their very existence.

My father had no stomach for my entering the convent, but at twenty-one I did it all the same. And later, he was very proud of my being a nun, so my sister told me. But for me, it meant that the distance between us grew wider. He wrote to me regularly, full of accounts of what was happening in the Valley, but entirely devoid of local gossip which he had always detested. But there was generally something there to make me laugh aloud. Once he was telling me his delight that a local boy, who had run off from home some years before, had got in touch with his father. It was a short letter, he said, and like the writer in 'Clancy of the Overflow' it looked at though it was written 'with a thumbnail dipped in tar!' But his joy was in the peace of mind it had brought to the boy's father. His own letters, written in his fine hand, had a certain formality about them and he always signed himself: Your fond pater, John O'Regan. He wrote his last letter to me when he was near to death. He told me not to grieve too much, that he had had a good life for which he was very grateful

251

and had entrusted himself into the hands of God.

Over the years, if I ever thought of it at all, I would have been certain that the parent who had the greater influence on me was my mother. From the perspective of seventy years, I'm not so sure of that. I see in myself my father's weaknesses and strengths. He's passed on to me his particular brand of humour. I have as many quotes as he ever had and I use them as freely. I have devised as many tricks as he, for my own convenience, many of them used once too often. I'm as certain as he was that everything in life happens for the best, and I'm a good storyteller — almost as good as my father.

✦ ✦

PAULINE O'REGAN was born in Reefton in 1922. She attended the Cronadun Primary School and received her secondary education at St Mary's High School, Greymouth. She entered the novitiate of the Sisters of Mercy in Timaru in 1942 and made her final profession of vows in 1947. She graduated MA in History from the University of Canterbury in 1953 and taught in Sisters of Mercy secondary schools for thirty years. During that time, she was Principal of Villa Maria College, Christchurch for seventeen years and of Mercy College, Timaru for two years.

In 1973, with Sisters Teresa O'Connor and Helen Goggin, she moved to live in a state house in Aranui, Christchurch to begin a new work. The book, *Community* (1989), which she co-authored with Teresa O'Connor, gives an insight into their experiences and outlines the methods they have used in building up community in the suburbs.

Pauline O'Regan has had two other books published: *A Changing Order* (1986) tells of the dramatic changes in the religious life in the sixties and shows how nuns in New Zealand courageously faced up to a massive disruption in their lives. *Aunts and Windmills* (1990) tells stories of her childhood in the twenties and thirties.

'He's passed on to me his particular brand of humour.'
Pauline O'Regan in 1991.

The Watch

The watch I carry in my pocket was my father's. A gift on his 21st birthday. It is a big-faced solid watch — ROAMER, 17 JEWELS, SWISS MADE, SUPER-SHOCK. The even numbers are very round and in place of the odd numbers are the shapes of slender arrow heads.

In the photographs this watch accompanies my father through his life. In the wedding picture of him and my mother I can see the winder edging out from under the sleeve of his dark suit. My mother's hand rests on his arm. Holding on to his other arm is his mother. To their right stands my grandfather — in the window behind there is a woman's hat and it looks as if it has just blown off his head. I realise that all the people in the photograph — except for my mother and father — are now dead. My two grandmothers, my grandfather and two smiling young men.

The watch is solid on his wrist as my father holds me — a tiny child almost covered over by his big hands. It is there as he balances my sister Jane on his shoulders and again as he holds Wendy against his knees.

This watch is my father as a young man still new to the world. Now he has a new watch and I have this old one. I carry in my pocket my father aged 21, his lean face ticking through the years.

JENNY BORNHOLDT

'The Watch' is an extract from 'From the Album' published in *Moving House* by Victoria University Press in 1989.

JENNY BORNHOLDT was born in 1960 in Lower Hutt and now lives in Wellington where she works part-time at Unity Books. She has published three books of poems with Victoria University Press: *This Big Face* (1988), *Moving House* (1989) and *Waiting Shelter* (1991), and has had work published in various New Zealand and international literary magazines.

Index of contributors

◆ ◆